Sandra Martin and Roger Hall

Where Were You?

Memorable Events of the Twentieth Century

Sandra Martin and Roger Hall

Where Were You?

Memorable Events of the Twentieth Century

Ⓝ Methuen

Toronto   New York   London   Sydney   Auckland

For our parents and for Jeffrey

Canadian Cataloguing in Publication Data

Martin, Sandra, 1947–
  Where were you?

ISBN 0-458-94310-X

1. History, Modern - 20th century. 2. Twentieth century. I. Hall, Roger, 1945– II. Title.

D422.M37   909.82   C81-094733-1

Printed and bound in Canada

1 2 3 4 5   81   86 85 84 83 82

Contents

Preface

Where Were You? is an attempt to write popular history from a slightly unusual angle. It is, in part, a narrative account of certain key "moments" in the twentieth century. But it differs from much popular writing by focusing on how a variety of people came to learn of these great events—in short, how they heard the news, and what impact that knowledge had on their personal lives. It is, then, a book of memory, recollection and reminiscence as well as narrative history. We think that the combination produces much insight into the nature of the century, especially when we recall the technological advances in mass communications that have permitted so many of us to share the news of these events simultaneously.

In preparing *Where Were You?* we have received generous help and cooperation from a large number of people and institutions. We are particularly grateful to the scores of busy individuals around the world who so generously took time to answer our queries: Col. Edwin (Buzz) Aldrin, Robert Thomas Allen, Isaac Asimov, Vladimir Ashkenazy, Margaret Atwood, Jean-Pierre Aumont, Sir Isaiah Berlin, Clark Blaise, Heinrich Böll, Sir Jack Brabham, Dave Brubeck, Anthony Burgess, General E. L. M. Burns, Barbara Cartland, Sammy Cahn, Lady Casey, Lord Kenneth Clark, Professor Manning Clark, Susan Clark, Senator Keith Davey, Lovat Dickson, Leon Edel, Arthur Erickson, Douglas Fairbanks Jr., Frederick Forsyth, Christina Foyle, Robert Fulford, Buckminster Fuller, Allen Ginsberg, Major-General Robert Gordon-Finlayson, Sir Alec Guinness, Stanley Holloway, Michael Holroyd, A. D. Hope, Donald Jack, the late Stan Kenton, Deborah Kerr, Eric Koch, David Lancashire, Ann Landers, Joseph Losey, the late John W. McCormack, Sir William McMahon, Raymond Massey, Pierre Mendès-France, the late Sir Oswald Mosley, Lord Olivier, Hal Porter, Escott Reid, Major-General Richard Rohmer, Chester Ronning, Josef Skvorecky, Georges Simenon, Gordon Sinclair, Howard K. Smith, Benjamin Spock, R. H. C. Steed,

David Suzuki, Lowell Thomas, Lord Tweedsmuir, Sir Edgar Vaughan, Gore Vidal, Judah Waten, the late Sir Roy Welensky, Katharine Whitehorn, Ernie Wise and George Woodcock.

We have also been greatly aided by the staffs at a number of public and private institutions. In Canada we should like to thank the Robarts Library at the University of Toronto, the Weldon Library at the University of Western Ontario, the Metropolitan Toronto Central Library, the Archives of Ontario and the Public Archives of Canada. In the United States we are grateful to the National Archives and the Library of Congress in Washington and the New York Public Library. In England we received much good service from the British Library and the Imperial War Museum. Special thanks go to Beatrice Schriever of CBC radio's "Morningside" and the program's Canadian and American listeners.

We should also like to acknowledge some personal debts: Don Sedgwick of Toronto, Professor W. M. Martin of Montreal and Dr. Guy Stanley of New York for their help in research; Professor John Dickinson of the University of Montreal, Professor Erich Hahn of the University of Western Ontario, and Beate Bowron, Jane Glassco, Charles Oberdorf and Mechtild Hoppenrath of Toronto for help with translations. Gordon and Marietta Dodds of Ottawa, Eric Haythorne in Washington, Susan Most in New York City, and Dick Shaw in London kindly took in itinerants. Sharon Gignac of Toronto typed the manuscript. And David Cobb's comments, as always, have been more than helpful.

SANDRA MARTIN
ROGER HALL

Introduction

CERTAIN DATES are benchmarks in all our lives. For example, most of us—whatever our age, station or nationality—know what we were doing when the news came of John F. Kennedy's assassination on November 22, 1963. And not only do we remember JFK's death, we talk about it. Indeed, exchanging reminiscences about the assassination has gone from a conversational gambit to a cliché.

The Kennedy murder was a horrible shock, and that accounts for much of our interest; but some of the explanation lies in the nature of mass communications: how we first heard the news. Invariably it came as a flash bulletin on an otherwise ordinary day, bursting into our consciousness as we worked in offices, studied in schools or libraries, listened idly to car radios, watched afternoon soap operas, sat in dentists' chairs or rode in elevators.

We found it fascinating that a piece of news could forge such tangible links among otherwise disparate individuals, and we decided to explore and chronicle people's reactions to a number of significant news events in the twentieth century—the century of mass communications—to see whether there were other "connectors." We isolated forty pivotal events, beginning with the death of Queen Victoria in 1901—an event which had been widely, albeit slowly, reported around the world by telegraph and newspapers—and finishing with the downfall of the late Shah of Iran in 1979—an event that had been flashed around the globe by satellite with the result that, because of time differences, the news was known in some parts of the world before it had happened.

Then we wrote to more than one thousand prominent people, individuals who had achieved recognition in the arts, the academy, government, business, entertainment and the military—people who themselves have had some impact on the media. We asked them to pick five events from our list of forty dates and to tell us where they were and what they were doing and thinking at the moment they heard each particular piece of news. We didn't want our correspondents to choose the events they considered to be important in the history of the world, but rather the events they remembered, the ones that were important in their own lives. We wanted to see how individual lives corresponded and coincided with the great conventional milestones of the century.

More than one-third of the people we contacted replied, and one-third of them contributed opinions and impressions which we were able to incorporate in *Where Were You?* Not everybody agreed with the events we had selected, and some people chose to suggest others. One man, for example, was distressed that we had not included the sinking of the battlecruiser HMS *Hood* by the German battleship *Bismarck* on May 29, 1941. To him, a Canadian serving with the Royal Navy during the Second World War, the destruction of the *Hood* marked one of the darkest days of his life, a date as significant as the stock market crash was to his father or the Cuban missile crisis to his children.

From our responses we selected the most frequently cited events and organized them into chapters; the remaining recollections we gathered into a miscellany. Once we had determined the "key" events, we searched through hundreds of autobiographies, memoirs, letters and diaries to see what other people had chosen to record about these dates. And finally, as a balance for the anecdotes and reminiscences and to set each event in historical context, we wrote general introductions to each chapter.

We wanted the human, personal aspects of historical statistics and our respondents certainly provided them, but we found that the events which crossed all socioeconomic and generational boundaries were not necessarily the obvious "top ten" on anybody's list of earthshaking dates. The very nature of the recollections made us wonder about the character of human memory and the factors that cause people to recall some events and not others. We began to question not only the role of the mass media in shaping our memories and reactions to world events, but also their function in actually creating the news, in producing what some have called "pseudo-events."

Why do we remember the Armistice, but not the end of the Second World War? Why can people recall Edward VIII's abdication in 1936, but not the more recent resignation of Richard

Nixon in 1974? Why did Lindbergh's flight across the Atlantic capture the public's imagination in a way that Neil Armstrong's lunar walk never did? And why did John Lennon's murder on December 8, 1980 generate such intense media and public interest, reaction so completely disproportionate to his artistic or political influence at the time of his death?

NOT SURPRISINGLY, we remember events principally in terms of how they affect us personally. If an event has no implication for the working out of our individual "life-dramas" then we tend to discard it from our memory files. People celebrated the Armistice more than the end of the Second World War because the Armistice was a single, climactic moment whereas in Europe the Second World War petered out in a series of surrenders and capitulations and in Japan ended only after the detonation of thermonuclear devices.

Another important factor in assessing memory is the impact on our society of the "information explosion." Television, with its ability to bring a mass audience to the scene of an event, to have us all "there," may have destroyed our need and our ability to imagine what it must be like to be "there." The trouble with being present via television is that we see only what the camera wants us to see. It's like observing the world through blinkers. We don't pick an event or an object to focus on—the decision is made for us. What we see is only part of the scene, and that part has been artificially intensified while everything on the periphery has been blurred.

When we watch television, we sit like lumps on an assembly line, ingesting information and opinions. After a while our ability to react to events is greatly diminished. Compare Edward VIII's abdication with the resignation of Richard Nixon. Edward spoke on the radio. We had only his voice; we had to supply the images. Nobody interpreted his speech either before or after he made it; we had to do that for ourselves. Richard Nixon's resignation received so much coverage, post-coverage, background and "analysis" that we were awash in information. The actual moment of his announcement was lost in a morass of talk and pictures, most of it a seemingly endless repetition of earlier broadcasts. Also, Edward spoke from a carefully prepared text, one that had been pruned and polished even to the addition of some Churchillian flourishes, while Nixon's final farewell was a tearful, rambling monologue. Electronic newsgathering has so radically increased television's scope that important news is not so much announced these days as delivered (and often even captured) in impromptu statements and off-the-cuff remarks. Such comments may promote spontaneity and even candor, but often they are so ungrammatical and so unleavened by wit or style as to be instantly forgettable.

The moon landing on July 20, 1969 reinforces our contention that more information and more technology results in less impact, less involvement, and ultimately fewer memories. That achievement, a goal which had grasped men's and women's imaginations for centuries—from Jules Verne to any number of other writers—fell flat. Some 723 million people watched it on television—one-fifth of mankind—but few "shared" the experience. Why? Because we all watched it in isolation. We didn't talk to our fellow observers; we didn't watch it with anybody. No matter how many people were in the room each of us was alone with the television set, communing with a device over which we have virtually no control, a machine with which we cannot converse. Nor was the achievement one man's romantic victory over the universe as Lindbergh's flight had been a triumph over the skies; rather it was the latest incident in the Cold War, an American technological breakthrough in which machines, not people, appeared to be in charge. The landing and the subsequent moon walk were far too complex for any individual to comprehend, and as a result the individual "self" felt alienated.

When asked about the moon landing, people generally remember that they were watching television and that it was summer—at least in the northern hemisphere—but very few can relate the moon landing to what else was going on in the world. For example, who ever connects the moon landing with Senator Edward Kennedy's car accident at Chappaquiddick in which Mary Jo Kopechne drowned? The two events seem centuries apart, yet they happened on the same weekend.

John Lennon's murder reflects a different media emphasis. Lennon was a pivotal figure in the most influential rock group ever, a group whose impact had splayed from music to popular culture to politics. But at the time of his death, Lennon, at forty, had just begun to emerge from a five-year retreat, and The Beatles themselves, the group that had been his vehicle to fame, had been disbanded for a decade. Upon reflection it is ironic that a cynical world, unmoved by the physical and political plight of thousands in Asia and Africa, went into general mourning over the death of one man.

In fact, a generation was mourning for itself or, at least, its lost youth. Lennon had swung to popularity and influence in the ripest years of the postwar baby boom. It had been the media that had made him and The Beatles better known than Jesus Christ—a fact that Lennon abhorred—and it was the media that celebrated a prolonged funeral mass to mark his passing. In fact, the baby boomies upon whom he had exerted so much influence in the 1960s were now in charge of the media front lines, as reporters and commentators, and even more important as editors determining how much space a story such as the Lennon murder should be given and in what order it should appear in the line-up. It was the media's decision to grieve on a mass scale that set both the pattern and the tone for people all over the world. In the end fewer tears were shed for Lennon's widow and his family than for the generation he represented.

TRADITIONALLY, historians have relied on documentary sources such as minutes and memoranda, personal letters and diaries to describe the past. Personal recollection has served at best only to provide a certain human coloring to the recreation of an event or as a check for other documentation. Of course, these sources themselves have been culled and ordered—either officially or unofficially—before the historian gets hold of them. Serious researchers have always considered autobiography suspect and oral history positively bogus. The distinguished historian A. J. P. Taylor wrote dismissively about the interview method: "In this matter I am almost a total sceptic. . . . Old men drooling about their youth—No." Nevertheless, thanks to this spontaneous tele-communications age, historians must rely more and more upon non-documentary evidence to reconstruct the past, particularly when they are dealing with social history. Perfect history, like perfect memory, is a thing of the past.

Before we can "learn" anything, we must understand it; once we have appreciated how information fits together, we can recon-struct it—or at least an approximation—at some point in the future. The same is true of our memory for events. Over time we dispose of certain components, but after the first few days of attri-tion, our memories remain pretty fixed or stable. Also, the more significant an event or fact is, the more likely it is we will remember it accurately.

There are dangers, of course. The "personal" link to an event can heighten recall or suppress it by the unconscious blockage of a memory. The Scottish psychologist Ian Hunter suggested that "the day lovers meet and war breaks out is memorable. But not so the humdrum, uneventful period of routine whose very lack of individuality ensures their being forgotten as unique events." Similarly, Tom Harrison, the founder of *Mass-Observation*, found in experiments conducted at the University of Sussex in England that, "We had people who [had] kept nightly diaries of the blitz (in London) . . . re-write from memory what they thought they felt and did then. There is usually little or no logical relation between the two sets of accounts 34 years apart. Memory has glossified and sanctified these finest hours." The same thing is true about French resistance to Hitler during the German occupation. Popular myth suggests that every Frenchman over the age of fifty was a maquis, with the result that a good number now recall their dreary wartime experiences and minor acts of resistance or defiance as heroic deeds. Marcel Ophuls' famous film *Le Chagrin et la Pitie* has helped to dispel that notion.

Because memory is a selective process, we asked people to choose the events that were significant to them, predicting that if people were interested enough to respond, a particular event must have a high degree of importance in their lives. Thus we attempted to increase the reliability of the responses, first by picking signifi-cant world events, and second by allowing the correspondents to choose amongst them. We assumed, too, that because the events we selected had each been widely disseminated by the mass media, there was a certain degree of consistency—and therefore reliability—in the manner in which our respondents heard the news of each event.

IT IS BOTH the consistency and the instantaneous nature of the mass media that are peculiar to our time. By the end of the nineteenth century, with the telegraph and the penny press in universal use, all the basic technology for fast and wide circulation of news was in place. The development of motion pictures with their larger than life impact was a mass phenomenon that occurred at the time of the First World War. After the war, broadcasting became the dominant media force. It had been given authority by the journalistic role it had played during the war, and its simple marriage of scientific theory and practical technology made radio an accessible and appealing innovation. All of this coincided with other "mass" developments, such as Henry Ford's production line, a considerable expansion of literacy, widescale advertising, popular phonograph records and the Hollywood star system.

A decline in the popularity of serious newspapers occurred about the same time, and tabloids emerged to fill the gap. America led the way in this process, and American isolationism between the wars doubtless strengthened the grip of its mass media. The scarcity of money in the 1930s gave commercial radio unquestioned preeminence, although it wasn't the golden age that some like to reminisce about. Radio also elevated the news to a new status, although sponsors were slow to be persuaded that it was worthy of their advertising dollars. With the outbreak of the Second World War, the news, controlled though it had to be, became an even more important programming feature. By the war's end most peoples' memories of significant events were memories of radio reports. Television and the introduction of further technological refinements—the transistor, the coaxial cable, the telecommunications satellite and electronic newsgathering—assured that the postwar world would be a wired-up media age.

Obviously there are substantial differences among radio, newspaper and television news coverage, and a substantial science has grown up to explain them. The late Marshall McLuhan's all-conclusive media theories, particularly his celebrated pronouncement that print is dead, have provoked violent and prolonged controversy among learned observers and ordinary watchers. In his peculiar language, McLuhan contended that radio, because of its singular appeal to the auditory sense, was a "hot" medium. Television, on the other hand, he called "cool" and suggested that, like face-to-face speech, it is multi-sensory and completely engaging. These theories are half-truths, not easily tested or disproved, but our informal view is that because radio and print are media which preoccupy a particular sense, they make a greater claim on our attention. Television solicits two senses at once with its indistinct, murky image and a mostly homogeneous sound. The result, McLuhan insisted, is engaging. We believe the reverse is true. Nor do we accept futurist Alvin Toffler's optimistic prediction that the new television sets—video terminals that users can program—will breed individualism within a stronger sense of community. Our view is that television—no matter how sophisticated—is disengaging, even alienating, isolating the viewer not only from the television set, but from fellow watchers. This leads us to suggest that the impact of news learned from radio or the press must be more substantial than that gleaned from television.

Recent research into the nature of brain hemispheres tends to support this opinion. We have both verbal and visual memories, as evidenced by the fact that often we can remember a person's face but not his or her name. And we have both verbal and visual parts to our brains. The left hemisphere which operates and controls verbal and analytical activities is considered the dominant sphere, while the right hemisphere which organizes spatial and visual activities is subdominant. However, hemisphere specialization is the mark of an adult brain. For babies, who are clearly non-verbal, neither hemisphere can be called dominant. Until they develop language, they can only absorb experience, and therefore memories, in non-verbal ways. Watching television is a non-verbal activity and there is evidence to suggest—notably the steady decline in verbal aptitude scores of high-school students writing college board examinations—that increased television viewing has produced a generation of largely right hemisphere thinkers, a generation for whom visual activities take precedence over verbal ones.

Since the purpose of journalism is business, the media have naturally and readily adapted themselves to this visual audience. There is nothing new in this accommodation. Fifty years ago newspapermen competed with "razzle-dazzle" stunts; today cameramen and photojournalists scour the world for winning film footage. Inevitably, the availability and quality of visuals has become a prime determinant in both the selection of items and the sequence in which they are presented on television news broadcasts. After studying the process at NBC Evening News, American writer Edward Jay Epstein concluded, "The chances of a film piece being used on network news increases with the amount of violent action it contains." Since, as public opinion polls consistently indicate, television is not only the chief source of news— nearly 65 per cent of American adults use television as their principal source of information—but the most believed source, whoever controls the tube goes a long way toward controlling the minds and hearts of the people.

Those with financial or political power have easy access to television; they produce commercials or they hold press conferences. Poor and disadvantaged groups can't afford to advertise, nor do they have the clout to demand legitimate air time. Instead they stage demonstrations. Hence this past decade's stark image of klieg-lit vigils around jumbo jets, banks, Olympic dormitories, trains and embassies.

Much of our present conception of the world seems based, then, on structured and fraudulent illusion. We live in a world shaped by media, a world which appears real only because everybody says that it represents the real world. Yet none of this is really new either. It is no more than an updating of what Walter Lippmann wrote almost sixty years ago in *Public Opinion*. In an essay entitled "The World Outside and the Pictures in Our Heads" he observed that most of us achieve our ideas about the world as a direct result of assumptions provided by interpreters of reality, in other words by journalists who are themselves part of that pseudo-reality. What is new is that the media, particularly television, have such an ubiquitous scope and a pervasive power that we have become virtual prisoners of an electronic environment. Worse, many of us are unprotesting inmates.

Moreover, in a world drenched in media values many of the real achievements of this century, seminal events such as the end of colonial rule in Africa and Asia, or the elimination of smallpox, have been lost in the general scramble for air time merely because they don't translate into gripping headlines or provide good visuals. In a way, the age of the great news event may have passed, and it is certainly ironic that the mass media which so carefully perfected the public announcement of "news" effectively have caused its apparent demise. What follows in this book, then, is a chronicle of a simpler time, when McLuhan's global village was curiously more akin to Goldsmith's deserted one:

> Where village statesmen talked with looks profound,
> And news much older than their ale went round.

1

1. Armistice celebration near Paris
   gate at Vincennes (*Imperial War
   Museum*).
2. Marshal Ferdinand Foch, carrying
   Armistice documents, leaves Forest
   of Compiègne for Paris (*Public
   Archives of Canada*).
3. Returning soldier (*Public Archives
   of Canada*).
4. Headline announces war's end
   (*William James Collection*).
5. Crowds celebrate around replica of
   Statue of Liberty, Philadelphia
   (*National Archives, Washington*).

2

CHAPTER 1

The Armistice

NOVEMBER 11, 1918

3

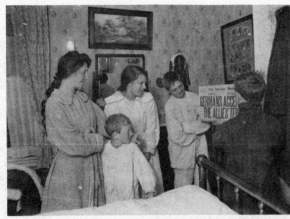

4

5

THE WAR TO END WAR ended on November 11, 1918. Ten million men had been killed in combat, twenty million had been wounded and millions of civilians were dead from disease and starvation. In four years of fighting, Europe and the world had been transformed: empires had collapsed, economies were in ruins, even the traditional social order had been destroyed.

It was cold and rainy in the Forest of Compiègne in northern France on that November morning when shortly after two o'clock a group of Germans—soldiers and civilians—disembarked from one railway car and proceeded to another two hundred yards away, where Marshal Ferdinand Foch, the commander-in-chief of the Allied Armies, was waiting. They talked for three hours. Then finally at five minutes past 5:00 a.m. the Armistice agreement was signed, and the belligerents acceded to Foch's suggestion that hostilities should cease later that same morning at precisely 11:00 a.m. on the eleventh day of the eleventh month.

The news was telegraphed around the world and the victorious Allies erupted in joyous and often drunken relief. It was not a time for moderation or reflection; that would come later. As it had unfolded, few had understood what the war was about—apart from the suffering—and its implications remained a mystery. For the moment it was enough that Germany was wracked by revolution, the Kaiser had fled and the German Army had surrendered. Victory for the Allies was sweet and all seemed peace and joy.

IN AUGUST 1914, war was still considered a sharp, exhilarating adventure, good for a nation's character and better still for its balance sheets. Few had heeded the bitter lesson taught by the first modern war—the vicious, protracted American Civil War of 1861–1865. Indeed, most senior European military men had been trained in an outmoded tradition that owed much to Napoleon and the nineteenth-century German military theorist Karl von Clausewitz. Their practical experience had been gained either in short European wars that were measured in weeks and months, or in imperial expeditions against poorly trained, ill-equipped native forces.

When imperial ambitions and a series of entangling alliances ensnared Europe in a general war, nobody believed it would be a prolonged conflict. "Business as usual" was the civilian motto, and the observation that the boys would be home for Christmas became a cliché.

Germany's Schlieffen Plan was designed to level a knock-out blow, a calculated right hook through Belgium which would devastate the French Army and permit the capture of Paris. Then the victorious Kaiser could turn his attention eastward to the lumbering Russians who would be slow to mobilize and slower to move. The French strategy was even simpler: French troops, propelled by their legendary *élan* would quickly and decisively plunge a steel wedge into the German center. Britain, too, relied on a traditional maneuver: an expeditionary force of 120,000 superbly trained and equipped professionals was sent to do the actual fighting while the magisterial Royal Navy ensured tranquility in the vital sea lanes. Confidence reigned in every capital, and the Kaiser told his troops they would be home "before the leaves have fallen from the trees." But they would not be home by then, nor by Christmas either. In the twentieth century, war would not be a cavalier adventure.

Germany's thrust through Belgium was weakened and delayed by the General Staff's decision to strengthen its left and center. It was held up further by the stout Belgium defense at Liège and the unexpected tenacity of the British Expeditionary Force. In the meantime, French *élan* had proven no match for the dour efficiency of German machine guns. The French troops in their vivid blue coats, red kepis and red pantaloons marched towards the Germans almost in parade-ground formation, and the Germans systematically mowed them down. The French did not retreat until they had lost a staggering 300,000 men—a figure that was suppressed until the end of the war. A near rout followed, and it was only disorganization in the German rear and the failure of their transport and communications systems that allowed French General J. J. C. Joffre to assemble a reserve army and stage a counterattack from the Marne, a few miles north of Paris.

The German drive had been broken, and Germany retreated north to the defensive line of the River Aisnes. Now both sides tried a series of desperate outflanking movements until the battle lines stretched from Switzerland to the North Sea. The war of movement had become a war of entrenched position. For the next three bloody years, the western front would not move more than ten miles in any direction.

Only in the east, against the ponderous Russians, was the German strategy at all effective. The Russians lost hundreds of thousands in their battles against the Germans and Austrians, but always there were more peasants to fill the ranks. And as the Germans drove ever eastward, they found (as Napoleon had learned earlier and as Hitler would discover later) that in Russia one had to fight the very land itself. They were confronted by seemingly endless stretches of forests, lakes and streams, all of which gave way onto even larger terrains.

After the Battle of the Marne it had become apparent that this war was like no other. It would be long, and more than just armies would be involved: civilian populations and entire economies would be dragged into the fray. The heady enthusiasm with which so many in the West had greeted the war waned, and nowhere was this more apparent than in France, the battleground for much of the fighting. In the first year, half of all French families received government telegrams informing them of the patriotic death of a husband or a son, while the British lost more officers in the first few months than in all their previous wars combined.

Traditions die hard and nowhere is that truer than on the battlefield. The notion that an entrenched defense is superior to an infantry attack—no matter how spirited—was painfully slow to register with the military strategists. Meanwhile, the trench systems became more complex and sophisticated and chlorine gas, which had been used first on a grand scale by the Germans at Ypres in 1915 (and quickly adopted by the British), proved as dangerous to offense as to defense, thanks to the capricious, shifting winds. It was roundly condemned, more for its novelty than for its atrociousness, because in the final analysis it was no more lethal than machine guns.

It took the staggering losses of 1916—Verdun: 700,000 deaths, roughly 350,000 on each side; the Somme: 400,000 British and Empire deaths (with 60,000 casualties suffered on the first day alone), 500,000 Germans and nearly 200,000 French—to destroy the old European order.

If 1916 was a seesaw year of stalemates and Pyrrhic victories, 1917 proved decisive thanks not to battles but to alliances. Russia signed a separate peace treaty with Germany, and the United States entered the war. These two events changed the entire nature of the conflict.

Throughout the war Russian military leaders had assumed that their peasant-soldier army would fight on regardless of appalling conditions and inadequate supplies. To the officers it was inconceivable that their troops would ever rebel, or throw down their arms—indeed if they had any—forget about the war, and march off to reclaim the country that was rightfully theirs. The officers were wrong. The people's long-festering discontent, stirred up by the incessant blundering of the Czarist government, erupted in St. Petersburg in March 1917 and was followed by the Bolshevik Revolution in October of that same year. The Bolsheviks, convinced that only by making peace with Germany could they assert control over a country that was fast slipping into civil war, signed the humiliating Treaty of Brest-Litovsk on March 3, 1917. It deprived them of the Ukraine, Poland, Finland and the Balkan Provinces. Russia now was neutralized.

The United States entered the war as a direct result of German naval policy. In 1915, German submarines had sunk the British liner *Lusitania* with the loss of 128 American lives. The American public was enraged and President Woodrow Wilson extracted a promise from the Germans that in future no neutral cargo or passenger ships would be attacked without warning. But in February 1917, the Germans, aware that they were being slowly strangled by the blockade maintained by the British, and confident that Britain could be cut off from its own supply routes, launched a campaign of unrestricted submarine warfare, sinking 1,870,000 tons between February and April. Britain was reduced to only six weeks worth of supplies.

The Germans now gambled that they could win the war on

land before the Americans, with their plentiful fresh troops and limitless resources, officially joined the Allied cause. They were wrong. Flushed with moral outrage, President Woodrow Wilson led his country into war in April 1917 with the promise that the United States would "make the world safe for democracy." The refinement of the convoy system, coupled with the rapid deployment of the U.S. Navy, reduced the submarine threat from menace to annoyance in a matter of months.

THE "GREAT WAR" changed everything, even warfare itself. Inevitably and inexorably it affected the "Home Front." For one thing it saw the demise of free enterprise—or, at least, the raw unbridled sort so beloved by nineteenth-century liberals. Since no one had expected the war to last so long, no country had devised an adequate industrial strategy. As time passed and the war continued, governments began to exercise more and more control over their economies in an attempt to direct all resources—moral, fiscal and natural—to the single purpose of winning the war. Luxury goods almost disappeared, stock and bond issues became tightly regulated, and business for mere profit, the motive that had fueled societies for centuries, became discredited as the concept of a "planned economy" was introduced.

Strikes were rare as with a dogged dedication workers accepted longer hours at low wages, although they did display a strong and growing resentment of the comforts still enjoyed by their social "betters." The war saw women replace many of the men in the labor force, which radically altered their perception of their role in society and awakened men to the idea that female suffrage was not an end in itself but merely a beginning. For the workers as much as for the soldiers, the postwar world was expected to bring not only change, but a world fit for heroes and heroines.

During the war America tripled its exports in part as a result of the British blockade and also due to the fact that the warring countries were busy manufacturing arms instead of their normal commodities. America as well moved from being a debtor nation, owing upwards of $4 billion to various European nations, but especially to Britain, to a creditor nation, being owed some $10 billion. Wars were expensive and all the cautionary procedures of another age were forgotten as governments printed stacks of paper money, cranked out bond and loan issues on a gigantic scale and borrowed heavily whenever and wherever possible. The problem of goods and supplies was toughest for the Central powers which had relied heavily on foreign trade and now, because of the blockade, were forced to be largely self-sufficient. Eastward conquests helped a good deal, especially in the acquisition of wheat and oil.

Freedom of thought and particularly freedom of expression were perhaps the greatest victims of the war. Modern censorship and the manipulation of the news so familiar to us today had its birth during that struggle. The press yielded to government pressure by glossing over battles that had been lost, failing to report heavy casualties, and distorting statistics. The British and the Americans at least had some independent news, whereas German, Russian and, to some extent, French readers learned only what their governments wanted them to learn. The loss of 25 per cent of all French *poilus* in the first few months of battle was never reported, nor the magnitude of the Russian defeat at Tannenberg, or the colossal scale of the British losses at the Somme. New words were coined—retreats became "strategic withdrawals," and mutinies were termed "collective indiscipline." Direct news from soldiers at the front was always censored— frequently by the senders themselves in an effort to protect the people at home from learning about the horrors of the battlefield. The truth was sacrificed because, as British Prime Minister David Lloyd George explained in 1917, "If people really knew, the war would be stopped tomorrow."

As the war staggered on with no end—and certainly no victory—in sight, propaganda reached a sinister and sophisticated level as each side blamed the other. Complex issues were boiled down to one or two essentials: the enemy was evil incarnate, and he had fomented the war in a maniacal campaign for world domination. This ludicrous deception was perpetrated to entice yet more people to enlist and to encourage those at home to work harder. Handbills, placards, postcards and posters all depicted the enemy as the very personification of sin and depravity. For the Allies, the Kaiser became a calculating, vicious demon and the German was the "Germ-Hun" who gleefully raped and pillaged innocent Belgium and boiled down his own dead for glycerine. To the Germans, the British were bloodsucking blockaders who delighted in starving children and the Russians were rampaging cossacks determined to ravage German womanhood. This propaganda, aimed at the emergent mass literate audience, was not restricted to print, but was spewed forth in lectures, sermons and patriotic plays.

THE WESTERN FRONT in 1917 presented a matrix of mud and death; French troops were so dispirited that mutinies erupted in more than half their divisions. By the spring of 1918 the Germans decided to risk all their remaining resources on a final massive offensive. They reached the Marne by May 30 and were pushing hard toward Paris when five days later the first American soldiers went into battle. By June 1918, 250,000 American troops were landing in France every month. Almost as crucial, the Allies had finally realized the need for an integrated command and had appointed France's Marshal Foch as their commander-in-chief. In July he counter-attacked on the Marne and the German offensive spluttered out.

Coordinated Allied assaults now pushed the Germans back to the Hindenburg Line, and by the end of September the German command urged an astonished Kaiser to arrange an Armistice. On October 4, 1918 Prince Max of Baden, a liberal constitutionalist, took control, but it was far too late for democratization to be imposed from the top. The Allied Armies, encouraged by the volte-face on the western front, broke north from Greece, silencing the Balkans and forcing Bulgaria to accept a separate peace; Turkey followed within a month and then, in late October, the Allied Italians vengefully shattered the Austrians at Vittorio Veneto. The Austro-Hungarian Army simply dissolved as each nationality in that ramshackle empire limped towards its homeland. November 3 saw the Armistice with Austria.

Revolution, not victory, came to Germany. The casualties of

nearly two million, disease, near-starvation, and four years of frustration combined to cause general disorder. The disturbances began at the naval yards at Kiel where sailors, learning that the fleet had been ordered to sea for one last effort, mutinied. Open revolt then broke out in Bavaria as the locals pressed the government to sue for peace now that Austria's collapse had left them open to attack.

At length Foch met German emissaries to arrange Armistice discussions. Then on November 10, 1918, with revolution gripping Berlin, the Kaiser abdicated, riding in a plush Royal train toward permanent exile in neutral Holland. The end came the next day. The final Armistice terms were harsh—exceedingly so— but it was difficult, if not impossible, to dispell the ideas that earlier propaganda had entrenched, particularly since every family had an empty chair as a reminder of the havoc Germany had wrought.

Germany glumly accepted the terms. They had little choice, and because of the peace treaty that followed, there would be few alternatives in the future, either for Germany or the rest of the world.

The Armistice shocked the German people. Government propaganda had downplayed America's involvement, juggled the casualty figures and exaggerated the country's fighting strength so effectively that few could believe the war had been lost. The last Allied victories had not been advertised widely even in England, for by now the press was preoccupied with a different cause: inciting the public to demand that the Kaiser's exiled neck should be stretched and that the bloody huns should pay. Because Allied concessions had allowed the German Armies to retire intact, a rationale emerged that for a time eased the shame of defeat and later provided Hitler with a slogan on which to ride to power. It went like this: since the army had remained inviolate, it couldn't have been defeated in the field; therefore it must have been civilian dissidents, the socialists, Jews and communists at home who had effected a "stab in the back" and arranged the mortifying Armistice. Such then was the state of affairs on November 11, 1918 when the world learned that the war had ended at last.

BRITAIN'S QUEEN MARY, herself German born, called it "the greatest day in the world's history." Few would have disagreed with her. At 6:50 a.m. British General Headquarters informed its armies that hostilities would cease precisely at eleven o'clock that morning; on the other side of the Atlantic, in Washington, the State Department released the same news to a sleeping continent at 2:45 a.m. Eight minutes later, the Statue of Liberty in New York was lit by searchlights—the first silent sign of peace. Then the *New York Times* building came alight, and the huge spotlight in its tower played over the city. Silence did not reign for long.

On the battlefields in France and Belgium it was very different. The weather that morning was fine although rather cold with mist in some places. Field-Marshal Sir Douglas Haig, commander-in-chief of the British Armies in France, wrote in his diary:

> The state of the German Army is said to be very bad, and the discipline seems to have become so low that the orders of the officers are not obeyed. Captain von Helldorf, who tried to get back to Spa from Compiègne with the terms of the Armistice by night, was fired on deliberately by the German troops marching on the road and he could not pass; while on another main road they broke up the bridges so that he could not proceed. . . .
> We heard this morning that the Kaiser is in Holland. If the war had gone against us, no doubt our King would have had to go, and probably our Army would have become insubordinate like the German Army [as in] John Bunyan's remark on seeing a man on his way to be hanged, "But for the Grace of God, John Bunyan would have been in that man's place!"

The madness at the front lasted until the final moment. Near Valenciennes a British batallion was told by a wounded German lieutenant, propped up against a wall, that the village behind him was empty since the rear guard had abandoned it two hours before. The English believed him—after all, the war was nearly over and the man had spoken with an educated English accent. They formed up in regular ranks and marched into the village square. German machine guns, from vantage points on all sides, cut down more than a hundred British soldiers. The enraged batallion broke ranks and, in a fierce battle, killed all the Germans in the village and then ran back and bayonneted the wounded lieutenant who, it was reported, was not surprised to see them. He died with an amused look on his face.

The insanity was not restricted to the Germans. At ten minutes to eleven, a British cavalry charge was ordered to capture a bridge over the River Dendre at Lessines. Officially, the purpose was to secure a bridgehead on the German side in case of truce violations. A squadron of dragoons in tight battle formation charged down a straight tree-lined road. German machine gunners methodically killed or wounded dozens of men until precisely eleven o'clock when, following orders, they stopped firing and the British peacefully took the bridge.

Shelling continued along the whole length of the front, and in some places American troops still went into action. Foolishly, their command had decided that the AEF should capture Sedan, to avenge a French defeat in 1870. Some of the men had no idea that the end of the war was only minutes away. They advanced bravely until their officers, watches in hands, ordered them to stop. Elsewhere, American artillery continued firing long after the magic hour had passed. Apparently, each of the gun crews wanted the honor of firing the last shot, and so order after order was ignored until finally one came from sufficiently high up in the chain of command that it had to be obeyed.

The French lines were quiet the whole morning. When news of the Armistice was announced, sentries were posted and the entire army sat down to wait. They would take defensive action only if attacked by fanatical, suicidal Germans. But there were few fanatics left on the German side that day, and so neither German nor French lives were lost on that section of the front.

And then it was over. Most would remember the silence—a silence bought with four years of noise. Little was said, out came the inevitable cigarettes, and a kind of shyness and uncertainty overtook men on both sides. Soon came the realization that steel helmets and gas masks weren't needed any more, and both were discarded without ceremony. Strict orders had gone out not to fraternize with the enemy. But the whole idea of "enemy" had blurred for the fighting forces. "Enemy" like "hun" was a favorite phrase of the propagandists. Germans at the front were nick-named "Heinies," "Fritz," or "Jerry," just as the British were called "Tommies." Both sides had a good measure of sympathy for the "poor bastards" whom they were assigned to kill. And so, despite the orders, men were drawn inexorably to the other side.

Captain Eddie Rickenbacker, the undisputed "American Ace of Aces" with twenty-six enemy planes to his credit, was with his squadron at the front. Orders came that all pilots should stay on the ground, but Rickenbacker was determined to witness the great moment.

It was a muggy, foggy day. About ten I sauntered out to the hangar and casually told my mechanics to take the plane out on the line and warm it up to test the engines. Without announcing my plans to anyone, I climbed into the plane and took off. Under the low ceiling, I hedgehopped towards the front. I arrived over Verdun at 10:45 and proceeded on towards Conflans, flying over no-man's-land. I was at less than 500 feet. I could see both Germans and Americans crouching in their trenches, peering over with every intention of killing any man who revealed himself on the other side. From time to time ahead of me on the German side I saw a burst of flame, and I knew that they were firing at me. Back at the field later I found bullet holes in my ship.

I glanced at my watch. One minute to eleven, thirty seconds, fifteen. And then it was 11 a.m., the eleventh hour of the eleventh day of the eleventh month. I was the only audience for the greatest show ever presented. On both sides of no-man's land, the trenches erupted. Brown uniformed men poured out of the American trenches, grey-green uniforms out of the German. From my observer's seat overhead, I watched them throw their helmets in the air, discard their guns, wave their hands. Then all up and down the front, the two groups of men began edging towards each other across no-man's-land. Seconds before they had been willing to shoot each other; now they came forward. Hesitantly at first, then more quickly, each group approached the other.

Suddenly grey uniforms mixed with brown. I could see them hugging each other, dancing, jumping. Americans were passing out cigarettes and chocolate. I flew up to the French sector. There it was even more incredible. After four years of slaughter and hatred they were not only hugging each other but kissing each other on both cheeks as well.

Star shells, rockets and flares began to go up, and I turned my ship towards the field. The war was over.

When the Armistice took effect Lt. General E. L. M. Burns was in the mud at Mons, Belgium, serving as acting staff captain of the 9th Canadian Infantry Brigade. He recalls the last moments of the war for the Canadian Corps.

> I was kept fully occupied with staff duties: . . . a victory march through the city square had to be arranged. The Mayor would take the salute alongside General Sir Arthur Currie, our Corps Commander. As many as possible of the units in the Corps would be represented in the march-past. The sun shone, and the troops, polished up as best they could after weeks of fighting, made a brave show.
>
> *Mons:* We Canadians felt that it was somehow a symbol and an honor that our part in the war should end where the first engagement between the British Army and the Germans had taken place in 1914. In the four years since, the Canadian Corps had been built up to what we felt was the most formidable offensive formation in the British Armies. There was no question of identity then; no one asked himself "What or Who is a Canadian?," whether one's mother tongue was French or English. Collectively in the Canadian Corps we were all Canadians and proud of it.
>
> Probably few of the men in the Corps were thinking this when the eleventh hour of the eleventh day in the eleventh month came. Many have told how they thought during the last few hours, after it had become generally known that the fighting would end, that before the guns finally became silent, it would be their fate to be killed by one of the last shots. Probably the commonest thought, when they looked at their watches and saw it was indeed eleven o'clock, was "The War is over, and I am still alive!"

By contrast the Home Front erupted with glee and abandon. Allied cities reverberated with a cacophony of bells, sirens, police whistles, fireworks and bands. There were no radios or televisions, of course, but the tinkle of piano keys was a common sound as families began celebrating.

In London, at a few minutes before 11:00 a.m., Winston Churchill stood at the window of his office looking up Northumberland Avenue towards Trafalgar Square while he waited for Big Ben to signal the Armistice. The war had seen Churchill's fortunes shift remarkably. At the outbreak he had been First Lord of the

Admiralty; then the Gallipoli disaster had forced his resignation,
and he had spent some time as an officer in the trenches in France.
His political resurrection began in 1917 with his appointment as
minister of munitions in David Lloyd George's coalition government. Although he was a member of the Cabinet, he was con-
siderably removed from direct control of the progress of the war.
"Not allowed to make the plans," he complained later, "I was set
to make the weapons."

> The minutes passed. I was conscious of reaction rather than
> elation. The material purposes on which one's work had been
> centred, every process of thought on which one had lived,
> crumbled into nothing. The whole vast business of supply,
> the growing outputs, the careful hoards, the secret future
> plans—but yesterday the whole duty of life—all at a stroke
> vanished like a nightmare dream, leaving a void behind. My
> mind mechanically persisted in exploring the problems of
> demobilization. What was to happen to our three million
> munition workers? What would they make now? How would
> the roaring factories be converted? How in fact are swords
> beaten into ploughshares? How long would it take to bring
> the Armies home? What would they do when they got home?
> We had of course a demobilization plan for the Ministry of
> Munitions. It had been carefully worked out, but it had played
> no part in our thoughts. Now it must be put into operation.
> The levers must be pulled—*Full Steam Astern*. The Muni-
> tions Council must meet without delay.
>   And then suddenly the first stroke of the chime. I looked
> again at the broad street beneath me. It was deserted. From the
> portals of one of the large hotels absorbed by Government
> Departments darted the slight figure of a girl clerk, distractedly
> gesticulating while another stroke resounded. Then from all
> sides men and women came scurrying into the street. Streams
> of people poured out of all the buildings. The bells of London
> began to clash. Northumberland Avenue was now crowded
> with people in hundreds, nay, thousands, rushing hither and
> thither in a frantic manner, shouting and screaming with joy.
> I could see that Trafalgar Square was already swarming.
> Around me in our very headquarters, in the Hotel Metropole,
> disorder had broken out. Doors banged. Feet clattered down
> corridors. Everyone rose from the desk and cast aside pen and
> paper. All bounds were broken. The tumult grew. It grew like
> a gale, but from all sides simultaneously. The street was now a

seething mass of humanity. Flags appeared as if by magic. Streams of men and women flowed from the Embankment. They mingled with torrents pouring down the Strand on their way to acclaim the King. Almost before the last stroke of the clock had died away, the strict, war-straitened, regulated streets of London had become a triumphant pandemonium. At any rate it was clear that no more work would be done that day. Yes, the chains which had held the world were broken. Links of imperative need, links of discipline, links of brute-force, links of self-sacrifice, links of terror, links of honour which had held our nation, nay, the greater part of mankind, to grinding toil, to a compulsive cause—every one had snapped upon a few strokes of the clock. Safety, freedom, peace, home, the dear one back at the fireside—all after fifty-two months of gaunt distortion. After fifty-two months of making burdens grievous to be borne and binding them on men's backs, at last, all at once, suddenly and everywhere the burdens were let down. At least so for the moment it seemed.

My wife arrived, and we decided to go and offer our congratulations to the Prime Minister, on whom the central impact of the home struggle had fallen, in his hour of recompense. But no sooner had we entered our car than twenty people mounted upon it, and in the midst of a wildly cheering multitude we were impelled slowly forward through Whitehall. We had driven together the opposite way along the same road on the afternoon of the ultimatum. There had been the same crowd and almost the same enthusiasm. . . .

Harold Nicolson was in Whitehall, at the Foreign Office working on plans for the coming peace conference.

I strolled to the window and looked down upon No. 10 Downing Street. A group of people stood in the roadway and there were some half a dozen policemen. It was 10:55 a.m. Suddenly the front door opened. Mr. Lloyd George, his white hair fluttering in the wind, appeared upon the door-step. He waved his arms outwards. I opened the window hurriedly. He was shouting the same sentence over and over again. I caught his words. "At eleven o'clock this morning the war will be over."

The crowd surged towards him. Plump and smiling he made dismissive gestures and then retreated behind the great front door. People were running along Downing Street and in a few minutes the whole street was blocked. There was no cheering. The crowd overflowed dumbly into the Horse Guards Parade. They surged around the wall of the Downing

Street garden. From my post of vantage I observed Lloyd George emerge into that garden, nervous and enthusiastic. He went towards the garden door and then withdrew. Two secretaries who were with him urged him on. He opened the door. He stepped out into the Parade. He waved his hands for a moment of gesticulation and then again retreated. The crowd rushed towards him and patted him feverishly on his back. My most vivid impression of Mr. Lloyd George derives from that moment. A man retreating from too urgent admirers who endeavour hysterically to pat him on the back. Ought he to have gone? Having gone, ought he to have retreated so boyishly? That scene was a symbol of much that was to follow thereafter. Having regained the garden enclosure, Mr. Lloyd George laughed heartily with the two secretaries who had accompanied him. It was a moving scene.

Within ten minutes of the announcement, five thousand people had gathered in front of Buckingham Palace to stand in the drizzle as thousands more streamed from all directions, particularly down the Mall from Trafalgar Square. Queen Victoria's monument was buried under Australian troops. Nobody knew where all the flags had come from, but everybody was waving one. People stood on cars, buses, taxis, and each other and began to chant for the King. When he finally appeared on the balcony no one could hear what he was saying, but it didn't matter.

The crowds took over the city for the rest of the day and effectively for a couple more besides. Among them were the playwright Noel Coward and the novelist Arnold Bennett, who at the time was deputy minister under Lord Beaverbrook in the ministry of information. Bennett complained in his diary about the jam in Piccadilly Circus and commented sourly that the rain was "an excellent thing to damp hysteria and bolshevism." As the day wore on the crowds emptied restaurants of food, bars of drink—there seemed to be plenty of money around—and jammed churches and theaters. Lamps and store fronts were stripped of their wartime shades and once again spilled light onto darkening streets. Effigies of the Kaiser were hanged, drawn and quartered hundreds of times, and his mock funeral processions contrasted horribly with the dozens of real mourners carrying the coffins of influenza victims who vainly tried to push through the throngs. Pickpockets and petty thieves had their best day for years. As night drew on huge bonfires blazed and searchlights criss-crossed the sky. The marks from one fire, set by rejoicing Canadians, can still be seen at the foot of Nelson's Column in Trafalgar Square.

Paris was more subdued than London; French losses had been the greatest of all, and poignant memories mixed with jubilation. At the Chamber of Deputies, Premier Clemenceau mounted the tribune and without introduction began reading the conditions of the Armistice. Applause and cheering interrupted him, and when he was done, the whole chamber erupted as the deputies sang the "Marseillaise." The anthem was picked up in the galleries, then spread to the crowds in the corridors, and finally to the throngs outside on the river banks and bridges.

Lowell Thomas, the American journalist and lecturer, had been a war correspondent and was in the city the day it ended.

> The city went wild, and streams of people jammed nearly all the boulevards. I watched most of it from a table . . . at the Café de la Paix. . . . I was especially interested in what the women of Paris did. They wore the most outlandish and picturesque hats. Why they celebrated with colorful headgear I don't know. But every woman was wearing an incredible hat which apparently she herself had designed. For American soldiers who were lucky enough to be in Paris it was a memorable experience. They were literally overwhelmed by the Parisienne girls.

By contrast, the staid *Times* of London boasted that British troops were "among the most kissed people in Paris." More than kissing went on in the streets that day, but the authorities turned a blind eye.

Marcel Proust, the French writer and author of *À la Recherche du temps perdu*, had just delivered the second volume of his masterpiece to his publisher, Gaston Gallimard. On the day of the Armistice he was, as usual, at home in Paris, where he wrote in a letter to a friend:

> The only kind of peace I want is the peace that leaves no bitterness anywhere. But since this peace is not of that sort, it might be wiser, now that a desire for vengeance has taken root, if we saw to it that it should never be allowed to find expression in action. Something of the kind *may* be in course of preparation,

but I rather think that President Wilson is a soft man. There is no question—because of Germany's guilt there can be no question—of a peace of conciliation, and, that being so, I should have preferred to see more rigorous conditions. My fear is that German Austria may be called in to swell Germany proper as some kind of compensation for the loss of Alsace-Lorraine. But this is all mere guesswork, and I may be wrong. Perhaps everything is all right as it is. General de Gallifet said of General Roget, "He speaks well, but he speaks too much." President Wilson does not speak very well, but certainly he speaks a great deal too much.

For Belgian towns and cities it was a day of freedom as well as of victory. Thanksgiving was more the theme in Ghent, for example, than unrestrained partying, and the following day, when King Albert reentered in triumph, white flowers showered from the balconies. In the hundreds of war-ruined villages near the front the celebrations were less formal. In response to Allied shouts of *"Guerre finie, guerre finie, Boche Kaput!"* the villagers covered the liberating soldiers with pink and white chrysanthemums, even stuffing them into gun barrels and under the straps of steel helmets.

Georges Simenon, in his autobiographical novel *Pedigree*, describes the effect of the news on a small town near Liège which had been occupied by the Germans for four years. The protagonist, Roger, is Simenon at the age of fifteen and a half. He was at The Palace, a music hall where on stage a burlesque private, dressed in a prewar French uniform, was leading the audience in song.

> Little by little the murmur in the auditorium, hesitant at first, became a vast roar accompanied by the orchestra, applause broke out, and the private skipped off behind a flat, coming back to take his bow.
>
> What happened then? They had caught a glimpse of a figure dressed in black standing in the wings. The comic, still half on the stage, started talking to him without taking any notice of the audience.
>
> They called for him. He came back to the footlights and bent down to speak to the conductor of the orchestra, who stood up, put his elbows on the stage, and, surprised, visibly hesitating, looked inquiringly at the man in black in the wings . . .

. . . and finally sat down again, said a few words to the musicians, raised his baton . . .

Then . . .

"*Allons enfants de la Patrie . . .*"

For a moment, nobody could believe his eyes or ears. With a magniloquent gesture, the soldier had snatched off his red wig and tossed back his brown hair. With the back of his sleeve he wiped away his silly mask. It was a young man with an intelligent face who roared at the top of his voice:

"*Aux armes, citoyens,*
Formez vos bataillons . . ."

Nobody stayed where he was. Everybody stood up without knowing why, because it was impossible to remain seated, because something carried you away. Eyes smarted. Trembling voices repeated the words of the *Marseillaise*:

"*Qu'un sang impur*
Abreuve nos sillons . . ."

The singer dashed over to the wings. Somebody handed him something which he brandished with a sweeping gesture, and a huge French flag unfurled in the glare of the floodlights.

Something else was handed to him, and the same gesture revealed the Belgian flag: black, yellow and red.

Then, while the orchestra struck up the *Brabançonne*, the man who was still wearing the costume of a music-hall soldier shouted to the two thousand people in the audience:

"It's the armistice! . . . The war is over!"

After that everything was chaos. Everybody was crying, laughing, embracing, pushing. There were some who rushed outside to shout the news to the passers-by, but the latter knew it already, the whole town had heard it within a few moments. The shopkeepers were on their doorsteps, women were leaning out of the windows, and some people, seeing the growing crowds, wondered whether it would not be advisable to lower the iron shutters.

The war was over! In spite of the rain, the streets were filling with an increasingly excited mob, singing could be heard, and then suddenly, like a signal, the sound of a window shivering into pieces.

It was a pork-butcher's shop whose owner had worked with the Germans. Men disappeared into the shop and started throwing out hams and black puddings. The furniture followed, hurled out of the first-floor and second-floor windows: wardrobes, beds, and bedside table, a piano. The police did not know what to do and looters ran off down the street with their booty.

"Destroy if you like, but don't take anything!" a police sergeant shouted.

Ten, twenty, fifty butchers' shops suffered the same fate and the crowd continued to become increasingly varied. In the Rue de la Cathédrale itself you could see whole groups of people from the poorer districts, certain cafés had begun serving free drinks and the others were forced to follow suit, for soon the mob insisted on it.

In a patch of shadow, a human figure was struggling with half a dozen determined men and Roger looked on uncomprehendingly. They were stripping a woman, tearing off every piece of clothing she was wearing. She was naked now, on her knees on the slimy pavement, and one of the men slashed her hair off with a pair of scissors.

"She can go now. We're going to do the same to all the women who've slept with the Huns. Like that, when their husbands come back from the front, they'll know what's what."

North America had celebrated the Armistice once before—on Thursday the seventh—when a false report had been flashed from Brest to New York. Nobody had thought to question the news because it was expected, and New York, Philadelphia, Boston, Chicago, Montreal, Toronto, San Francisco and everywhere in between cut loose in joyous abandon. Trading on Wall Street stopped, Enrico Caruso sang from a window of the Knickerbocker Hotel, and in Washington, President Wilson waved uncomprehendingly at a huge crowd gathered outside the White House. Few seemed to mind when the afternoon papers announced it had been a hoax and, indeed, many of the merrymakers carried on. Gordon Sinclair, the Canadian journalist and broadcaster, remembers the "whooping" and "hollering," and the delight of riding on the roof of a streetcar: "I was 18 and every time I got off that car some girl kissed me. . . . When the *real* Armistice came a few days later," he recalls, "life was more orderly and cynical."

My boss was a bulky Irishman with red hair. I told him I should go home and get into uniform. I was a private in the 48th Highlanders with a kilt a bit short for me and thus rather daring. When I got into uniform a lot of people started offering me things as if I were a war hero. I'd never been out of the country; never heard a shot fired except in the basement of

Hart House at Toronto Varsity where we did target practice in the dark.

Downtown every soldier, even skinny kids like me, was being hugged and kissed and slapped on the back. I had a girl whose father so hated soldiers that he would never let me into the house. She lived at the beach so I decided to go there in uniform on Armistice Day and see if that made a difference.

The street railway had brought out some of the open summer cars and made no try at collecting fares. I went down Broadview Avenue on a regular enclosed car and got off at Queen to get an eastbound car to Scarborough. It was November, but not cold, and the first car to come along was one of the open cars. It was crowded with some people standing on the side steps.

I got standing room at the back and as the car started to bump its way across the switch lines, a tall dragoon with a silver helmet came running to get on the moving car. His spurs jangled and the shiny helmet fell down over his eyes so that he couldn't see. Regulation cavalry spurs at that time were rounded and smooth but some troopers bought their own western style spurs—sharp and cutting. They made a louder noise. Very macho.

This dragoon had oversize spurs and as he swung on to the street car heading for the beach, one raked across my bare knee causing a spurt of blood that was more spectacular than dangerous. There was commotion. "A wounded highlander on Armistice Day!" It was joy for some of the people. Me too, because of all the attention I got.

People on the car which had stopped between streets seemed to feel that they were now part of the war. The dragoon called for handkerchiefs and was offered a dozen. A man tore a sleeve from his shirt. This fallen highlander must be helped! . . .

The first motor car to come along was flagged to a halt and a variety of people screamed about the wounded kiltie. I was lapping it up. The motorist, with three willing helpers in case I fainted, drove me to St. Michael's Hospital where I was washed and bandaged. There was a soldier's hostel right near the hospital and after they turned me loose with a gallant bandage, I walked there. Nobody made a fuss over me in the hostel. That was girl stuff for civilians.

I have the scar to this day. It is long and slim and white— as if cut by a knife. But it was a cowboy's spur on the boot of a trooper in the Royal Canadian Dragoons.

Each city had its special way of celebrating. New York dumped an estimated 155 tons of ticker tape onto its streets, and in a packed Times Square a tall fresh-faced English girl, "with the Devonshire bloom still fresh on her cheeks," climbed to the platform of "Liberty Hall," raised a hand to hush the crowd, and in a "clear silvery voice" sang the doxology—"Praise God from Whom all Blessings Flow." The *New York Times* reported that a churchly calm spread over the square; heads were bowed and hats doffed. Then a roar of approval followed as she went on to sing the "Marseillaise," the "Star-Spangled Banner" and "God Save the King."

Montreal favored talcum powder which coated everyone in snowy white dust; huge bonfires were lit in the streets of Toronto, and everywhere there were flags—not just American, British and French but flags of all the Allies. If people had been "war mad," said one reporter in Toronto, they now became "peace mad." The stores ran out of confetti, talcum powder, toilet paper, and every other sort of paper. Patients left hospitals, judges released prisoners, and in some places, such as Montreal, fashionable restaurants quickly sported patriotic menus and served "Potage à la Victory Bond" and "Pudding à la Wilson."

And so it went across the continent and throughout the British Empire. New York's six million might have mustered bigger crowds, but other cities' celebrations were just as enthusiastic. Extra editions announced the news and people poured into the streets, some near-naked or in night clothes, while others called jammed switchboards to confirm the news. An old word was revived—"mafficking," a term once used to describe the joyous crowds that filled the capitals of the British Empire when word came of the fall of Mafeking during the Boer War. The phrase was heard everywhere from Sydney, where spring-time crowds celebrated in shirt sleeves and light dresses, to New York.

Hal Porter, the Australian novelist and short story writer, was staying with his aunt and uncle on a farm near Sale, a country town about 140 miles east of Melbourne. He was seven and considered, not unnaturally (nor inaccurately for some), that the end of the world might be at hand.

I was sitting on the orchard gatepost. Except for rose-like left-overs here and there on an apple tree, blossom-time was over for fruit trees. However, the hawthorns surrounding the orchard were deeply coated with chalk-white blossoms that smelt of mingled honey and pepper, and simmered with bees busy at a prolonged and gentle growling.

As I drowsily listened, this husky reverberation seemed to change pitch, to intensify and multiply. A supernatural announcement of the End of the World? No—the town, streets away, was making all the noise it could. That day I recognized only the nearest bell, that of Notre Dame de Sion Convent, clattering unreligiously. Today I know that every bell, whistle, siren, drum, and brass band in Sale would have been deafen-ingly supporting the human hallabaloo—singing and cheer-ing—of Armistice being celebrated. Mr. Smith [a sulphur-crested cocatoo] could be heard screeching at God.

Whether I understood that the Great War was over is doubtful. I think I'd have preferred to know instead that the extravaganza known as the End of the World was beginning. I was not, however, displeased with the distant din of revelry on that divinely sunny day; and absolutely delighted with the bonfires and fireworks that night. I had, in fact, experienced my first mafficking—and from the sidelines, the wisest place to experience any occasion on which humanity loses its head.

Actually in most Allied cities in late 1918 large gatherings or demonstrations were strictly against the law—and for good reason. 1918 marked not only the ultimate year of the greatest war in human history, but also the outbreak of the most virulent plague since the middle ages—the dreaded Spanish influenza. By the Armistice, the pandemic had been raging for eight months. It fed on a war-weakened world and before the final wave passed in the spring of 1919 nearly twenty-two million died—twice as many as had been killed in the war.

Joseph Losey, who in later years would direct such films as *The Servant* and *The Go-Between*, recalls:

I was recuperating from a severe and near fatal influenza at the age of nine, in bed at my home in La Crosse, Wisconsin, with a twenty-four hour a day nurse. My family, with the sanction of my grandmother and nurse, got me up at four in the morning, bundled me up in blankets, took me around the town in the antique (then very new) Ford touring car to witness the burn-ing in effigy of the Kaiser, an experience I will never forget.

The Canadian writer George Woodcock, author of *Anarchism* and *The Crystal Spirit*, remembers a similar incident. He was six years old and living in the little town of Marlow besides the Thames.

> It was a little place of four or five thousand people, and most of its energetic inhabitants were off on various war missions, but we had to make our demonstration, with a procession down the High Street of the local military (crocks too sick or old for active service) and the Boy Scouts and the Salvation Army Band and the local dignitaries. We gravitated to the procession route, I with my mother. I had just escaped dying from Spanish influenza by the skin of my teeth, and must have been a skinny pallid little creature trying to see between the legs of the people in front of me. My mother was starting to lift me up, when a tall white-maned man beside her bent down and lifted me on to his shoulder, and I saw the marching and heard the songs, and at the end of it all the white-maned man took my mother and me off to drink coffee and eat wartime cakes, and charmed my mother with his politeness, and always talked to me whenever afterwards he saw me in the street. He was Jerome K. Jerome, author of *Three Men in a Boat*, and my first literary acquaintance. The child's eye view of historic events tends to be very narrow and personal.

The pacifist literary and artistic mafia of Bloomsbury, which was to dominate British intellectual life in the first decades of this century, celebrated the Armistice in its own fashion. Writer Virginia Woolf had a dentist's appointment in London's Harley Street. She had met her husband, Leonard Woolf, in Wigmore Street and they slowly strolled to Trafalgar Square. He later wrote:

> The first hours of peace were terribly depressing. The Square, indeed all the streets, were solid with people, omnibuses, and vehicles of all kinds. A thin, fine, cold rain fell remorselessly upon us all. Some of us carried sodden flags, some of us staggered in and out of pubs, we wandered aimlessly in the rain and mud with no means of celebrating peace or expressing our emotions of relief and joy. Our emotions of joy and relief ebbed, our spirits flagged. All, or nearly all of us, decided at the same moment to go home, and at once it became impossible to go home, for the buses, the trains, the stations became a solid mass of people struggling to go home. Eventually we managed to get to Waterloo and some two hours later to Richmond.

Not all of Bloomsbury found the peace celebrations so dreary. Painters David Garnett and Duncan Grant were working as laborers on a farm in Sussex and lived nearby in a farmhouse rented by Virginia Woolf's sister, Vanessa, and her husband Clive Bell. As soon as they heard the news, they grabbed their bicycles and pedaled furiously to the station to catch the London train.

> By the time we arrived, it had already gone mad. The streets were thronged with crowds, singing and laughing, dazed with happiness. Lorry loads of girls—munition workers in their working overalls, straight from Woolwich Arsenal, or the factories, their young faces stained bright yellow with the fumes of picric acid, were driving slowly along, singing and yelling. Some of them exchanged catcalls and badinage with passing soldiers, but most of them seemed to be in a religious trance. There were more than the usual number of motorbuses—in some places the roads were blocked with them. They no longer ran on their accustomed routes, but loaded with a full and permanent complement of cheering passengers, they explored new neighbourhoods, such as the squares of Mayfair and Bloomsbury, at the whim of the driver. Every taxi had half a dozen passengers inside and a couple more on its roof.

In the afternoon the two painters made their way to a flat near the Adelphi Theatre where barrister and art patron Montague (Monty) Shearman was hosting a party attended by London's political, literary and artistic elite. Among them were Maynard Keynes, Lytton Strachey, Osbert and Sacheverell Sitwell, D. H. Lawrence and his wife Frieda, Roger Fry, Clive Bell, Mark Gertler, Diaghilev, Massine and Lady Ottoline Morrell. Osbert Sitwell described his friend Lytton Strachey's dancing as being like "a benevolent but rather irritable Pelican." Despite the gaiety and general hilarity of the party, David Garnett remembers that D. H. Lawrence, who looked "ill and unhappy," said to him prophetically:

> I suppose you think the war is over and that we shall go back to the kind of world you lived in before it. . . . Very soon war will break out again and overwhelm you. It makes me sick to see you rejoicing like a butterfly in the last rays of the sun before the winter. The crowd outside thinks that Germany is crushed forever. But the Germans will soon rise again. Europe

is done for; England most of all the countries. This war isn't over. Even if the fighting should stop, the evil will be worse because the hate will be dammed up in men's hearts and will show itself in all sorts of ways which will be worse than war. Whatever happens there can be no Peace on Earth.

For the poet and novelist Robert Graves, Armistice night was a time of mourning and remembrance. He had served in France with the Royal Welch Fusiliers. At one point he had been reported killed by shell-fire and subsequently had the disconcerting experience of reading his own obituary in *The Times*. For him the Armistice had brought melancholy news:

> I heard at the same time of the deaths of Frank Jones-Bateman, who had gone back again just before the end, and Wilfred Owen, who often used to send me poems from France. Armistice-night hysterics did not touch our camp much, though some of the Canadians stationed there went down to Rhyl to celebrate in true overseas style. The news sent me out walking alone along the dyke above the marshes of Rhuddlan (an ancient battlefield, the Flodden of Wales), cursing and sobbing and thinking of the dead. Siegfried's [Sassoon] famous poem celebrating the Armistice began:
>> Everybody suddenly burst out singing,
>> And I was filled with such delight
>> As prisoned birds must find in freedom . . .
> But "everybody" did not include me.

Raymond Massey, the actor, had been wounded in France and shipped back to Canada to convalesce. The war's end found him halfway round the world, in eastern Siberia, as part of the Allied effort to get Russia fighting the Germans again. It soon became apparent, however, that the real purpose of the Allied presence was to help the White Russians crush the Bolsheviks. Emotions were mixed.

> We had been in Vladivostok a month when the Armistice in Europe was declared. The news was two days old when we heard it. On November 15, elements of all allied troops in the area marched along Pushkinskaya in what was proclaimed to be a peace parade. It wasn't too happy a description. Many of the thousands who watched us pass were refugees for whom peace was a meaningless word.

But the parade confirmed what we had been told many times by people who knew the facts of the revolution: that the presence of allied troops, however small in number, made possible the growth and spirit of resistance to the Bolsheviks. Without us, the newly organized White Russian troops would "melt away," as Sir Robert Borden, Prime Minister of Canada, wrote just about this time.

As our little collection of odds and sods of the advance party marched by the crowds, we heard wild cheers. The American regiment of infantry, a British infantry battalion of the Middlesex Regiment, and the French instructors all got the same reception. But a battalion of Japanese passed to resentful silence. The crowd was cool even to the Czech battalion.

It was understandable that the Japanese would get the cold shoulder. After all, it was just fifteen years since they had given the Russians one of the most humiliating lickings in history. But the Czechs had literally saved Siberia from the Red revolution.

In Berlin and the other capitals of the Central powers, the scene was bleak. Defeat had made the prospects of a cold winter even more cheerless as people sadly contemplated their meager provisions. There was very little fuel and almost no food. Returning soldiers were a mixed blessing. Nobody needed more mouths to feed, and what would the men do, anyway? The government and the economy were in chaos. When news of the Kaiser's abdication was formally released, mobs began assaulting officers, tearing off their epaulettes and decorations. Prince Max had retreated to Baden, leaving the new socialist Premier Friedrich Ebert to sort out the mess. It would take some time.

Theodor Wolff, the influential editor of the *Berliner Tageblatt*, was an informed observer at the confused center of Germany's hastily assembled new government. He recorded the chaotic scene in the old Imperial Chancellery in his diary:

In the afternoon I went with Otto Nuschke, editor of the *Volkszeitung*, to the Chancellor's palace, where we were to discuss the coup of Adolf Hoffmann and the Independents with Scheidemann and other "Commissars of the People"— the members of the improvised Socialist Government have considered this the proper title for the moment. The same well-drilled, noiseless old attendants who had opened and closed the doors here in the time of William II, took us to the room on the ground floor which had been Bethmann's ante-room. The first to join us was Herr Kurt Baake, formerly on the staff of *Vorwärts*, now Head of the Chancellory: he bore all the outward signs of doing very well indeed. Then Scheide-mann came in, bothered and nervous. While we were reporting the case he shook his head now and again to show his disap-proval. Before Scheidemann actually said anything, Kurt Baake interposed softly, simply oozing wisdom: he could only advise giving way and accepting things as they were. Rather astonished at this, I asked Scheidemann:

"Is that what you think too?"

He threw up his arms in perplexity. "Yes, the Independ-ents now have the power; I have no soldiers, what can I do?"

I pointed out that after all, at yesterday's meeting of representatives of the Workers' and Soldiers' Councils in the Busch Circus, the soldiers voted with the Majority Socialists; but the argument failed to move him; he merely repeated: "I have no soldiers," and gazed into the distance, evidently look-ing for more soldiers.

Landsberg came in: a very clever lawyer, representing the Majority Socialists, with Ebert and Scheidemann, in the Provisional Government: the other three members represent Hugo Haase's radical wing. We put the matter to him.

"Yes," he said, "we are in an impossible situation. Haase is much stronger than we are. If things go on like this we shall have no alternative but to resign."

At that moment a grey-haired attendant announced, in the same tone in which he used to announce Ambassadors:

"The Supreme Soldiers' Council."

It was obviously an unwelcome announcement, and there was general agitation and perplexity. Landsberg said under his breath: "More trouble!" Scheidemann jumped up in annoyance—"That lot again!" We quickly departed. The impression given by the scene was almost that the executioner and his men were at the door.

Outside in the vestibule the Supreme Soldiers' Council were waiting impatiently. As far as I remember there were four or five of them, all in faultless officer's uniform, well brushed, with broad red armlets. They were all tall, thin men, and all doing their best to maintain an expression of severity and grimness—the pose of a Saint-Just delivering sentence. I recognized the writer Colin Ross, the ex-Prussian Deputy

Cohen-Reuss, and Brutus Molkenbuhr. In themselves they were entirely decent and agreeable men, but now they were statues, they thought it the right thing to ignore my presence, and only Cohen-Reuss shook my hand—coolly and in a very reserved manner. Brutus Molkenbuhr was rather shorter than the rest, but he had the surname of a father with a long and honourable record as a Social Democrat, and on top of that he had been christened Brutus—a huge piece of luck with a revolution in progress.

There was a shout of "Captain von Beerfelde!" and Beerfelde came out of another waiting room, tall and erect, stiff, majestic, magnificent, exceedingly grave. He has an uncommonly interesting head: bushy eyebrows, with hairs sticking out like needles, and he has the stride of the young Napoleon. I have met Beerfelde (he was an officer on the General Staff) several times in the course of his strange spiritual journeyings; he first came to me with a mission from the Theosophical salon of Frau von Moltke. Some of his activities, well-meant as they were, did not appeal to me, and at times I was obliged actively to oppose them, but I have always had for him, as most people would, the sympathy naturally aroused by a fine specimen of a zealot born out of due time. No enthusiast and dreamer could be more selfless and sincere and single-minded than he, and none was so ill-suited to our age as this Knight of the Grail and child-minded Quixote, mystic and social idealist. He always stood outside all parties, and now, too, is just as remote from all the various revolutionary camps. But this afternoon he has gone with the other members of the Supreme Soldiers' Council to the Provisional Government, looking straight ahead, with a stern and commanding expression, from under his bushy eyebrows, to call the Government to account in the name of the people. I can still see him as the door was opened to admit him and he entered the room at the head of the group, with the firm step of a ruler of men. Then I went away from that house, in which I have had many interesting experiences, but none more surprising.

Some miles north of Berlin at Pasewalk, in Pomerania, not far from Stettin, a young soldier was in a military hospital convalescing from the effects—both physical and emotional—of a British mustard gas attack. He had been in the front lines near Werwick, south of Ypres, when the bombardment had begun and the gas had made him painfully, but temporarily, blind. Most of his sight had returned by November 9 when he heard the shattering news that the Kaiser had abdicated. Once again his vision faded. Later, he wrote, "That night I resolved that, if I recovered my sight, I would enter politics." The medical authorities could find no apparent reason for this second bout of blindness and concluded that their patient, Lance-Corporal Adolf Hitler of the 16th Bavarian Reserve Infantry Regiment, was hysterical.

On Armistice night, or possibly the next night, Corporal Hitler experienced what he called a "supernatural vision." He said that voices had called upon him to rise and save Germany. Suddenly his blindness disappeared. Solemnly, he reaffirmed his vow to enter politics and direct all his energies to carrying out his sacred trust.

CLEMENT ATTLEE, later to become Britain's first Labour prime minister, celebrated the Armistice in an English hospital, being treated for boils.

In Paris, PABLO PICASSO and his wife Olga had spent the previous evening with the poet GUILLAUME APPOLLINAIRE, who was dying from Spanish influenza. Later Picasso said that he had painted his last self-portrait on the Armistice, the day that his dear friend Appollinaire had died.

LOUIS ARMSTRONG, the jazz trumpeter, was shoveling coal in New Orleans. He quit on Armistice Day.

CHAPTER 2

The Wall Street Crash

OCTOBER 24, 1929

1

1. Effects of the Crash, New York, 1929 (*United Press International*).
2. Facade of the New York Stock Exchange (*Miller Services*).

2

"**W**ALL ST. LAYS AN EGG," shrieked *Variety*, the American entertainment trade paper, on October 30, 1929 in a headline that for once proved an understatement. Wall Street hadn't merely laid an egg; it had killed the goose. The assault had begun six days earlier on what has come to be known as Black Thursday, the day of the great New York Stock Market Crash. October 24, 1929 ruined many—$9 million were lost in the first hour of trading alone—but more than that, it marked the end of America's cocky postwar prosperity. As well, the Crash blew a hole in the American dream, that lofty fantasy of affluence and opportunity that had lulled Americans through the bubbly, buoyant 1920s. Black Thursday, and the even more calamitous Black Tuesday which followed five days later on October 29, proved that the great economic pie had a circumference after all, and no, everybody couldn't be rich, and what's more, maybe the business of America wasn't just business. Although the financial fallout from the Crash eventually contaminated almost every country in the world, the story of the Crash is uniquely American. World War I had catapulted the United States to the forefront of power and influence. Only America had emerged a clear winner from that long and bloody conflict. She had suffered the fewest casualties— 50,000 battle deaths—and had reversed her economic position so that by war's end most European countries were in her debt.

IN 1919 THE ALLIES gathered at Versailles, not so much to discuss an equitable peace settlement with Germany, but to wreak revenge. Maybe they couldn't hang the Kaiser, but they *could* make Germany pay. And they did. By the terms of the peace treaty, Germany was burdened with the heaviest reparations in history— 132 billion gold marks (U.S. $33 billion). Germany (and indeed the other European nations) could only settle their enormous debts by selling goods abroad, particularly to the newly rich United States. But the United States made it difficult to pay up.

The America of the 1920s was stubbornly isolationist. Returning "doughboys" had first voiced the sentiment with the slogan "We've paid our debt to Lafayette; who the hell do we owe now?" The Republican-dominated Senate had agreed and refused to ratify Democratic President Woodrow Wilson's idealistic peace treaty and consequently threw out the whole idea of the League of Nations as well. America returned, in the words of the new president, Warren G. Harding, to "normalcy." And "normalcy" meant a kind of quarantine that slammed the door on anything foreign.

In 1920 the Republicans erected a lofty tariff wall which was pushed progressively higher until the Smoot-Hawley Tariff was enacted in 1928. As a result, foreign goods and materials became prohibitively expensive, and Germany and the other European countries, unable to sell their products to America, followed her lead by erecting their own protective barriers. Soon they were forced to borrow large sums on short terms—from America—just to meet the installments on their colossal debts.

By 1924 another Republican president, Calvin Coolidge, had declared that the business of America was business; it wasn't only businessmen who believed him. Money was the measure of success and the successful business giant the ultimate folk-hero or, in the case of Henry Ford, a demi-god. To be sure, there were other heroes in this new age—sports figures, movie and radio personalities—but the most tangible definition of success was the prosperous businessman. He personified the hardy American ideals of confidence, pragmatism, openness and optimism. To help him flourish, Andrew Mellon, the millionaire secretary of the treasury, repealed income, estate and excess-profits taxes. Business, it was argued, was hampered by these restrictions.

In the resulting scramble, some of the oldest businessmen— the farmers—were forgotten. Farm incomes declined from a postwar high of $15½ billion in 1920 to $5½ billion twelve years later. The squeeze almost put agriculture out of business. Organized labor didn't fare much better. President Coolidge once had stated grandly that "the man who builds a factory builds a temple. . . . The man who works there worships there." Certainly, American workers benefited financially—their wages shot up, and their working day was reduced to an eight-hour shift—but in other ways money was an easy and effective bribe. For example, employers tried to divert employees from joining unions by establishing benefits such as cheap cafeterias, group insurance, medical clinics and some small profit-sharing.

Technological innovations, not a burgeoning work force, were the key to the boom in American productivity. By 1925, Henry Ford could boast that his assembly lines produced a finished car every ten seconds. Wages proceeded at a more leisurely pace. While workers' earnings increased 11 per cent between 1923 and 1929, corporate profits zoomed by 62 per cent. And although auto workers worshiped at the right church, there was no prosperity for coal miners and textile laborers. At the end of the decade 71 per cent of American families made less than $2,500 per annum, the sum thought to represent the "minimum standard for decent living."

By contrast, the upper fringes of American society lived very decently indeed. For them materialism was a sacred creed and businessmen were its high priests, closely followed by engineers, advertisers and movie stars. America loved cars, films, jazz, Lindbergh, flappers, a chicken-in-every-pot, and more than anything else, America loved itself. The 1920s was an age of American narcissism. Nativist intolerance roared out against socialists, Blacks, Jews and radicalism of any sort. The narrow provincial decade saw the flourishing of the Ku Klux Klan, prohibition and fundamentalist religious fervor.

It was to this fat and sassy land that Herbert Hoover came as president in 1928. All the barometers registered prosperity and the forecasters heralded even greater times. Consumer goods, especially radios, automobiles, household appliances and cosmetics, were produced and, thanks to wide-scale advertising, purchased in steadily increasing volume. The new president, an engineer by profession, seemed the perfect man to run the country's political and economic machinery.

Americans believed they had a God-given right to get rich quickly, and in their naivete they swallowed any number of sucker schemes such as the Florida real estate bubble of 1925-26. There was money to be made from Florida's undoubted attractions—all of which suddenly had been made accessible by the automobile—but many of the thousands who flocked to the orange-juice state dreaming of a "fast buck" bought fantasies consisting of stinking swamps and shifting sands. Frequently they bought their land on "binders," that is, agreements to buy secured by a fraction of the purchase price. This scheme was profitable as long as there was a steady demand for land. But in the winter of 1926 a hurricane swept the state, and in its wake many of the skimpy developments lay destroyed. Overnight the Florida real estate bubble burst. Many investors were burned, but nobody heeded the warning.

Next came the nationwide craze for playing the stock market. "Buying on margin" was the new fad. In simple terms this meant buying stock by putting up a certain amount of cash with a broker (usually 25 per cent, but frequently less). The broker then bought the stock for the investor, but could call on him to cough up "more margin" at any time. The trouble was that the broker himself was forced to borrow huge sums to cover *his* advances. Demand by speculators also caused stock promoters to organize enormous investment trusts and holding companies which, unlike solid manufacturing concerns, had no real basis for their existence other than the making of speculative profits. As long as the market kept going up, and more and more people bought in, all seemed well. Soon "solid" companies were lending money at a good return to the extended brokerage houses, and by the end of 1927, brokers' loans stood at $4 billion.

A minor recession occurred in 1927, but once again few chose to recognize the signs of an ailing economy, particularly since prosperity soon returned, burying the unfortunate statistics in a further rash of stock market enthusiasm. America had a population of 125 million in 1928 and it was estimated that twenty-five million of them were playing the market. That figure seems a crazy exaggeration and could probably be quartered. Nevertheless, everybody from gardeners to bishops, movie stars to elevator operators, had a tip or knew an insider. "We in America," Herbert Hoover declared, "are nearer to the final triumph over poverty than ever before in the history of any land. . . ."

Rumblings of discontent shook the market during the summer of 1929. Production was down, consumer spending dropped off, and construction slumped. But the market went up and up, reaching its height on September 3. The gains were remarkable. Radio Corporation of America (RCA) stood at 505, up from 94¼ in one year; General Electric had climbed from 129 to

396 in the same period; A.T. & T. had jumped from 180 to 336.

Now a few voices began to call for caution. By the end of the month, stocks had fallen and margin calls had gone out. By Wednesday, October 23, something was clearly amiss. Six million shares had been traded and the fifty leading railroad and industrial stocks tabulated by the *New York Times* were off 18.24 points. "Normal—quite normal," said the experts. "The market is merely shaking out." The next day, many predicted, would tell the tale.

WALL STREET RUNS only eight short blocks. Because it is lined with tall buildings, it is known as the place where the sun never shines. An old saying skewers it nicely: "Wall Street begins in a graveyard and ends in a river." The New York Stock Exchange stands ten storeys high at the corner of Broad and Wall Streets. It has an imposing marble facade that is graced by six Corinthian columns, half the height of the building. They support a pediment where ten massive marble figures toil, each representing a different aspect of America's industry and commerce. In the center stands the outstretched figure of Integrity, the symbolic guiding light of all that goes within.

On that mild, cloudy morning of Thursday, October 24, 1929, the gong to signal the start of trading sounded promptly at 10:00 a.m. For a few moments all seemed well. Then pandemonium erupted as brokers and traders began dumping thousands of shares, at far below the closing prices of the previous day. More than two thousand people were wedged onto the trading floor, shouting and screaming at one another and into the telephones that linked the exchange to the rest of the country and the world. The stock tickers beat a melancholy rhythm, minutes and then hours behind the transactions, as stockholders shoveled their shares into the market at any price rather than produce the cash needed to cover the margin. The vast shaky edifice built on credit was collapsing under its own weight; the "leverage" had simply disappeared.

IN AUGUST, 1929 Winston Churchill had embarked on a two-month speaking tour of Canada and the United States. Like almost everybody else, he had been speculating in the American market and his letters home told of the small fortune he was making. However, when he arrived in New York on October 24 he quickly learned that all his money was lost. Fortunately, he had sold or arranged for £40,000 worth of articles to be published in American newspapers and magazines and so managed to write his way out of his difficulties. His account of Black Thursday for the *Daily Telegraph* is interesting, not the least because it is at variance with so many other reports.

> I happened to be walking down Wall Street at the worst moment of the panic, and a perfect stranger who recognized me invited me to enter the gallery of the Stock Exchange. I expected to see pandemonium; but the spectacle that met my eyes was one of surprising calm and orderliness. There are only 1,200 members of the New York Stock Exchange, each of whom has paid over £100,000 for his ticket. These gentlemen are precluded by the strongest rules from running or raising their voices unduly. So there they were, walking to and fro like a slow-motion picture of a disturbed ant heap, offering each other enormous blocks of securities at a third of their old prices and half their present value, and for many minutes together finding no one strong enough to pick up the sure fortunes they were compelled to offer.

The visitor's gallery was cleared at 11:00 a.m., but not before one man screamed and another bellowed that it was the end of the world. That morning a pall of ominous silence hung over North America and Europe; nothing was heard from the stock wizards, the securities kings, the soothing, confident experts. Outside the crowds gathered. They were orderly and quiet, but the expressions on their faces were grim as mourners.

There had been panics before, most notably in 1873 and in 1907. Then the great bankers had intervened and stopped the distress selling. They tried again now. At noon the senior city bankers met at J.P. Morgan and Co. to pool their resources (more than $6 billion in assets) and stem the hysteria. True, some were speculators, but that day they were moved more by public and corporate responsibility than by individual gain. Richard Whitney, exchange vice-president and a frequent agent for the Morgan interests, was placed in charge of more than $20 million. With these assets he went on to the floor of the exchange and with a singular sangfroid started buying U.S. Steel and other key stocks. A thin cheer went up as news of the bankers' bold action was flashed to the world. Slowly the market was soothed. By the end of the day some stocks actually made slight gains. The stock ticker banged four hours late that night, totting up the staggering rate of trade. Thirteen million shares had been bought or sold. Unbelievable. Thank God for Richard Whitney and the bankers, the heroes of the day.

British journalist Claud Cockburn, then a young reporter for *The Times* of London, was based in New York. On October 24, he was invited to lunch at the home of financier Edgar Speyer and his wife Leonora, a poet:

> We had swallowed no more than a mouthful or two of lamb when the noise in the passage became so loud that nobody in the dining room could even pretend to ignore it. A woman shouted, "Go on—or else!" and then the door was burst open and the butler, very red in the face, nearly bounced into the room as though he had been pushed violently from behind at the last moment. He closed the door and as collectedly as possible marched across the room to Speyer and in low apologetic tones begged him to come outside for a moment. Listening with an air of astonishment, Speyer, after a few seconds' amazed hesitation, left the room with him. Almost immediately Speyer came back again looking a little dismayed. He begged us to excuse him. The staff, he explained, had of course their own ticker-tape in the kitchen premises and of course they were all heavily engaged on the Stock Market. And now the ticker was recording incredible things. In point of fact the ticker was by that time running just over an hour and a half late, owing to the enormous volume of trading, so that the prices which the Speyer staff were reading with horror at a quarter to two were the prices at which stocks had changed hands at the very worst moment of the morning before the bankers had met and the formation of the bankers' pool had been announced.
>
> The staff saw their savings going down in chaos; since they were certainly operating on margin, they might at this

The Wall Street Crash / 39

moment already have been wiped out. Among the stock in which all of them had speculated was that of Montgomery Ward, and that had dropped from an opening price of 83 to around 50 before noon. And all this was going on before their eyes while their employer, reputedly one of the shrewdest financiers in New York, was calmly sitting upstairs eating pompano and saddle of lamb. They absolutely insisted that he go at once with them to the kitchen, study the situation, make telephone calls if necessary, and advise them what to do for the best.

Speyer left the rest of his lunch uneaten, and his wife and her guests finished the meal under conditions of confusion and makeshift which probably had never been seen in the Speyer household before. I left as soon as I decently could and did not see Mr. Speyer to say good-bye. He was still in the kitchen. I hurried to the office to write my story, beginning at last to be aware of what the great crash meant.

The next morning everybody knew something had happened, but nobody quite understood what. The newspapers thought the slippage had been spectacular, but not too troubling. One called it a "gambler's panic." President Hoover observed that the "fundamental business of the country—that is the production and distribution of goods and services—is on a sound and prosperous basis." One Boston firm placed a large ad in several newspapers that telegraphed the letters of every investor's hope: "S-T-E-A-D-Y." And steady it was on Friday and during the short session on Saturday when, for the most part, prices held.

The fat Sunday papers heaved a sigh of relief. Nevertheless rumors persisted. Eleven speculators had committed suicide; the stock exchanges in Buffalo and Chicago had closed; troops had quelled riots on Wall Street. The hidden reality was worse: thousands and thousands of speculators—large and especially small—had been ruined on the Thursday, and thousands more passed a nervous weekend in fearful anticipation. Churches all over the continent were packed.

Monday saw the market digest a huge backlog of selling orders and prices dove: A.T. & T., 34 points; General Electric, 48; U.S. Steel, 18. The most common statement was that things had to get worse before they were going to get better. They got worse the very next day. "Black Tuesday" became a standard against which to measure all other terrifying days. In the first hour of business three and a quarter million shares were traded, an amount equivalent to a normal day for the exchange. If the little man had been wiped out on the previous Thursday, it was the huge traders who were in trouble now. They dumped everything they had. More than sixteen million shares were traded in the panic, and this time the bankers did not come out.

Sidney J. Weinberg, a senior partner of the Goldman-Sachs Company, a leading American investment house, stayed in his office for one whole week beginning on Black Tuesday.

The tape was running, I've forgotten how long that night. It must have been ten, eleven o'clock before we got the final reports. It was like a thunder clap. Everybody was stunned. Nobody knew what it was all about. The street had general confusion. They didn't understand it any more than anybody else. They thought something would be announced.

Prominent people were making statements. John D. Rockefeller, Jr. announced on the steps of J.P. Morgan, I think, that he and his sons were buying common stock. Immediately, the market went down again. Pools combined to support the market, to no avail. The public got scared and sold. It was a very trying period for me. Our investment company went up to two, three hundred, and then went down to practically nothing. As all investment companies did.

Over-speculation was the cause, a reckless disregard of economics. There was a group ruthlessly selling short. You could sell anything and depress the market unduly. The more you depressed it, the more you created panic. Today we have protections against it. Call money went up—was it twenty per cent?

No one was so sage that he saw this thing coming. You can be a Sunday morning quarterback. A lot of people have said afterwards, "I saw it coming, I sold all my securities." There's a credibility gap there. There are always some people who are conservative, who did sell out. I didn't know any of these.

Winston Churchill saw a more dramatic scene:

Under my very window a gentleman cast himself down fifteen storeys and was dashed to pieces, causing a wild commotion and the arrival of the fire brigade. Quite a number of persons seem to have overbalanced themselves by accident in the same sort of way. A workman smoking his pipe on the girder of an unfinished building 400 ft. above the ground blocked the traffic of the street below, through the crowd, who thought he was a ruined capitalist, waiting in a respectful and prudently withdrawn crescent for the final act.

That brokers jumped en masse from windows is a myth. But some did, and many others swallowed pills, shot themselves, or revved up the family car in the garage. Most of the victims, big and small, however, lived with their losses. The late Groucho Marx was one of the losers. In October 1929 he was appearing on Broadway in *Coconuts*, making $2,000 a week, which he regularly plunged into the market.

All I lost was two hundred and forty thousand dollars. (Or one hundred and twenty weeks of work. . . .) I would have lost more, but that was all the money I had. The day of the final, convulsive crash, my friend, sometime financial adviser and shrewd trader, Max Gordon, phoned me from New York. In five words, he issued a statement that I think will, in time, compare favorably with any of the more memorable quotations in American history. I'm referring to such imperishable lines as "Don't give up the ship," "Don't fire until you see the whites of their eyes," "Give me liberty or give me death!" and "I have but one life to give to my country." These words sink into comparable insignificance alongside Max's notable quote. Never the frilly type of conversationalist, this time he ignored the traditional "Hello." All he said was, "Marx, the jig is up!" Before I could answer, the phone was dead.

Possibly the most succinct comment about the stock market came from singer Eddie Cantor:

Before the crash I had a million dollars, a house, three cars, and four daughters. Now all I had left was five daughters.

On September 3, 1929 the *New York Times* average of leading stocks had stood at 542, up 200 points since 1928. By November 1929 it rode at 224. Even so, who would have guessed that by July 1932 it would sink to 58? The fear and frenzy of New York had its equivalents in San Francisco, Boston, Chicago, Winnipeg, Toronto and Montreal—wherever there was a stock exchange and wherever there were investors.

Cab Calloway, the band leader, had just arrived in New York from the Midwest. He made the rounds of the clubs and finally found work at the Savoy, opening shortly after the Crash.

> By the end of the year, investors had lost $40 billion and more than 6 million people were out of work, 5,000 banks had failed, and 32,000 businesses were bankrupt. There were breadlines everywhere and near-riots in New York. Everybody was angry with poor old Herbert Hoover. Everybody except people in the entertainment world, I guess. It's a funny thing, when things get really bad, when the bottom falls out of the economy, that's when people really need entertainment. . . . The movie industry was making a mint, Broadway was having its best season in years, the record industry was cleaning up, and the number of concerts increased. I suppose that people figure, what the hell, let's go out and have a ball. It's one way to get away from the gloom.

Of course, some people survived. Among them was the financier Bernard Baruch who had come back to New York at the end of September from a shooting holiday in Scotland and had begun to sell stock immediately. "The condition of the market could be measured by its wild fluctuations, followed by assurances from every direction that all was well," he wrote in his memoirs *Baruch: The Public Years.* "But I had heard this lullaby before. I knew that the continuity of confidence was beginning to break."

Another who escaped with his fortune intact was the canny film-maker Charlie Chaplin:

> During the filming of [City Lights] the stock market crashed. Fortunately I was not involved because I had read Major H. Douglas's *Social Credit*, which analysed and diagrammed our economic system, stating that basically all profit came out of wages. Therefore, unemployment meant loss of profit and diminishing of capital. I was so impressed with his theory that in 1928, when unemployment in the United States reached 14,000,000 I sold all my stocks and bonds and kept my capital fluid.
>
> The day before the crash I dined with Irving Berlin, who was full of optimism about the stock market. He said a waitress where he dined had made $40,000 in less than a year by doubling up her investments. He himself had an equity in several million dollars' worth of stocks which showed him

over a million profit. He asked me if I were playing the market. I told him I could not believe in stocks when 14,000,000 were unemployed. When I advised him to sell his stocks and get out while he had a profit, he became indignant. We had quite an argument. "Why, you're selling America short!" he said, and accused me of being very unpatriotic. The next day the market dropped fifty points and Irving's fortune was wiped out. A couple of days later he came round to my studio, stunned and apologetic, and wanted to know where I had got my information.

In Europe it soon became apparent that nobody had realized how dependent everything was on the United States economy. Americans might have preached isolationism politically, but the capitalist system they advocated was based on a precise, interlocking global mechanism. Soon after the Crash United States investors called in their short-term loans. American capital export ceased abruptly as Americans dumped their European securities and stopped buying foreign goods. Thus the economic rug was wrenched from under Europe's wobbly feet.

The American journalist Janet Flanner, who under the nom de correspondence Genêt wrote a regular "Letter from Paris" for *The New Yorker*, described the effects of the Crash in Paris:

In the Rue de la Paix the jewelers are reported to be losing fortunes in sudden cancellations of orders, and at the Ritz bar the pretty ladies are having to pay for their cocktails themselves. In the Quartier de l'Europe, little firms that live exclusively on the American trade have not sold one faked Chanel copy in a fortnight. A wholesale antiquaire in the Boulevard Raspail has a cellar bulging with guaranteed Louis XIV candlesticks which are not moving. In the Rue La Boëtie a thrifty young Frenchwoman, who as a Christmas gift bought herself a majority of stock in the art gallery where she works, finds that all the forty-nine blue Dufys are still hanging on the wall and that it is not likely her stock will pay a dividend. In real estate circles certain advertisements have been illuminating: "For Sale, Cheap, Nice Old Château, 1 Hr. frm Paris; Original Boiserie, 6 New Baths; Owner Forced Return New York Wednesday; Must Have IMMEDIATE CASH; Will Sacrifice."

Generally, the French people's sympathy in our disaster has been polite and astonishingly sincere, considering that for the past ten years they have seen us through one of the worst phases of our prosperity—which consisted of thousands of our tourists informing them that we were the richest country in the world, that they should pay their debts, that we had made the world safe for democracy, that we were the most generous people in the world, that they should pay their debts, and that we were the richest country in the world. Only in a few malicious French quarters has it been suggested that now certain small American investors can afford to paste Wall Street stocks on their suitcases or toss them to the crowd, as they pasted and tossed five-franc notes here that marvelous summer when the franc fell to fifty.

The continuing strain on European banks became enormous, and in May 1931 the Austrian *Creditanstalt* suspended payments. Now the whole European system began to totter. Banks fell, industries laid off workers. Nobody could sell; nobody would buy. The crisis soon paralyzed Britain. In an attempt to restore her balance of payments, she abandoned the gold standard in September 1931. That year stock market prices in London were halved.

For countries which were primarily agricultural producers, the prospects were dire. The war had caused a sharp rise in agricultural production and prices, and farmers had taken out mortgages on land and bought expensive machinery on credit. But in the 1920s with Europe producing again, the opportunities for new agricultural markets vanished. Wheat was the hardest hit of all the commodities. The western world had more than enough wheat, but it couldn't (and wouldn't) sell its surpluses to the starving masses elsewhere because they couldn't pay the prices. Countries like Canada and Australia were devastated. In 1930 a bushel of wheat sold, in relative terms, for the lowest price in four hundred years.

The prescription for paralysis was simple: the lack of markets was bad not just for the farmer but for the transportation companies and the farm machinery industries. Reduced sales meant lower production which led to unemployment and small dividends. This in turn meant no reinvestment of capital and, of course, a concomitant reduction of goods and services. It was the classic vicious circle. No country, not even the vast, brave new U.S.S.R. could be completely insulated. The Depression, or

"World Slump" as some euphemized, was on; it wouldn't be shaken off for a decade.

What had happened? Folklore has indicated greed—both corporate and individual—as the arch villain who killed the prosperity of the 1920s. Certainly that is true, but it was more than that. The surge of credit, the gap between the rich and the poor, government intransigence, inadequate corporate structure, banking over-confidence and a sick world trade balance all played their parts. Perhaps if governments and bankers had taken swift, responsible action to control and stabilize the market in the months following the Crash, the devastating impact of the Depression might have been lessened.

The Crash has become a scapegoat for all the narcissistic fantasies of speculators in the great bull market, for the frenzied foibles of the giddy 1920s, and the naive and vaulting ambitions of all those who put nickels and dimes into the margins. The Crash said bust to an attitude. The businessman ceased to be a hero. Wall Street no longer symbolized the pinnacle of success, but became equated with foolish, irresponsible gambling. The Crash became the proverbial emblem of the Depression and helped to create a kind of "Depression psychosis" which moulded the thoughts and actions of a generation.

Could the Crash happen again? The conventional answer is no. Government controls prevent the rampant speculation that nurtured the bull market of the 1920s. Anyway, if the cynics are correct that you have to have a boom in order to bust, we should be safe for some time to come. As John Kenneth Galbraith, America's best known economic translator, wrote in *Harper's* in 1969, "What is necessary for a new disaster is only for the memories of the last one to fade and no one knows how long that takes."

On the night of Black Tuesday New York Governor FRANKLIN DELANO ROOSEVELT was guest speaker at a political dinner in Massachusetts. Everyone laughed when a bogus telegram arrived asking if the Crash would be blamed on the Democrats.

1

INSTRUMENT OF ABDICATION

I, Edward the Eighth, of Great
Britain, Ireland, and the British Dominions
beyond the Seas, King, Emperor of India, do
hereby declare My irrevocable determination
to renounce the Throne for Myself and for
My descendants, and My desire that effect
should be given to this Instrument of
Abdication immediately.

In token whereof I have hereunto set
My hand this tenth day of December, nineteen
hundred and thirty six, in the presence of
the witnesses whose signatures are subscribed.

SIGNED AT
FORT BELVEDERE
IN THE PRESENCE
OF

2

3

1. Edward leaving Buckingham Palace
   (*Miller Services*).
2. Crowds gather outside palace gates at
   height of abdication crisis (*National
   Archives, Washington*).
3. The abdication document (*Miller
   Services*).
4. Edward with brothers the Duke of York
   (on left) and the Duke of Gloucester (on
   right) at funeral of their father, King
   George V (*Miller Services*).
5. Marriage, June 3, 1937 (*Miller Services*).

CHAPTER 3

The Abdication of Edward VIII

DECEMBER 11, 1936

GEORGE V OF Great Britain, Ireland, and the British Dominions Beyond the Seas, King, Emperor of India, died on January 20, 1936 at Sandringham in Norfolk. For two days his body rested in the little church there, watched over by servants and gamekeepers. Then it was brought to London. At King's Cross Station, the coffin, draped in the Royal Standard and with the Imperial Crown resting on top, was placed on a gun carriage for the solemn procession to the Great Hall of the Palace of Westminster for the lying-in-state. As Edward VIII, the former Prince of Wales, and his three younger brothers marched behind their father's coffin through the streets of the capital, the Maltese cross atop the Imperial Crown worked loose, and when the Royal party turned into the gates of Palace Yard, the cross fell off and rolled into the gutter. "Christ! What will happen next?" the new king was heard to mutter as a Grenadier Guard quickly bent down and scooped it up.

Although Edward VIII was the most popular monarch ever to ascend the British throne, there were some who had misgivings about him and who were willing to see in the fallen cross a dangerous portent for his reign. Only a couple of days before, at the Accession Council that had proclaimed Edward king, Prime Minister Stanley Baldwin had wondered aloud to Clement Attlee (then leader of the opposition) whether Edward would "stay the course." Baldwin's remark was prompted perhaps by a comment George V had made a few months earlier: "After I am dead the boy will ruin himself in twelve months."

THE ARCHBISHOP OF CANTERBURY, Cosmo Gordon Lang, was also apprehensive, for the new king, who carried the title "Defender of the Faith," rarely went to church and often went to night clubs. What bothered father, cleric, and politician alike was that Edward, at forty-one, was unmarried, defiantly outspoken, and pro-German. Worse, Edward had a decided predilection for married ladies, particularly Mrs. Wallis Simpson, a twice-married American socialite.

Edward realized all their fears. Within eleven months of his accession, he abdicated in favor of his brother Albert, Duke of

York, because, as he explained to the world via a radio broadcast from Windsor Castle, "I have found it impossible to carry the heavy burden of responsibility and to discharge my duties as king as I would wish to do without the help and support of the woman I love." That said, he drove to Portsmouth, boarded the destroyer HMS *Fury*, and sailed to France and voluntary exile. He had fulfilled his father's prediction one month early, and by so doing made 1936 the "year of the three kings."

Ironically, Edward left England on December 11, the same date on which James II had sailed into exile 247 years earlier. But there the comparison ended. James II, because of his autocratic assumptions and his "Popish" ways—he had his son and heir baptised a Catholic—so alienated his subjects that they staged the "bloodless" revolution of 1688 and invited William of Orange and his wife Mary (James II's daughter) to become the new monarchs. By contrast, nobody, least of all the king himself, wanted Edward to abdicate.

BY THE MID-1930s it was apparent that the European postwar settlements had collapsed. The international economic community could still quibble about whether the world faced a "depression" or merely a prolonged "slump," but the reality was certain: continuing trade paralysis, scarce capital and high unemployment. The only palliative for national economies were massive government work projects. In America President Roosevelt introduced his innovative New Deal; in fascist regimes the initiative came from rearmament programs.

The first manifestation of fascist territorial ambitions occurred in 1935 when Italy invaded Abyssinia. The League of Nations, by failing to introduce effective sanctions, abandoned its principles and with them its effectiveness as an arbiter of international affairs. Then, less than two months after King Edward's accession, Germany repudiated the Locarno Treaty and boldly reoccupied the Rhineland. By May of the same year, Italian troops were in the Abyssinian capital of Addis Ababa and Mussolini could offer his sovereign, Victor Emmanuel III, the appellation "emperor" to add to his other titles. As if Europe were not in enough turmoil, on July 17, 1936 a garrison in Spanish Morocco rebelled, signaling the beginning of the vicious tangle of ideologies and emotions that marked Spain's agonizing and lengthy civil war. It would be a horrible and bloody preview of the larger conflict that many observers now saw as inevitable.

In the meantime the romance of Edward VIII and Mrs. Simpson had become headline news everywhere but in England; the newspaper barons, suffused with patriotic concern and led by Lord Beaverbrook of the *Daily Express* and Lord Rothermere of the *Daily Mail,* had agreed to a press black-out. It wasn't until December 3, 1936, one week before the abdication, that speculation about the king's marriage plans appeared in the British press.

But if the people were unaware of their sovereign's affairs, the government wasn't. As Neville Chamberlain, chancellor of the exchequer in Stanley Baldwin's Conservative Cabinet, complained bitterly, "For two precious months, while the Duce's son-in-law Ciano was at Berchtesgaden, while Germany signed the anti-Comintern pact with Japan, and while Fascist soldiers entered Spain, our ministers could attend to only one thing, the determination of King Edward VIII to marry an American citizen, who was bringing divorce proceedings against her second husband."

Edward might have been able to have his crown and Mrs. Simpson too. An English monarch, after all, had the right to marry anybody he or she chose as long as that person was not a Catholic. But Edward, although not as is frequently thought Head of the Church in England, did carry the title Defender of the Faith, and was sworn to keep communion with the Church. To the Church (and its ruling bishops) marriage was indissoluble; divorce and further remarriage therefore was impossible. What Edward proposed in marrying Mrs. Simpson—commoner, American and divorcée—had the potential to divide British and Commonwealth society absolutely, and to throw into doubt the whole institution of the monarchy. All sifted down to a power struggle between Edward and his prime minister, Stanley Baldwin. That Edward VIII lost the fight says much about his character, that of his intended, and even more about the prime minister's determination.

EDWARD VIII was born June 23, 1894 and christened Edward Albert Christian George Andrew Patrick David; his family called him David. He had a wretched childhood. His austere and aloof mother was quite devoid of maternal qualities, and his father, despite his public image as a kindly, devoted family man, was something of a bully. Both parents were determined to instill a seriousness of purpose and character in their children, but neither had any talent for the task. They concentrated so hard on character that they neglected intellect, and as for psyche, it was a meaningless and probably unknown word to George V and Queen Mary.

The future king was educated first in the Royal Nursery, then by a governess and later by a tutor. From this insulated environment David and his brother Bertie—two boys who had never known any children other than their siblings—were despatched to Osborne and later Dartmouth to be inculcated in the rough communal life of the navy. Abruptly in 1912, George V decided the senior service was too specialized for his heir and sent the boy, by now trained only to be a naval officer, to Oxford. Fortunately, David was spared the entrance examinations.

The First World War arrived two years later and it both saved and made him. The Prince of Wales—a title his father had conferred on his sixteenth birthday—loved exercise and had a reckless physical courage. He used both to advantage when he was finally allowed (by his father and Lord Kitchener) to go to France in November 1914. The prince wanted nothing more than to serve in the horrible squalor of the trenches as though he were an ordinary young man of his generation. This privilege he was, of course, denied. Nevertheless, he grabbed every opportunity to escape his relatively safe ADC duties and make his way, usually by bicycle, to visit the troops at the front. The men noticed and they remembered, and those who came back from the war carried with them an image of the Prince of Wales as a courageous, golden being.

The war sparked the myth, but the extended Dominion tours which the prince began in 1919 established it. He toured Canada, the United States, the West Indies, Hawaii, New Zealand, Australia and India, and everywhere he was swarmed over by young men who wanted to be his friend and young women who dreamt of him as a lover or, better still, a husband. He was the stuff of fantasy and no matter where he went he was cheered and grabbed and adored. The prince gave himself unstintingly to the people— at one point on his Canadian tour his right hand became so bruised that he had to shake hands with his left—although increasingly he chafed at the inexorable round of official duties.

His visits were so successful that he won even his father's grudging approval. More important, Edward saw the undeniable results of his personal diplomacy, and it fostered an abiding faith in the rightness of his instincts and opinions and a contempt for official advice. The tours had proven that there was an immediate and deep rapport between Edward and his people. He thought it was irrevocable. And it was—as long as Edward embodied the Prince Charming fantasy that his subjects demanded.

But what the people got when Edward finally became king in 1936 was not Prince Charming, but a middle-aged man given to severe bouts of melancholia, one who had no intellectual pursuits, no interest in or aptitude for the minutiae of diplomacy, and not much appreciation or understanding of his role as a constitutional monarch. Moreover, he was obsessed by Mrs. Simpson.

The Prince of Wales first met Wallis Warfield Simpson in the autumn of 1930 when Lady Furness—his current married friend— introduced them. About that time the romantic novelist Barbara Cartland and a friend met Lady Furness in the street:

> She was a close friend and I knew that she and the Prince of Wales had been in love with each other for a long time. He went nowhere without her. She was looking very lovely and elegant.
>
> "I'm off to America," she told us.
>
> "The Prince won't like that," my friend said. "What will he do without you?"
>
> Thelma Furness smiled.
>
> "I've asked Wallis Simpson to look after him. He will be safe with her."
>
> We walked on.
>
> "Wallis may not be beautiful," I said reflectively, "but I have known her ever since she married Ernest (Simpson) and she has bloomed fantastically—I think now she has an extraordinary fascination!"

It wasn't until six months later that Mrs. Simpson and her husband Ernest made the first of many weekend visits to Fort Belvedere, the prince's country retreat. By the spring of 1934, however, she was in the ascendant and soon London society was whispering and buzzing about her splendid jewels in their smart new settings.

Mrs. Simpson was neither beautiful nor brilliant. Neither was she young, being forty the year Edward came to the throne. Still, she had a rather vulgar wit and a vivaciousness and a magnetism that attracted people. Her background was genteel but poor and she saw in Edward's attentions, as she wrote in her autobiography *The Heart Has Its Reasons*, "an open sesame to a new and glittering world that excited me as nothing in my life had done before. . . . His slightest wish seemed always to be translated instantly into the most impressive kind of reality." For his part, the king was mesmerized.

By 1936 the Simpsons were so much a part of the new king's life that their names were published on official guest lists given to the Court Circular—indeed Mrs. Simpson had been invited to watch the Accession Ceremony from a room in St. James's Palace. Then in the summer of 1936, despite the unrest in Europe, the king and Mrs. Simpson took a leisurely Mediterranean cruise aboard the yacht *Nahlin*; Mr. Simpson had pressing business elsewhere. In October Mrs. Simpson divorced her husband, which meant, assuming her absolute decree was granted six months later, she would be free to marry the king before his scheduled coronation in May.

The king's ministers and his family were willing to accept a liaison such as Edward VII had had with Mrs. Keppel fifty years earlier, but it soon became apparent that what this Edward wanted was to marry the twice-divorced Mrs. Simpson and, what's more, to have the blessing of the state, the church and his mother. He was no match for such a triumvirate. If the king had been ruthless and insisted that there would be no coronation unless there were a marriage, he might have succeeded in his scheme. Unfortunately, he was so politically inept and so falsely convinced of the sagacity of his own counsel that he was doubly damned even before he began the struggle.

He had good advice, principally from Lord Beaverbrook, Winston Churchill and his legal advisor and friend since Oxford days Walter Monckton, but largely he ignored it. Instead, acting on a suggestion made to Mrs. Simpson by Esmond Harmsworth (Lord Rothermere's son), Edward asked his prime minister, Stanley Baldwin, to request that the Cabinet sanction a morganatic marriage, that is, one in which Mrs. Simpson would become the king's wife, but wouldn't share his rank; nor would any children of the union have any right to succession.

The morganatic marriage proposal required special legislation and the approval of the British and Dominion Cabinets. By taking this course the king was asking Parliament to sanction his marriage. It was a mistake, and Lord Beaverbrook strenuously advised him to withdraw the proposal, but as Beaverbrook wrote in *The Abdication of Edward VIII*, "When the King telephoned me late at night and told me Mrs. Simpson preferred morganatic marriage to becoming Queen, I knew my urgings were in vain. A morganatic marriage was what Mrs. Simpson wanted, and what Mrs. Simpson wanted was what the King wanted."

Vincent Massey, who later became the first native-born governor-general of Canada, was Canadian high commissioner in London at the time.

I had become aware of the crisis-in-the-making long before it became a matter of public knowledge—even before it was thought good manners to mention it at a luncheon table; Alice [his wife] and I had met Mrs. Simpson in the company of the Prince of Wales at Lady Cunard's house. The high commissioners were all kept closely informed of the course of events. My diary first mentions the crisis in an entry for November 23: "Geoffrey Dawson (*editor of The Times*) with me at 12 H.P. Gardens. Conversation on *l'affaire du Roi* which is nearing a crisis. . ." Three days later I was summoned by the Prime Minister, Stanley Baldwin, to Downing Street:

The King is determined to marry Mrs. S. What would Canada think? I told the P.M. that Canada would not like the marriage—that it would make a very bad impression—but I warned the P.M. about the King's great popularity in Canada which made it necessary that the whole matter should be handled with great delicacy & care if a collision took place on this issue between the King and his Ministers . . .

The P.M.'s attitude seemed entirely sound except in one particular. He doesn't seem to attach enough importance to the necessity of using the press as an all-important ally. He hates the press in rather a foolish way & even seemed to blame the newspapers for their (in my opinion) most admirable silence up to date.

Two days later, the British Prime Minister sent a cable to Mackenzie King, and to the prime ministers of the other Dominions, setting out the situation as it had developed and requesting their views. Mackenzie King replied on November 29, and on December 1 I called at the Dominions Office to hear the telegram from my P.M. in answer to the wire from Baldwin on the subj. of the King and Mrs. Simpson. It rejected both a regular marriage as well as the proposal for a morganatic union. But pointed out that the King's popularity in Canada was such that a collision between the King & his Ministers on the issue would have the effect of dividing opinion dangerously.

Inevitably the British and Dominion Cabinets all rejected the morganatic marriage proposal, and since the king resolutely refused to give up Mrs. Simpson, he was left with no choice but to abdicate. On December 5, 1936 he informed Mr. Baldwin of his decision, and the mechanics of the succession were set in motion.

The British press which had been silent for so long finally broke the news first in the provinces on December 2 and a day later in London. When the public at last learned the king's intentions, they separated into a rough-hewn division: those who didn't count much were for the king; those who did were against him. Baldwin set great store on the "official" opinions he received from the Dominion governments in response to his carefully worded telegrams, but nothing really was known of the average person's view. That would be seen only in the aftermath.

As the political machinations of the abdication and succession ground on and as Edward vacillated and Mrs. Simpson fled to France, the crowds in the streets generally seemed to support the king's cause. "God Save the King—from Stanley Baldwin" declared the signs held high over the heads of the well-dressed throng in front of Buckingham Palace. Newspapers were sharply divided over the issue. The provincial press and most of the London dailies—particularly *The Times*—remained solidly behind the prime minister, while the large, popular Beaverbrook and

Rothermere papers backed the king and called for morganatic marriage. Winston Churchill vainly tried to rally the king's cause in Parliament, where it was widely estimated that a King's Party of sixty members could be mustered.

Opposition to the king hardened, however, as people learned more about the lady from Baltimore. The idea of *their* king marrying a twice-divorced American became too much for many ordinary English men and women. That Sir Oswald Mosley and his British Union of Fascists on one hand, and the Communist Party on the other supported the king's cause confused and bewildered them. Members of Parliament who had returned to their constituencies that weekend of December 5-6 discovered, especially in the North, that the public mood, particularly among the working classes, was moving against Wallis Simpson. Then, as the new week wore on and the king hesitated further, public opinion moved against him. For many of his subjects the problem was simple: the king had to choose between them—his people—and her—the woman he loved. "Duty Before Divorce" became a popular slogan. Increasingly, the opinion was that the only honorable course for the king to reject Wallis.

Finally at Fort Belvedere on the morning of Thursday December 10, 1936 Edward VIII signed the abdication instrument—seven copies—and the King's Message to the Parliaments of the Dominions—eight copies—in the presence of his Royal brothers. Now there could be no turning back. That afternoon Stanley Baldwin addressed the House of Commons, outlining his view of the events. In the course of his speech, as H.G. Wells later noted, Baldwin cunningly transferred what should have been political disaster into a personal triumph.

All week Edward had requested a radio broadcast to appeal directly to his people, but Baldwin refused to allow it. Once Edward became a private citizen, however, the prime minister could no longer intervene. So Edward planned to broadcast a farewell message on the evening of Friday, December 11, 1936 before he left the country.

He spent the morning of the eleventh packing and working on his broadcast. Winston Churchill lunched with him, read his draft and added some flourishes to the text. They were still eating at 1:52 p.m. when the instrument of abdication was given final assent by Parliament and Edward VIII ceased to be king. He had reigned for 326 days. Later that afternoon Churchill, with tears in his eyes, recalled Andrew Marvell's lines on the execution of Charles I: "He nothing common did or mean/Upon that memorable scene."

The news of the abdication was accepted calmly in London, although the afternoon newspapers screamed the announcement in the largest type since the end of the war. Edition after edition was sold out, and as people gathered in pubs and clubs or massed in the underground or in train stations, the solemn talk was all the same. In cinemas the news was flashed across the screen. Invariably there was silence until the announcement was made that the Duke of York would succeed. Then applause and cheering broke out. Some theaters and cinemas substituted "Land of Hope and Glory" for the normal recital at the end of the day's business of "God Save the King."

That evening Edward dined with his mother, his brothers and other close friends and members of the family at the Royal Lodge, Windsor. Then, accompanied by Walter Monckton, he was driven to Windsor Castle, where they were met by Sir John Reith, director-general of the BBC.

> The former King seemed to be in a different mood from usual. "Good evening, Reith," he said. "Very nice of you to make all these arrangements and to come over yourself." . . . the civil war in Spain had not prevented Madrid ringing up to ask permission to relay his talk. That amused him. . . . In a little sitting room the microphone had been installed. Next door the engineers had their apparatus. . . . At half a minute to ten I sat before the microphone at the table waiting for the signal— the tiny red light that would bring the ears of the whole world into that little room. A thousand million people were there to hear what the man standing beside me was about to say. I thought with quiet satisfaction of the vast and flawless efficiency of the organization behind the now dull circle of glass. . . . "This is Windsor Castle. His Royal Highness the Prince Edward."
>
> I slipped out of the chair to the left; he was to slip into it from the right. So slipping he gave an almighty kick to the table leg. And that was inevitably and faithfully transmitted to

the attendant multitudes. Some days afterwards I was invited
to confirm or deny a report that, having made the announcement, I had left the room, slamming the door. It was even
suggested that, by so doing, I was not just forgetful of microphone sensitivity, but was indicating disapproval of what was
to follow. I had left the room, but no microphone would have
noted it. . . .

Then the ex-king began to speak:

At long last I am able to say a few words of my own.

I have never wanted to withhold anything, but until now
it has been not constitutionally possible for me to speak.

A few hours ago I discharged my last duty as King and
Emperor, and now that I have been succeeded by my brother,
the Duke of York, my first words must be to declare my
allegiance to him. This I do with all my heart.

You all know the reasons which have impelled me to
renounce the throne. But I want you to understand that in
making up my mind I did not forget the country or the Empire
which as Prince of Wales, and lately as King, I have for twenty-
five years tried to serve. But you must believe me when I tell
you that I have found it impossible to carry the heavy burden
of responsibility and to discharge my duties as King as I would
wish to do without the help and support of the woman I love.

And I want you to know that the decision I have made has
been mine and mine alone. This was a thing I had to judge
entirely for myself. The other person most concerned has tried
up to the last to persuade me to take a different course. I have
made this, the most serious decision of my life, upon a single
thought of what would in the end be the best for all.

This decision has been made less difficult for me by the
sure knowledge that my brother, with his long training in the
public affairs of this country and with his fine qualities, will
be able to take my place forthwith, without interruption or
injury to the life and progress of the Empire. And he has one
matchless blessing, enjoyed by so many of you and not
bestowed on me—a happy home with his wife and children.

During these hard days I have been comforted by my
Mother and by my Family. The Ministers of the Crown, and in
particular Mr. Baldwin, the Prime Minister, have always
treated me with full consideration. There has never been any
constitutional difference between me and them and between
me and Parliament. Bred in the constitutional tradition by my
Father, I should never have allowed any such issue to arise.

Ever since I was Prince of Wales, and later on when I occupied the Throne, I have been treated with the greatest kindness by all classes, wherever I have lived or journeyed throughout the Empire. For that I am very grateful.

I now quit altogether public affairs, and I lay down my burden. It may be some time before I return to my native land, but I shall always follow the fortunes of the British race and Empire with profound interest, and if at any time in the future I can be found of service to His Majesty in a private station I shall not fail. And now we all have a new King. I wish him, and you, his people, happiness and prosperity with all my heart. God Bless you all. God save the King.

By 1936 "everybody" had a radio, as political leaders (including Stanley Baldwin) were well aware. Edward's broadcast, however, was neither the ceremonial Christmas message that his father had initiated in 1932 nor was it the fireside chat that President Roosevelt had made famous in the United States. Edward's broadcast was poignant, dramatic, sincere—and news. Simply, it was the most effective use of radio to date.

The broadcast was aired, relayed around much of the world and repeated countless times. Like millions of others, Mrs. Simpson was in tears as she listened to a radio in the villa in Cannes where she was staying. In Australia, India, New Zealand, Canada, South Africa and every other British colony, an audience of some five hundred million waited to hear their king's explanation. His own family listened at the Royal Lodge and his mother, Queen Mary, recorded her impression of the talk: "Good and dignified."

Others were equally moved. Ex-Prime Minister David Lloyd George was vacationing in Jamaica. He said he was "deeply affected" by the broadcast and suggested that "we had got rid of a King who was too progressive." He was certain, "the new one would give them no cause for anxiety."

Helen Keller, the blind and deaf American lecturer and author, was in Scotland at the time. "The whole world," she wrote in her diary, "has listened to the King's farewell broadcast. I sensed a noble ring of veracity in his words and honored him for the frankness with which he spoke out his mind." But still she felt, "looked at from every angle, Edward VIII's surrender of a power he could have wielded is hard to understand. No doubt he has encountered a mass of difficulties that require constant thought and ingenuity. So much greater would have been his triumph in solving them.''

Lord and Lady Baden-Powell, were journeying to France, for the celebration of the 25th anniversary of the founding of French scouting, and both were apprehensive about their reception. On arrival they "were amazed at the way the news of the abdication was received.'' "You English are a wonderful nation,'' they were told. "You can change your king overnight without losing your *savoir faire.*''

Diplomat and historian Sir Edgar Vaughan was then part of the British legation at Barcelona. He remembers a certain "period of calm and order had been reached after the turbulence of the summer, with the militiamen in their overalls now at the front and a more regular Republican army coming into being.'' But Spain was still a country locked in vicious civil war, a cauldron of Nazi and fascist aggression. "When I did become aware of the Abdication crisis,'' he remembers, "it seemed to me to be an irrelevance beside the issues being decided in Spain, from which it tragically was turning away the attention of the British people.'' Nevertheless, as Sir John Reith noted, Radio Madrid, in a city under siege, had contracted for the link.

The Canadian author Lovat Dickson, who in the 1930s ran his own publishing house in London, was surprised to find himself feeling enormous gratitude to the king for leaving the throne without fuss, and with dignity, in order to avoid a constitutional crisis.

Perhaps he would never have made the great King we all hoped he would be after his golden years as Prince of Wales. I had driven him for three days in the Rockies in 1927 when I was a student working summers at Jasper Park Lodge. Our exchanges had been limited to a few words. Perhaps adoration for someone so supremely placed blinded me, but I fell for him hard. And he remembered me, for he recognized me three years iater in London when he almost ran me down as I was crossing Rotten Row in a daydream, and he had put his horse to a gallop. I had had a possessive love for him which I thought nothing would ever destroy. But I had become a publisher, and such judgment as I had now outweighed romantic notions.

He would certainly not be remembered as one of the world's great lovers. Was there to be no lasting place for him in the memory of men? No, only that glint of beauty and promise. There had been a million such, a whole generation, his, who had been shattered in the mud of Flanders. He came, only a little late, to that Nirvana.

We the survivors, grey-hued men not golden, were to reach ours later at Munich.

Donald Jack, the Canadian humorist, showed the insouciant innocence of a pre-teenager.

I was twelve years and four days old that day, so the event in itself did not mean much to me except insofar as it affected my parents and their friends. . . . There was an unnatural hush that Thursday [*sic*] in our house in my hometown, Radcliffe, near Manchester. Before the broadcast it was as if somebody had died, and us kids—two brothers and two sisters—weren't allowed into the drawing room where the radio was, as if to be spared the sight of the corpse. So we subduedly scuffed the Axminster runner in the corridor outside and listened through the door; but lost interest shortly after the voice started speaking. . . .

Later, however, I was the cause of a certain relief in the tension when I went into the room where father and mother and two or three friends were gravely discussing the speech. I piped up, "I heard a good poem about him in school, Daddy."

"Who, Edward?"

"Yes. It goes,

There was a young fellow named Ted,
Who took Wally-Wally to bed.
As they bobbed up and down,
He said 'Bugger the Crown,
I'll have Mrs. Simpson instead.'"

And that was my principal reaction to the abdication—bewilderment at the roar of laughter that followed after about ten seconds. I'd had no idea what the "poem" was about. Children of that age were a good deal less knowledgeable than they are today.

Of course, Americans had more than a casual interest in the affair. The incidence of courtship and even marriage between British aristocrats and American women was common, although normally the woman involved was rich, young and beautiful and

the man—of course—never before had been a reigning monarch.
Douglas Fairbanks, Jr. remembers that he was in London in his
flat in Grosvenor Square during the crisis:

> Earlier, I had been mixing with the crowds around the Palace
> and watching, as well as feeling, the anxious, confused and
> sad mood of the mass of people. By a fortunate accident, I had
> been spending a few days prior to the abdication in the
> country with a friend who was closely connected with the
> King and the Royal Family. Each evening I would, through
> him, get a fairly detailed report of how things were progress-
> ing at Fort Belvedere. . . . It was certainly an emotional
> moment to witness the improbable happen, which, even for
> an American (or, indeed, anyone of any nationality) was an
> incident of history not easily forgotten. . . . It was, after all, the
> King-Emperor of the British Empire, the largest empire
> known in the world's history . . . abdicating, reluctantly but
> voluntarily, for personal reasons rather than challenge either
> the constitution or the mores and faiths of his peoples
> throughout the world. It was a uniquely memorable moment.

Dame Fanny Lucy Houston, the British eccentric and phil-
anthropist, wrote in her *Saturday Review* that Edward should go
into politics as a private citizen and "do for Britain what Hitler
and Mussolini have done for their countries." *Le Figaro* in Paris
suggested, as did many others, that Princess Elizabeth would rule
with the aid of a Regency Council presided over by the Dowager
Queen Mary.

A Hollywood actress thought the event "out-Hollywooded
Hollywood," and made "Greek tragedy seem trivial." In New
York the stock market climbed, and taxi drivers ignored their fares
and pulled over to the side of the road to listen. Gore Vidal
remembers:

> I listened to the . . . speech while sitting on my mother's bed at
> Merrywood in McLean, Virginia. My stepfather H. D. Auch-
> incloss sat on the other side of the bed (the bed's owner was *in*
> the bed). All three of us wept. Later, I came to know the Duke
> of Windsor fairly well. He was uncommonly stupid even for
> his position in life; hardly worth a tear.

Dr. Benjamin Spock was a young instructor in pediatrics at
Cornell Medical College in New York.

I had been a worrier about national and international problems for some years. But when so many Americans became emotionally involved in the questions whether the King should marry Mrs. Simpson and whether Churchill [*sic* Baldwin] had the right to force his abdication, I was delighted to find this an issue of no importance, about which I didn't have to take sides.

Jazz pianist Dave Brubeck was sixteen and living on a cattle ranch quite isolated from the rest of the world.

My mother and her English relatives were quite astir with the Edward and Wally gossip. My older brother, who has since gone on to greater things, came home from college to play for us on the living room piano his first and only pop tune, "I Would Abdicate For You." I was more impressed with my brother's song than the event that inspired it.

Toronto businessmen were worried about the souvenir medallions, plaques, calendars and china plates they had ordered and stocked for the upcoming coronation. Some feared they would be rendered worthless; others were convinced the junky mementoes would rise in value and become collectors' items. They were, of course, right. Canadian newspapers fretted about the legitimacy of postage stamps and coins bearing Edward's image. In the province of Manitoba the minister of natural resources stayed up most of the night signing land grants to avoid the expense of printing new documents.

Lord Tweedsmuir—the son of the Scottish novelist and then governor-general of Canada, John Buchan—was himself living in Canada and working for the Hudson's Bay Company.

I was travelling with an RCMP Dog Team Patrol in North Saskatchewan, and had spent the night in a then remote Hudson's Bay Company Trading Post. There was one Mountie and a Special Constable besides myself. . . . We put the dogs in harness, and tied the team to the flagpole. . . . Then we went indoors to listen to the radio. . . . We heard the speech through and then went back to the dogs, whose breath was now rising in orange clouds in the light of the gathering dawn. Both my companions were in tears.

The Canadian painter Emily Carr wrote:

> We have just said goodbye to Edward VIII, our beloved King.
> Who is to condemn him, who to praise him? I do not think any
> public national event has ever moved me so deeply. I am glad
> no one was here at my radio. I cried from the deep of me.

By and large, the imperial press deplored the abdication but
applauded the new king. The Duke of York chose the name
George VI to remind people of the stable reign of his father, and
to minimize the inconvenience of his accession he took his
brother's proposed coronation date, May 12, 1937, as his own.
(His first act as king was to create his older brother H.R.H. the
Duke of Windsor. No such Royal rank was ever conferred on the
Duchess.)

In India the masses were probably unaware that they had lost
one emperor and gained another—nevertheless the press was as
much agog with the news as any newspaper in Britain. Occasionally, it offered an unusual and refreshing twist: *The Leader* in
Allahabad saw "no other" possibility to explain the "sad historical event," except the intervention of "Karma, or Fate if you
prefer. . . ." Rangoon, in Burma, was reported "profoundly
shocked," with "knots of people" gathering on street corners
arguing about the event. Some Asians saw danger signals. The
Bombay Chronicle labeled Edward as a "victim," suggesting that
he was forced to abdicate in "a denial of democratic principle.
King Edward's sacrifice at the altar of the undemocratic and
imperial prestige of the throne," the paper warned, "is a lesson for
India."

The *Australian Worker* saw the former king as the "Worker's
Friend." Indeed, Australia's Labour Party had been the first
imperial political group to rally to his side. The *Worker* wondered what Edward might do now. "Will he stand and fight with
brain and voice and pen for a larger measure of right for the mass
of his fellow men?" The Toronto *Globe and Mail* speculated that
he and Mrs. Simpson might live permanently on the Canadian
ranch he had bought in 1919.

Gregory Clark, a reporter for the *Toronto Star*, recorded the
reactions of the crowd in his newspaper's offices clustered around
loudspeakers especially set up for the event. He thought Edward's
voice sounded "absolutely shattering in the surprise of its tone:

slow weighted, filled with humility, sincerity and neighborly distress. . . ." When Edward declared "with all my heart," Clark observed,

> the girls in the packed room lifted small fists to mouths. The older women bowed their heads, the elder men's heads began to tremble on their stems. The ironic young men fixed their eyes upon the walls. As Edward intoned "as I would wish to do, without the help and support of the woman I love" all the young girls turned their heads suddenly. Now the older women lifted their fists to their mouths. Smiles of absolution appeared, strangely, on the faces of the older men. The young men's mouths moved as they muttered unknown somethings under their breath.

It was the kind of feature story that reporters lust after, and if they were like Clark, they made the most of it. On Saturday the major department stores took out full-page advertisements proclaiming the new king; but on the next publishing day all was back to normal and Christmas specials occupied the space.

The final word came from H. L. Mencken, the American critic and essayist from Mrs. Simpson's own Baltimore. He contended that Edward had been "an idiot" to give up the throne. However, since he had, Mencken thought "he ought to go to Hollywood. If he is too dumb to make good there, then he could go to Washington and become a member of the Cabinet."

Instead, Edward married Mrs. Simpson at the Château de Candé, in the Loire Valley in France on June 3, 1937 and spent the rest of his life in an aimless, wandering exile.

MRS. GEORGE KEPPEL, Edward VII's longtime mistress, was lunching with Victor Cunard at the Ritz. Somehow the text of the abdication speech Edward VIII was to make on the radio had been leaked and it quickly circulated among the fashionable diners. Mrs. Keppel was heard to remark, "Things were done better in *my* day."

1

2

1-2. British Prime Minister Neville
   Chamberlain returning from Munich,
   September 30, 1938 (*National
   Archives, Washington*).
3. Adolf Hitler declares war against
   Poland, September 1, 1939, in the
   Reichstag, Berlin (*National Archives,
   Washington*).
4. German officers interrogate Polish
   prisoners (*National Archives,
   Washington*).
5. German command post (hidden
   behind haystack) on first day of drive
   into Poland (*National Archives,
   Washington*).

3

CHAPTER 4

The Coming of the War

4

5

MUNICH: TO MANY THE WORD is synonymous with surrender and betrayal, for it was there on September 29, 1938 that British Prime Minister Neville Chamberlain and French Premier Edouard Daladier signed the infamous conciliation pact that ceded the Czechoslovakian Sudetenland to Germany. In the shadow of later events, it is easy to see Munich as the penultimate way-station on the road to war, but at the time, the Munich Pact was enormously popular and those arch-appeasers Chamberlain and Daladier were fêted and congratulated as the saviors of civilization—not just in Britain and France, but in Germany and Italy as well. In truth Munich did not guarantee that war would follow. Rather, it provided the poisoned atmosphere in which a general conflict could gestate.

Munich is important for another reason. It was a pioneer form of the summit diplomacy that has become commonplace since the Second World War. At Munich negotiations were carried out, not by representatives, but personally, by heads of government. Ironically, neither Czechoslovakia—nor its ally the Soviet Union—was even invited to the conference that transferred one-third of its population to Germany.

And, thanks to radio, Munich became the first international conference to be reported live to millions of people. During the two weeks of meetings, radio did more to alert the world to the implications of rampant fascism than any number of newspaper editorials or parliamentary debates. Radio brought the sound and the tone of Hitler's fevered exhortations, Mussolini's shameless bombast, and Chamberlain's wearisome accommodations right into people's living rooms.

Munich demonstrated as never before radio's ability to capture and sway a mass audience. A month later the full impact of that dramatic, day-by-day coverage reverberated throughout the United States when, on the night before Halloween, a radio dramatization of H.G. Wells's *The War of the Worlds* gripped a war-scared, depression-weary American public. Six million people heard at least part of the program, and one million actually believed that the world had been invaded by Martians, that thousands had been killed, and that large sections of New York and

New Jersey had been destroyed. They were terrified. The result was the largest display of civilian hysteria in American history as people fled from their homes and jammed roads in their panic to escape from the monsters. Surprisingly, nobody was killed.

The War of the Worlds showed that radio could be used to provoke and manipulate people's thoughts and emotions. More importantly it proved that the person in charge of the microphone could cajole, persuade, intimidate—in fact control—vast numbers of listeners. As communications theorist Marshall McLuhan concluded later, "Orson Welles's broadcast about the *War of the Worlds* was a simple demonstration of the all-inclusive completely involving scope of the auditory image of radio." Then he added, "It was Hitler who gave radio the Orson Welles treatment for real."

Ever since there have been mass media, politicians have grappled to control them as the easiest means of reaching and therefore swaying their constituents. During the Depression, American President Franklin Delano Roosevelt soothed and encouraged an impoverished nation through his fireside radio chats. Later, during the Second World War, British Prime Minister Winston Churchill broadcast hope and courage to the British public, but nobody exploited radio more effectively or ruthlessly than Nazi propaganda minister Josef Goebbels who controlled, among other cultural forms in the Third Reich, the complete broadcasting system.

THE SAME ALLIES who so generously and nobly had allowed Germany to march its armies off the battlefields in November 1918 convened only two months later in January 1919 determined to crush their former enemy at the bargaining table. Their bludgeon was the Treaty of Versailles. By its terms Germany was stripped of its colonies and of such valuable possessions as Alsace-Lorraine and, as if that weren't enough, handed a massive reparations bill totaling not only the costs of the war, but the peacetime occupation as well. Finally, and most hatefully, under article 231, Germany was forced to acknowledge guilt for the war. Germany signed the treaty only under protest and never accepted its terms as just or final.

Not only was the treaty vengeful and humiliating, it proved to be a catalogue of blunders, a settlement that failed to protect France from a remilitarized Germany and, by its clumsy dismemberment of the Austro–Hungarian Empire, created a power vacuum in central Europe leaving ethnic rumps in many newly created states. It was Marshal Ferdinand Foch, commander of the Allied Forces, who bitterly and prophetically declared: "This is not peace, it is an armistice for twenty years." Nevertheless, the Allies firmly if naively believed that the League of Nations, their newly created international forum, could and would settle any disputes arising from the realignment of peoples and territories. But America never joined the League and the Soviet Union was not invited.

The Wall Street Crash in 1929 and the slump that followed it dashed any hope that the fragile European postwar settlement could be upheld. The Depression threw between twenty and thirty million out of work, cut international trade in half, and toppled banks like straw huts in a hurricane. The failure of the interdependent international financial system saw European nations scrambling to shore up what they could of their national economies. In the end all they salvaged were their nationalist ambitions.

The German economy was in tatters in January 1933 when the aged President Paul von Hindenburg appointed Adolf Hitler chancellor and invited him and his National Socialist German Workers' Party to form a government. Only a dozen years before, Hitler and the National Socialists had been a mere fragment of the intricate German political scene—one of twenty-six recognized political parties—but through the 1920s they gained popular support from the depressed, inflation-racked middle class. The Nazis, as they came to be called, were a disciplined bunch commanding a mammoth and efficient propaganda machine which capitalized on rising unemployment and communist scares. They condemned the humiliating and crippling Treaty of Versailles and offered the people a convenient and universal scapegoat for the political and economic ills afflicting Germany: the Jews.

Once in office Hitler staged incidents such as the Reichstag Fire in February 1933 and the Röhm Putsch in June 1934 to assume emergency powers, first against left-wing parties and then to crush all opposition. On Hindenburg's death in August 1934 Hitler had himself proclaimed "Führer of the German Reich" and thus became head of state, prime minister and supreme commander all rolled into one.

Hitler believed that all of Germany's economic and social problems, particularly unemployment and inflation, could be obviated through rearmament, and in this conviction he was actively supported not only by key German industrialists but by the public-at-large. Less than a week after having been named chancellor, he declared his intention of using a restored German military might to grab new territories in the east. To a nation battered by the Depression, to a dispossessed middle class, to a proud race convinced it had been "stabbed in the back" at Versailles, there was an immediate appeal in Hitler's simplistic solutions.

ELSEWHERE, OTHER NATIONS were finding that aggression and totalitarianism served as economic spurs at home and as steam-rollers abroad. In 1931 Japan tested its super-charged militarism in a blatant attack on Manchuria. While the League of Nations remonstrated, Japan expelled the Chinese authorities and in 1932 established the puppet state, Manchukuo. Only Germany and Italy recognized the new regime, and Japan resigned from the League in protest. Germany followed a few months later.

In 1935 Germany, against the express terms of the Treaty of Versailles, reintroduced conscription. That same year Italy attacked Abyssinia. Once more the League yelled foul and indeed it even imposed economic sanctions, but as with Japan a few years earlier, bluster proved ineffective against armed aggression. Even now, nearly fifty years later, the questions remain why League members did not cut off Italian trade, embargo iron and steel and particularly oil, and why the Suez Canal was left open for Italians to supply their troops in Abyssinia. More important, why didn't England and France, who each had colonies to protect in Africa and Asia, rally more effectively against Italy?

In a shameful connivance, the British foreign minister, Sir Samuel Hoare, and his French counterpart, Pierre Laval, offered Italy almost two-thirds of Abyssinia in exchange for ceasing the hostilities. Abyssinia would be left a narrow strip of land giving access to the sea, something *The Times* later dismissed scornfully as a camel corridor. The plucky but doomed Emperor Haile Selassie appeared before the League of Nations and in an impassioned speech won admiration—but nothing more tangible. In parting he warned, "Us today, you tomorrow." One thing was certain, the League was moribund and the concept of collective security died with it. Italy, long departed in spirit, quit formally in 1937 and, with other ex-members Japan and Germany, formed a Rome-Berlin-Tokyo axis.

In the meantime, while events elsewhere screened his actions, Hitler sent 22,000 men into the demilitarized Rhineland on March 7, 1936, again in direct contradiction to the Versailles Treaty. France denounced the move, but did not mobilize. Had she done so, Hitler would probably have withdrawn. However, in the general uncertainty, France was not assured of Britain's support and she was fearful of the domestic consequences of engaging in a confrontation with Germany. So Hitler reoccupied the Rhineland, unopposed. But by now he had tipped his hand. It was obvious that his strategy was to bite off bits of territory here and there, first promoting an atmosphere of war by confronting and confusing his opponents, and then alternatively screaming and soothing until he was allowed to keep his spoils.

At home the Führer's racial decrees, cloaked in the jargon and practice of pseudo-science, had created a police state. In September 1935 he had enacted the Nuremberg Laws which divested Jews of their citizenship and forbade their intermarriage with Aryans. Jews were publicly baited, hounded from official positions, driven from their businesses and beaten in the streets by Nazi thugs. All of the other trappings of totalitarianism soon slid into place: a secret political police (the Gestapo); "Peoples' Courts"; concentration camps; fanatical youth movements; and the censorship of churches and the labor movement. These abuses, coinciding with a new prosperity and a massive propaganda campaign reinforcing traditional nationalist sentiments, combined to give the Nazis a kind of legitimacy.

Then in 1936 the Spanish Civil War broke out, and in England Edward VIII abdicated. Britain, France, Germany, Italy and the Soviet Union agreed not to intervene in Spain; only Britain and France honored their pledges. Germany and Italy saw Spain as a potential ally which could challenge France on two fronts (thus dividing her land forces) while threatening British naval supremacy in the Mediterranean. The situation in Spain soon slumped into a slow vicious grinding contest promoted by Germany and Italy on one side and the Soviet Union and scores of international volunteers on the other.

While war raged in Spain, Japan launched a full scale invasion of China in 1937 and threw back both communist and Kuomintang forces. The League again remonstrated, but America—since no war had been declared—did not adhere to her official neutral stance and provided loans to the Chinese government while selling war supplies to Japan. Then in February 1938, Hitler, emboldened by his alliance with Italy, determined once and for all to create the "Anschluss," the long brewing issue of the union of Austria and Germany which had been expressly forbidden by the Treaty of Versailles.

He summoned Austrian Chancellor Kurt von Schuschnigg to Berchtesgaden and demanded concessions and government positions for prominent Austrian Nazis. Schuschnigg, fearing a German invasion was imminent, acquiesced, then stiffened and announced he was calling a plebiscite on the question of Austrian status. Hitler, himself an Austrian, responded on March 12, 1938 by pouring German troops into Austria and then holding his own plebiscite. The Anschluss was confirmed by 99.75 per cent— Hitler had scored another bloodless victory, netting as a prize six million ethnic Germans. There were three million more in Czechoslovakia, in an area called the Sudetenland, an untidy remnant of the Versailles settlement.

Czechoslovakia was the only democracy left in central Europe. She was in a firm alliance with France. Together with Rumania and Yugoslavia she comprised the so-called "Little Entente," France's main prop in Eastern Europe. Moreover, she was rich in resources and possessed a well-trained army and strong fortifications.

Hitler began a loud campaign for the Sudeten Germans, whom he argued were ruthlessly persecuted by the Czech majority.

Germany, he thundered, was ready to go to war to protect this dissociated minority. The Soviets called for a strong stand, but the western powers, anxious about Soviet intentions and worried about Soviet abilities, vacillated. In the summer of 1938, the Czechs, under pressure from the French and British, made some concessions to the Sudeten Germans, but this did not satisfy Adolf Hitler, and by September 1938 the world was traumatized by "the Czechoslovakian question." Hitler's bluster became a daily test of British and French diplomatic and political nerves.

One person who listened to the radio and was frightened by what he heard was Lester Pearson, who would become Canadian prime minister in 1963. He was an official in the Canadian High Commission in London, which at the time was headed by Vincent Massey, brother of actor Raymond Massey. Vincent Massey and his prime minister, William Lyon Mackenzie King, were both strong advocates of appeasement. The other Dominion governments also favored this policy and would continue to do so until after Munich.

Pearson recalls how on the late afternoon of September 27, 1938,

> . . . when things looked very bad, as I left to go home to Fairacres in Roehampton, I noticed that the *Evening Standard* hoarding outside Canada House said in bold red type: "Keep calm and dig." It would be easier to dig than to keep calm. We had sent for our son at boarding school as we had decided that he and his sister should sail for Canada and safety on the first boat. That night Neville Chamberlain broadcast to the nation in such gloomy terms that the Pearson family was weeping as they were packing.

Charles Ritchie, another Canadian diplomat attached to the Canadian embassy in Washington, wrote in his diary on September 28:

> We are now on the very edge of war. Already my feelings have changed since I last wrote. Perhaps I am already beginning to suffer from war blindness. I feel more and more part of my generation and my country and less an individual.
>
> The war offers us no ideal worth dying for—we make no sacrifice for a noble cause. We fight with no faith in the future. It is too late to pretend (though we shall pretend) that we are

defending the sanctity of international obligations or the freedom of individuals. We are fighting because we cannot go on any longer paying blackmail to a gangster. Whoever wins, we who belong to what we call "twentieth century civilisation" are beaten before we start. We have had our chance since 1918 to make a more reasonable and safer world. Now we have to go and take our punishment for having missed that chance. We have willed the ends but we have not willed the means to attain those ends. That must be our epitaph.

Here in America it is "business as usual." Tonight I have been listening to the radio for hours. It reflects the stream of normal American existence, the advertising, the baseball games, the swing music, but every few moments this stream is interrupted by a press bulletin from Europe. More mobilisations. Hitler may march before morning. These warnings from another world give Americans shivers down their spine, make them draw the curtains closer and huddle around their own fireside thanking God that they are safe from the storm outside.

The retrospective diary entry written on Friday, September 30 by Harold L. Ickes, Franklin Roosevelt's secretary of the interior and a self-styled "curmudgeon," outlines the American position and shows that country's growing dependence on radio for news:

Late Sunday night [September 25] the President addressed an appeal to the involved nations of Europe in the interest of peace. He pointed out the serious social and economic results that would follow a general European war such as threatened. He called attention to the repercussions that a war would have even in such a country as the United States. He argued that differences between Germany and Czechoslovakia should be resolved at the council table and he urged that negotiations be continued until a solution could be found.

Following this appeal by the President, Hitler went on the air in a speech that came into this country the middle of the afternoon. I did not hear him, but, according to common opinion, he ranted and raved for over an hour. At times he seemed to be almost incoherent. He shrieked his defiance to the whole world, bragging of the prowess of Germany and its ability on the basis of its own resources not only to withstand any assault from without but to reach its objectives beyond its borders. He had made his demands and he would not abandon them by one jot or tittle. War seemed to be inevitable, with every tick of the clock bringing it closer.

On Tuesday at two o'clock Eastern Standard Time, Chamberlain went on the air. He talked for less than twenty minutes. A radio had been set up in the Cabinet room and the Cabinet sat there listening to the British Prime Minister. His words were carefully measured and several times his voice was at the breaking point. He spoke slowly and feelingly. He gave the impression that the tears were just beneath the surface. He declared that he was a man of peace who would not cease to struggle for peace until the very end. He would not pit the British Empire against Germany for the sake of Czechoslovakia alone if the issue between those two countries could be adjusted by negotiation. He would fight Germany if it were in Germany's heart to attempt to dominate the world. While he made it clear that he would leave nothing undone to preserve the peace, it could be seen that he felt utterly hopeless.

For Neville Chamberlain, who had succeeded Stanley Baldwin as British prime minister in May 1937, appeasement was the only means of avoiding a general war. Certainly it had been an honorable enough pursuit in the 1920s. Then it had represented an effort to be fair to a defeated enemy, reconstituted as a democratic Germany, by systematically slicing the reparations bill and compensating Germany for the more blatant injustices of the Treaty of Versailles. But by the 1930s appeasement had disintegrated into a shameless means of buying off aggression, of shielding one's own country from the costs of German, Italian, and even Japanese expansion at the expense of moral responsibility.

Neville Chamberlain and other leading politicians simply failed to realize that Adolf Hitler was not an ordinary statesman with "normal" goals and ambitions. They assumed he was a reasonable, logical fellow, one who could be swayed and mollified. Worse, Chamberlain, who had no experience in foreign affairs, was not willing to accept any opposing view—whether from Winston Churchill or Anthony Eden in the House or from professional diplomats or the intelligence services. Rather, he was driven by a strong moral conviction that he was—*right*. He listened only to those who reinforced his own opinions: Lord Halifax, Sir Samuel Hoare (rehabilitated since Abyssinia) and his personal adviser, Sir Horace Wilson.

Anthony Eden was in his seat in the British House of Commons on Wednesday, September 28 as members crowded in to hear Chamberlain deliver his version of Munich Week. Eden had resigned as foreign minister early in 1938 because he could no longer cope with his leader's personal style of diplomacy and because he opposed extending a conciliatory policy towards Italy without some form of compensation, such as the removal of Italian troops from Spain.

> A scrap of paper was passed along to [Chamberlain]. He glanced at it and then announced that Hitler had invited Mussolini, Daladier and himself to Munich. Members of all parties rose to their feet, cheered and waved their order papers. I did not feel I could take part in this scene, neither did Churchill, neither did Mr. Leopold Amery. As one who witnessed it all from a seat under the gallery wrote, "there doubtless were others." This was so.

And so the stage was set for summit diplomacy at Munich.

WILLIAM L. SHIRER was the best-known American broadcaster covering Nazi affairs. He kept a diary during the years he was based in Germany (1934–41).

> *Munich, September 30.* It's all over. At twelve thirty this morning—thirty minutes after midnight—Hitler, Mussolini, Chamberlain, and Daladier signed a pact turning over Sudetenland to Germany. The German occupation begins tomorrow, Saturday, October 1, and will be completed by October 10. Thus the two "democracies" even assent to letting Hitler get by with his Sportpalast boast that he would get his Sudetenland by October 1. He gets everything he wanted, except that he has to wait a few days longer for *all* of it. His waiting ten short days has saved the peace of Europe—a curious commentary on this sick, decadent continent.
>
> So far as I've been able to observe during these last, strangely unreal twenty-four hours, Daladier and Chamberlain never pressed for a single concession from Hitler. They never got together alone once and made no effort to present some kind of common "democratic" front to the two Caesars. Hitler met Mussolini early yesterday morning at Kufstein and they made their plans. Daladier and Chamberlain arrived by separate planes and didn't even deem it useful to lunch together yesterday to map out their strategy, though the two dictators did.

Czechoslovakia, which is asked to make all the sacrifices so that Europe may have peace, was not consulted here at any stage of the talks. Their two representatives, Dr. Mastny, the intelligent and honest Czech Minister in Berlin, and a Dr. Masaryk of the Prague Foreign Office, were told at one thirty a.m. that Czechoslovakia would *have* to accept, told not by Hitler, but by Chamberlain and Daladier! Their protests, we hear, were practically laughed off by the elder statesman. Chamberlain, looking more like some bird—like the black vultures I've seen over the Parsi dead in Bombay—looked particularly pleased with himself when he returned to the Regina Palace Hotel after the signing early this morning, though he was a bit sleepy, *pleasantly* sleepy.

Daladier, on the other hand, looked a completely beaten and broken man. He came over to the Regina to say good-bye to Chamberlain. A bunch of us were waiting as he came down the stairs. Someone asked, or started to ask: "*Monsieur le Président*, are you satisfied with the agreement?" He turned as if to say something, but he was too tired and defeated and the words did not come out and he stumbled out the door in silence. The French say he fears to return to Paris, thinks a hostile mob will get him. Can only hope they're right. For France has sacrificed her whole Continental position and lost her main prop in eastern Europe. For France this day has been disastrous.

How different Hitler at two this morning! After being blocked from the Führerhaus all evening, I finally broke in just as he was leaving. Followed by Göring, Ribbentrop, Goebbels, Hess, and Keitel, he brushed past me like the conqueror he is this morning. I noticed his swagger. The tic was gone! As for Mussolini, he pulled out early, cocky as a rooster.

In the final analysis what pleased Chamberlain most about Munich was not the agreement over Czechoslovakia. After that issue had been resolved, Chamberlain returned to see Hitler on the morning of September 30 and asked him to endorse a pledge that Britain and Germany would not go to war again. Hitler signed enthusiastically. It was this scrap of paper attesting to "peace for our time" and "peace with honor" that Chamberlain waved so ostentatiously at the new BBC television cameras and to the crowds at Heston airport welcoming him back from the Munich conference.

As Chamberlain's plane landed, the famed Lutine Bell of Lloyd's, rung only to tell the fate of ships at sea, pealed to symbolize that "the ship of state, foundering on the shoals of war, had been saved from disaster." The Lord Chamberlain greeted the prime minister and handed him a letter from the king which Chamberlain announced was a command for him to go to Buckingham Palace for a personal commendation. Cars were parked double for a mile along the road leading to Heston and two hundred Eton boys in their traditional black jackets, striped trousers, and silk hats formed an honor guard. At Whitehall crowds stood ten deep and many observers were reminded of Armistice Day. Londoners had been terrified and now they were delivered. They had expected war, not from the sea, but from the air, in the guise of German bombers, incredible machines which would wreak devastation like those seen in the currently popular film of H.G. Wells's *The Shape of Things to Come*. Plans for the evacuation of London were well advanced. Trenches were being dug in the parks and gas masks were ready for distribution. Leaves were canceled and the military and the fleet mobilized. All this horror and death and deprivation had been avoided as a result of one man—Neville Chamberlain. With his scrap of white paper he was a conquering hero, home without a fight. "The country has cheered Mr. Chamberlain to the echo, the country has thrilled to his German visit as a sporting and courageous step," wrote Lester Pearson. "It's a great picture; that of a 69-year-old Premier, taking his first trip in a plane, starting out to face Hitler, Ribbentrop, and the strutting ranks of Nazidom, dressed as if for his morning stroll in St. James Park, complete with black hat and rolled umbrella."

Television journalist Howard K. Smith, then studying at Oxford on a Rhodes scholarship, was on vacation in London.

> Unlike most Londoners I met who felt relief, I was outraged. I soon returned to Oxford and joined the only organization opposing Munich, the Oxford Labour Party (then the biggest student organization, with 1,000 members out of a university enrollment of 5,000). Such was my agitating zeal, that I was soon elected to head that organization, the first American to

do so. But my zeal died and the party fissioned into many parts
a year later when the Hitler–Stalin pact was signed.

Clement Attlee, leader of the British Labour Party, did not
want war but was most concerned that Czechoslovakia, the only
real democracy remaining in central Europe, would be swallowed
up. Personally, he didn't think that Hitler could be bought off,
but publicly he saluted the peace.

> It was on the 3rd October, 1938, that Chamberlain reported to
> the House of Commons on his visit to Munich. I recall that
> before the Prime Minister made his statement, Duff Cooper
> (later Lord Norwich) made a personal explanation of the
> reasons that had led him to resign from the Government the
> previous day. Following immediately after Chamberlain, I
> spoke at some length and perhaps the line I took can be
> summed up in a couple of sentences early in my speech: "The
> events of these last few days constitute one of the greatest
> defeats that this country and France have ever sustained.
> There can be no doubt that it is a tremendous victory for Herr
> Hitler."

Lord Louis Mountbatten was also embittered by Munich. He
was thirty-nine, a captain in the Royal Navy, and a vigorous
opponent of appeasement anxious that the Navy rearm with the
most modern equipment. He wrote to Duff Cooper after he
resigned as First Lord of the Admiralty.

> "I expect it is highly irregular of me, a serving naval officer,
> writing to you on relinquishing your position as First Lord,
> but I cannot stand by and see someone whom I admire behave
> in exactly the way I hope I should have the courage to behave
> if I had been in his shoes, without saying 'Well done.'"
>
> Even now people who thought as Duff Cooper and I did
> were few and far between. However, there was a certain
> awakening. Such rearmament as we managed to achieve really
> began now, after Munich—but there was not much time left.
>
> It was in this year that the Navy at last won its battle to get
> back the Fleet Air Arm from partial control by the Royal Air
> Force, which gratified me. It was too late in the day to get the
> new aircraft and all the things we needed before the war
> came—but better late than never!

H.E. Bates, the English novelist and short story writer, also opposed appeasement. He disdainfully described Chamberlain as "one who looked half like a Baptist church deacon and half like a provincial commercial traveller trying to sell sewing machines." With such a man in power he felt Munich was inevitable.

> For me it merely represented the culmination of almost a decade of foreboding, fear and finally fright. I was at a football match when I heard its cruel, sanctimonious, funereal knell and I wasn't far away from an impulse to shoot, if not myself, at least the guardians of "peace in our time." I thought greatly, then, of my children: my two beautiful daughters and my young son, impeccable as always in his cream shantung jacket. My world, which had at last seemed about to blossom to the full, was instead about to be blighted, together with that of unlimited millions of others. I conceived and shared no illusion whatever about this. War's inevitability had been as predictable as an eclipse of the sun. This was the eclipse and I was mightily, bitterly angry.

Writer George Woodcock, by the time of Munich, also believed that war would come,

> . . . and that when it came it would immediately destroy the world I knew. For the sake of that world, and for my own sake just as much, I longed for the day of reckoning to be postponed. And that was why, when Chamberlain went to Munich, I hung on the news; I got home on the crucial night, and found the radio had broken down, so that we—my mother and I—had no means of knowing what had happened until I went to the station on my way to work in London the next morning, and I learnt that Chamberlain had been successful in postponing the inevitable. I shall never forget the strange mingling of joy and guilt with which I and my friends faced each other on that day. We were relieved—and for the moment we did not care at whose expense we were relieved! And then we felt that we were betraying all we had said about resisting the Nazis. I suppose as a pacifist I was able to square my conscience a little more easily than the more violent socialists who expressed the same relief. It was Jimmy Maxton, the fiery left-wing Clydeside revolutionary, who spoke for us all on that

morning, when he thanked Chamberlain for having given the
young a few more months of life. But under all the guilty
euphoria was the sense that this was the last reprieve, and I do
not think any of us doubted that war would come or expected
it to be later than 1939. Munich gave us the pause that enabled
us to see the reality of history, so that the declaration of War a
year later was a definite anti-climax.

David Ben-Gurion was in London and greatly fearful of the
repercussions of Munich for Jewry. The problem of Palestine was
not likely to be settled by the appeasement policy, but it was
influenced by it. It is not too much of an exaggeration to say that
the British mandate in Palestine at the time was locked in civil
war—among Arabs, Jews and their nominal masters, the British.
On October 1, 1938, he wrote:

> There is no news from Palestine today. People here in
> England are rejoicing over the Munich agreement, which they
> think has averted a war. But I'm not happy about it. It's
> certainly good that there's no war. But this peace will cost us
> dear. Hitler has won a great victory, and his influence will
> increase all over the world. Nothing good will come out of this
> for the Jews and the workers.

Josef Skvorecky, the Czech novelist and film-maker who now
lives in Canada, was a boy living in Bohemia, close to the German
border.

> On the day of the signing of that agreement which started all
> consequent sellouts, first to the Nazis, then to the Communists,
> I was admiring the concrete fortresses on the Czech-German
> border about one mile east of my native town of Náchod, in
> north-eastern Bohemia. We, at fourteen, were fascinated by the
> tales of vast subterranean labyrinths hidden under the network
> of these Maginot-like giants that changed the cozy skyline of
> the mountainous countryside into Lovecraftian Mountains of
> Madness. With our mandatory gasmasks on we played at men
> from Mars—looking rather like flies from Mars—and sincerely
> hoped that the big guns encased in the ominously grey shapes
> would soon start spitting fire at the Germans on the other side
> of the border. To our great joy, the war eventually came, one
> year later, but the beautiful fortresses had been destroyed by
> then. Not in battle; by the German *Sprengkommandos* who
> were after their iron turrets. I understand these were then

melted and remade into tanks and *Panzerjägers*. I stood, under
the majestic ruins, with my father, at the highway leading
through my native town into Glatz (then Germany) and
further on to Poland, watching endless columns of German
army lorries packed with SS-men in a jolly mood who were
rushing into the *Blitzkrieg*. My father, a giant of a man, who
had been crippled in World War One (the battle of Zborov on
the Eastern front) lifted his walking stick and shouted at the
singing SS, in obscene Czech, the equivalent of, I think, "Up
yours!" They took him for an enthusiastic old *Frontkamerad*
and cheered back their "Haitlas!" and "Sieg heils!" Two years
later they were where my father had wished them to be. And
during that other campaign, further to the East, I saw my
demolished, beautiful, useless, fortresses again: on the screen
of my father's cinema. They were presented there, in the
German newsreel, as Soviet fortifications which could not
withstand the barrage of the long German railway guns. But I
recognized the graceful silhouette of the black mountain of
Dobrosǒv in the background, looming over my native town,
and was introduced to what Kuleshov used to call "creative
montage," whereby you create a convincing lie out of little
disconnected truths. The basic artistic method of any official
art.

Thousands of miles distant, Mahatma Gandhi wrote:

Czechoslovakia has a lesson for me and for us in India. The
Czechs could not have done anything else, when they found
themselves deserted by their two powerful allies. And yet I
have the hardihood to say that if they had known the use of
non-violence as a weapon for the defence of national honour,
they would have faced the whole might of Germany with that
of Italy thrown in. They would have spared England and
France the humiliation of suing for a peace which was no
peace; and to save their honour they would have died to a man
without shedding the blood of the robber.

Gandhi's countryman, Jawaharlal Nehru, talked with a
correspondent of *The Daily Worker* on September 30. He used the
opportunity to stress India's struggle for independence and gave
an imperial opinion very different from Canada, Australia and
the other white dominions.

Of all the people of the world, none is better able to understand and sympathise with the feelings of the Czechoslovakian

nation than the masses of India. India has followed this tragic drama of betrayal with intense interest.

From long experience her people have learned not to trust the promises of the British Government, and yet recent developments in British foreign policy have amazed and shocked them.

Apart from the final dramatic statement, Chamberlain's speech in Parliament was more remarkable for what it left unsaid than for what it said. Except for his perfectly right insistence on peace, his talk said nothing about the high principles and policies involved or about the international right and morality or about the maintenance of democracy.

Czechoslovakia is to be sacrificed, the Soviet Union isolated, and a clear field left for Nazi expansion, despite Hitler's promises towards the south-east of Europe.

Mussolini will no doubt ask for his pound of flesh in Spain and elsewhere, and Chamberlain and Daladier might, in the name of peace, agree to this gift.

Peace at any price—at the price of the blood and suffering of others, the humiliation of democracy, and the dismemberment of friendly nations.

Even so it is not peace, but continuous conflict, blackmail—the rule of violence, and ultimately war.

The British Government has been repeatedly talking about self-determination and even Hitler and Mussolini were laying stress on it. So are the people of India. Three hundred and seventy millions of them want this self-determination and independence. The people of the Indian states from Travancore to Kashmir are also struggling for their freedom but are being ruthlessly suppressed.

Future French Premier Pierre Mendès-France had been vacationing in a small, isolated Swiss village together with his wife, his children and some friends.

My most striking memory of this period is of Hitler's radio speeches. Even after the agreements were signed, the violence and fury of his tone of voice were significant and we all understood that he was leading us down the road to war.

I returned to Paris right after the signing of the agreements and was able to sense that strange atmosphere which Léon Blum later characterized as "cowardly relief." I had the opportunity of meeting Daladier who, even if he later accepted somewhat begrudgingly the popularity this event was to bring him, was not deceived by Hitler and told me that those who were happy with the peace were fools.

It became clear that henceforth anything was possible, that war was almost certain to break out and that we had better start preparing ourselves for this eventuality. I took the necessary measures to protect my family and started getting the town of Louviers (I was its mayor) organized for the worst possible calamity.

Edouard Daladier had indeed returned to France half expecting to be lynched. Instead he was fêted the way Lindbergh had been celebrated when his plane landed at Le Bourget in 1927. A great chant of *La Paix! La Paix!* went up from a crowd estimated at more than 200,000. Half a million more lined his route into the city strewing flowers in his path. Munich, everyone declared, was "the pact of peace." Finally, nobody proclaimed peace more joyfully than the happy Germans of Munich itself who, among their cries of *"Duce"* and *"Führer,"* also gratefully shouted *"Friede!"* over and over again.

· THE DECLARATION OF WAR—SEPTEMBER 1, 1939 ·

THE REAL TEST of peace, of course, was time, and through that autumn and winter of 1938, time passed quickly. The shoddy structures of appeasement and "peace for our time" were exposed in all their fatal weaknesses when Hitler annexed Bohemia and Moravia, the truly Czech parts of Czechoslovakia, and made them into a German protectorate. Finally, Chamberlain and Daladier were convinced that Hitler's promises—broken in fewer than six months—were worthless. At the same time the Spanish Civil War, after causing 600,000 deaths, ended with a fascist victory. Then on Good Friday, April 7, 1939 Hitler's Italian ally, Benito Mussolini, annexed Albania. The Munich Pact clearly appeared to be what one American journal, *The Nation*, derisively had labeled it: "The Peace to End Peace."

Britain now scrambled to redress the arms imbalance. Conscription was introduced, for the first time ever in peacetime, and massive rearmament programs were pushed forward in earnest. Finally, when a dispute arose over Germany's eastern frontier with Poland—the next logical step in Hitler's eastward ambitions

—Chamberlain and Daladier determined to take a stand. Britain and France both solemnly pledged to guarantee Poland's borders.

Having abandoned democratic, powerful Czechoslovakia, drawing the line at Poland was astonishing. Poland had no defensive borders—the stout Czech defenses had staggered Hitler when he visited them—and rather inferior armed forces. Besides, Poland was an oligarchical dictatorship run by a tightly knit politico-military clique. Moreover, in their disgraceful arrangement over Czechoslovakia, Britain and France had foolishly spurned the Soviet Union, thus alienating an essential ally in the defense of Poland.

Now in the fidgety spring and summer of 1939 France and Britain attempted a reconciliation with the Soviets. But Stalin, whose suspicions of western intentions ran deep, feared the West wanted to lure him into a war where Germany and the Soviet Union would batter themselves to pieces while France and Britain looked on. He was also miffed that the British had not sent a full cabinet minister for the talks and recalled that at Munich Chamberlain himself had flown to see Hitler. For their part, the fiercely nationalistic Poles wanted nothing to do with their Russian neighbors, and the British were unable to persuade them to give the Soviets free passage through Poland to engage the Germans. When the Soviets learned this, the talks stumbled and were broken off, and instead, on August 23, the Soviets signed a non-aggression and friendship pact with Nazi Germany. Stalin had bought time and an option on half of Poland. The world was stunned: those sworn enemies, fascist Germany and communist Russia, were in alliance.

The pieces were now all in place. Abyssinia had made war probable, Munich made it possible, and the Nazi–Soviet pact made it inevitable. Hitler now had only to choose the time. He didn't wait long.

LIKE THE FIRST, the Second World War broke out in high summer. September 1, 1939 was a Friday, the date of the Feast of St. Giles, appropriately the patron of the crippled, the poor and the insane. The incident which triggered the hostilities—the German invasion of Poland—was imaginative and ruthless. Hitler had a squad of S.S. troops, dressed in Polish uniforms, "capture" a radio station at Gleiwitz, a German town near the Polish border. They overpowered the local staff and then broadcast vague but menacing declarations in Polish announcing the Polish invasion of Germany and the capture of Gleiwitz. As the Germans withdrew from the radio station, they scattered about the bodies of some German concentration camp victims—the supposed Polish invasion force. In truth the hapless inmates had been dressed in Polish Army uniforms, injected with poison and shot full of holes. When the police arrived, closely followed by journalists, the incident was clear: Germany had been attacked and invaded by Poland.

Thus cruelly provoked, German forces struck Poland in the early dawn in a classic example of the blitzkrieg (lightning war) technique. Armored units acted as spearheads to punch holes in the Polish defense, and supported by the massed air strength of the Luftwaffe, more than a million men and their machines rapidly outfought, outflanked and outdistanced the unfortunate Poles. The outcome was clear even in the first few hours of the fight, and within a month the Polish government had collapsed and all resistance, even the valiant struggles of the Warsaw Jews, had been extinguished.

Neither France nor Britain moved quickly that first morning of September 1939 to support their Polish ally. Indeed it was difficult to do otherwise. Britain, at least, was bolstering a country half a continent away, and one to which she had no direct access.

In London, writer Gore Vidal recalls seeing Chamberlain:

> I stood in front of 10 Downing Street and watched Neville Chamberlain come out; he waved to a small crowd which moaned curiously instead of cheering, got into his car and drove to Parliament to say that war was at hand. Two days later came the declaration. He looked to me like a butler in an MGM film; the head was too small for the body.

Not far away diplomat Charles Ritchie was working at his office at the Canadian High Commission. Later he wrote in his diary:

A day which may have lasted a week or a year. It began when that severely black-clad spinster in my office handed me the *Evening Standard* with the text of Hitler's proclamation to the German army. Until then I suppose I had not really taken in that there would be a war. There followed an interminable period of sitting about. It was like waiting for a train that would not turn up. People made their appearances in my office, stayed and disappeared. Voices from what seemed to be every part of my life spoke to me on the telephone. It was like the anteroom to Hades in which one expects to run into an ill-assorted variety of company. . . . At seven in the evening Mr. Massey [the Canadian High Commissioner] came back from the House of Commons. By then there was a black-out. Three or four of us gathered in his huge office, its walls marked where the oil paintings had been removed to safety, its windows curtained. Mr. Massey stood under the vast chandelier. He was excited—unnatural or too natural, "We shall be at war some time tonight."

I dined in the candlelit gloom of Boodle's Club dining-room. All but two waiters had been called up. It was the first time in history that members were permitted to dine in the dining-room in day clothes. After dinner I emerged into the coal-black St. James's Street of Pepys or Dr. Johnson. Through the driving rain I walked along the Mall. I half expected to see a crowd outside the Palace, but its grey mass did not show a light. I hailed passing cars, unable in the blackout to see whether they were taxis or private cars. As I squelched through the mud by the park railings I thought that this compact city civilisation, inter-related like a switchboard, is overturned. One's friends join up or go to the country, sail to America, or evacuate school children. If you see a friend you cling to him. For when he is gone he is swept away, and God knows when you will see him again. Telegrams are not delivered, telephones not answered, taxis do not run. I suppose once the war gets under way we shall get back to more normal conditions.

Inevitably more than soldiers and citizenry needed attention as war approached. Biologist Sir Julian Huxley was secretary of the Zoological Society of London. He had been attending a conference in Dundee, Scotland in late August when "the news came over the radio that the storm had burst." He took the night train back to London and had his first experience of the blackout.

The first thing I did on my return was to see that the black
widow spiders and the poisonous snakes were killed, sad
though it was, for some snakes were very rare as well as beautiful. I closed the aquarium and had its tanks emptied; and
arranged that the elephants, who might well have run amok if
frightened by the expected bombing (elephants are very
nervous creatures) be moved to Whipsnade. I had previously
set up an air-raid squad of keepers, allowed by special dispens-
ation to carry rifles, to be on guard during the night to deal
with bombs and, as I had told Winston [Churchill], to shoot
any dangerous animals that might escape. There were, of
course, all sorts of minor but necessary details to attend to: for
instance, we had now to breed our own mealworms for feeding
insectivorous birds and mammals, instead of importing them
from Germany.

Officially, for the British, the war began on September 3, two
jittery days after the Germans invaded Poland—days of indecision
and uncertainty, of stalling and suppressed hopes. A British
ultimatum demanding German withdrawal from Poland expired
at 11:00 a.m. that morning and a similar French ultimatum
elapsed at 5:00 p.m. that afternoon. Australia and New Zealand
backed up the mother country immediately. South Africa declared
war on September 6, and the Canadians, to show their independence, waited until the tenth. Most people remember September 3
as the start of the war, and particularly 11:15 a.m. London time
when British Prime Minister Neville Chamberlain made a radio
broadcast that was heard around the Commonwealth and Empire
and even in isolationist America. He spoke in a low wavering
voice, in a tone of weary sadness:

> This morning the British Ambassador in Berlin handed to the
> German government a final note stating that unless we heard
> from them by eleven o'clock that they are preparing at once to
> withdraw their troops from Poland, a state of war would exist
> between us. I have to tell you that no such undertaking has
> been received and in consequence this country is at war with
> Germany.

Chamberlain's words weren't remembered nearly as well as
the voice in which he spoke them. Reaction to his announcement
represented less a triumph of radio's ability to inform than its

technical capacity to capture human emotions.

British journalist Katharine Whitehorn was eleven at the time.

> My task was listening to the radio bulletins and writing down all the stuff about blackout and evacuation which might concern us. And it was *exciting*. We were all dutifully praying for peace of course; but peace meant back to London in the same old way; war meant something different happening— my father was a schoolmaster in Mill Hill and they were to be evacuated to St. Bees in the event of war. And I realised that morning when the wireless announcement came (we were all in the big drawing room listening to that one) that I would have been disappointed if it had been peace. And was appalled at myself. But that was how it actually was.

Lord Kenneth Clark was sitting in a café in London's Charing Cross Road when he heard Chamberlain's "tired old voice" make the declaration.

> At last he had acknowledged the reality of evil which had been dumbly recognised by his countrymen for the last two or three years. I walked aimlessly through the dark, empty streets and found myself standing in Waterloo Place. I looked past the Athenaeum Club towards the park, and then up Regent Street. Piccadilly Circus, without its vulgar illumination, achieved a kind of pathos. The large, dull, office buildings took on a grandeur and fatefulness that I had never felt before. The banal thought passed through my mind that even if they were not destroyed by bombs that night they would before long be deserted and crumble to the ground. It gave me a curious feeling of elation. The social system of which these featureless blocks were an emanation was a worn-out monster founded on exploitation, bewildered by a bad conscience. It would be better to start afresh. At this point the figure of an air raid warden materialised beside me and flashed a tiny torch to see if I was carrying the regulation gas mask. "O.K." and he vanished into the night. The gas mask, of course, was never used, and not a pane of glass was broken in the buildings that had been the object of my philosophic reflections.

Canadian General E.L.M. Burns was touring France during a break in his studies at the Imperial Defence College in London. He was in Paris when he heard the news of the invasion of Poland.

Next day the roads were filled with tourist cars making for Calais, Boulogne, the Channel and hoped-for safety. Waiting overnight in Boulogne for the morning's embarkation, I looked from the hotel window shortly after dark, and saw groups of French soldiers marching to their rendezvous in the scheme of mobilization. But they trudged along in silence. No crowds to cheer the brave defenders of the country, as in 1914, hardly a passer-by to give them a glance. My impression was that the hearts of those men were certainly not in the war; the French sentiment for *la patrie* and *la gloire* had died in the barbed wire and machine-gun fire, the mud and blood in the trenches from 1914 to 1918.

Burns was back in England—at Eastbourne—in time to hear Chamberlain's announcement.

His melancholy accents, and the image we had of him as the umbrella-waving dupe of Hitler after the Munich agreement, all combined to depress. We were at war because Britain had to keep her word to an ally, but the deeper reason was that it was realized that Hitler had to be faced and fought, otherwise he would take over Europe piece by piece, with each bite making it harder to resist him.

There was nothing in Chamberlain's words or voice to make the heart beat faster, to instil a fighting spirit. That had to wait for disaster and for Churchill. The First World War had ended only twenty-one years before, and though victory had come in the end, in the years since 1918 it was of the victory's costs in men killed and crippled, of wealth and the means of creating it destroyed that most Englishmen thought. Pacifism seemed the voice of reason, and few thought it would be drowned by the bellicose oratory of dictators.

Like General Burns, Manning Clark, the Australian historian, was a commonwealth student in Britain. And like Burns he found nothing to cheer about in Chamberlain's words.

My wife and I were sitting in our basement room in 13 Bradmore Road, Oxford. We had very little money. She was expecting a child. We listened on the radio to the voice of Neville Chamberlain telling us, and millions of others sitting in rented rooms, that His Majesty's Government was now at war with Germany. I remembered afterwards his words: ". . . evil things we will be fighting against." What I could not understand was Chamberlain's smugness. I had been studying briefly in Bonn eight months before that and had some idea of the strength of the German Army. I also had seen what the Nazis had done to the Jews on the night of 7-8 November 1938 (Kristallnacht) and so knew at first hand all the evil the Nazis had "done under the sun." What gave me pause that Sunday morning in September in Oxford as Neville Chamberlain used the language and the pronunciation of the English governing classes for what should have been a people's occasion was to wonder then what was the answer to all the evil under the sun, labouring then, as Chamberlain was labouring, under the delusion that it was something outside me, and not knowing then the meaning of the words ". . .wherein we are all guilty."

Most Londoners listened to Chamberlain's broadcast calmly enough, but a good number soon began searching the skies for the Luftwaffe. There was an overriding fear that war would come from the air, showering destruction upon the city, blowing millions to bits or poisoning them with gas. In a cottage in Sussex, Lovat Dickson, the Anglo-Canadian publisher, and his wife were afraid.

> We sat on the steps of the cottage in the Sussex Weald, listening to the voice of the old man, broken with emotion, complaining that his trust had been misplaced, and that we were at war. If we felt anything besides a well-founded apprehension of what was to come, it was annoyance with the silly old fool for having been taken in by such a charlatan. We looked up at the blue sky, half-expecting to hear the rumble of an approaching air armada, which in ten minutes might pound Southeast England into submission.
>
> On the washing line the baby's nappies flapped in the gentle breeze. The small object slept peacefully in his pram in the orchard. Calm prevailed while life hung suspended.
>
> Then no sooner had the old voice ceased droning than the air raid sirens blasted their warning. It was a sound we were not yet used to. We heard later that at Westminster the members of Parliament gathered for the Prime Minister's speech dutifully trooped down into the air-raid shelters in Parliament Square, their gas masks at the ready.
>
> We sprang into action. We could hear the engine of an approaching plane. My wife rushed to the pram to snatch up the sleeping baby. I rushed to the clothes line to tear down the

line of nappies, the tell-tale of human habitation. Five minutes later the All Clear went. No explanation was given. Twenty million families all over England from the Wash to the Channel must have been caught in some ridiculous posture. Baldwin had said that the bomber always gets through. The press had prepared us for a massive bombing attack which would be bound to follow the declaration of war.

That false alarm served its purpose. We were in no state to fight, and for the heavy drama promised a farce was substituted. *Charley's Aunt* instead of *Lear*. There was no certainty of there being a breathing-space. But the mood veered. If these were to be the last months of life they should be lived with zest.

Loading up the old car, we started back to London. Waiting for a gap in the traffic where we joined the Folkestone Road, we saw that everyone was laughing.

Between 5:30 p.m. on that first day of September and midnight on the third, some 600,000 London children and teachers were evacuated to safe billets in the country. For most it was an exciting adventure, an unusual mixing of the social classes, and a confused journey with a strange bed at the end. That same weekend, thirty-eight million gas masks were distributed, buildings and walls were shored up with sandbags, windows were taped to minimize the hazards from flying splinters and fragments. Antiaircraft guns were set up in Hyde Park and on Hampstead Heath, and the trenches that had been dug during the Munich crisis and subsequently boarded over were opened up again. In makeshift hospitals doctors and nurses awaited the victims of air attacks, firemen stood by their equipment, air raid wardens manned their posts, and in towns and cities all over England blackout curtains were draped unceremoniously over windows. But only barrage balloons floated lazily in the calm, clear September sky. The Luftwaffe did not come that first day of the war, nor for some time afterwards. In a sense it had already won its greatest victory—it had terrified Neville Chamberlain at Munich.

Anthony Burgess was a young student at Manchester University at the time. He put his thoughts into a poem, hitherto unpublished:

The night before last was Saturday night —
The cinema queues were excited.

The newsboys yelled "Special!" with all their might;
Some gloated: "Going to be war all right,"
Elated, dilated, delighted.

Yesterday morning after mass
Chamberlain spoke on the wireless.
My brother was screaming of poison gas:
"Seal all the windows!" And while I was
Tired from the start he was tireless.

I had never seen it so dark before:
The streets had invisible craters.
Talk in the pub was about The War.
I drank until I thought no more
Of democracy and dictators.

I drank until I thought no more
Of death's impending dominion,
And so I said when a beersoaked bore
Complacently turned and asked me for
My own considered opinion:

"The King is only a cinema slide.
The soldier puts cunt before country.
Last night a drunk was run over and died,
A neurotic abandoned suicide,
And a child was raped in an entry."

Society photographer Cecil Beaton wrote in his diary:

I feel frustrated and ashamed. This war, as far as I can see, is
something specifically designed to show up my inadequacy in
every possible capacity. I am too incompetent to enlist as a
private in the army. It's doubtful if I'd be much good at
camouflage—in any case my repeated requests to join have
been met with, "You'll be called if you're wanted." What else
can I do? I have tried all sorts of voluntary jobs in the neigh-
bourhood, helping Edith Olivier organize food control, and
the distribution of trainloads of refugee children from White-
chapel. I failed in a first aid examination after attending a
course given by a humorous and kindly doctor in Salisbury.
Now I start as night telephonist at the ARP centre in Wilton.

American journalist Howard K. Smith desperately wanted to
get involved. He was in London when war was declared,

. . . living at Number 1, University Street, where Indian students from Oxford usually lived when in London—and I grew close to the Indian landlord's radio. I resigned my Rhodes Scholarship and got a job at U.P., which sent me on January 1, 1940 to Berlin, because I had learned German and had made Nazi Germany my central study. On the U.P. staff in Berlin, I replaced a young reporter named Richard Helms, who wanted to go home to the U.S. and seek a different career, which eventually climaxed in his becoming head of the CIA.

On that Sunday, Berliners too looked up at the sky and tried on their gas masks. Thousands of them headed for the city's urban lakes to soak up the sun or gathered in jammed cafés along the Kurfürstendamm. Their mood was somber, however. The man-on-the-spot for the British was Sir Nevile Henderson, His Majesty's Ambassador to Germany.

Up to those last twenty-four hours I had gone about freely in the streets of Berlin, either on foot or in my motor with its British flag; and I am glad to take this opportunity to bear witness to the fact that throughout those anxious weeks, and up to the very end, when we crossed the German frontier, neither I nor any member of my staff was subjected at any time to any discourtesy or even a single gesture of hostility. It was a very different eve of war from that of August 1914. Then a howling mob had surged in front of the Embassy, had broken its windows and hurled abuse at its inmates and at Great Britain.

    My impression was that the mass of the German people—that other Germany—were horror-struck at the whole idea of the war which was being thus thrust upon them. It is true that I could only judge of Berlin itself, and that I was not in a position to witness the reaction of German youth or of the soldiers in the troop-trains which were leaving for the Polish front. It is true also that the trial black-outs, the bread-cards, and the strict system of rationing, which was already in force, were not exactly cheerful beginnings to a war. But what I can say is that the whole general atmosphere in Berlin itself was one of utter gloom and depression. Every country has the government which it deserves, and the German people must share the responsibility for the present war with those to whose authority they so meekly and readily submitted. But they have a share also of the immense pity which I feel for all those who have got to suffer because the Nazi war party, which had been foiled in September 1938, won the day in Germany in August 1939, and because one man was ready to sacrifice their united happiness to the satisfaction of his individual lust for military glory, which must be greater even than that of Frederick the Great.

In order to see for myself the mood of the people after the attack on Poland, I went that last Saturday afternoon for a walk down Unter den Linden, the main street of Berlin. Few people were about, and everyone seemed completely apathetic. I happened to want a drug called "Codeine," and went into a shop to buy it. The chemist glumly told me that he could not give it to me without a doctor's prescription. I mentioned that I was the British Ambassador. He repeated that he was sorry, but the regulations on the subject were quite definite. So I said again, "I don't think you understand; I am the British Ambassador. If you poison me with your drug, you will get a high decoration from your Doctor Goebbels." The chemist's lugubrious face lit up with pleasure at this feeble joke and he at once gave me all the Codeine that I wanted. But there was something very pathetic about it. I had the same sensation when I left the Embassy for the last time. . . . About a hundred yards from the door there was always a policeman on point duty where the Wilhelmstrasse crosses Unter den Linden. At that particular corner the policemen, who were not members of Himmler's Gestapo, but mostly old soldiers of the municipal police force, used generally to salute me when I passed. That morning, when he saw me approaching, he carefully turned his head the other way and pretended to be preoccupied with the traffic coming in the other direction. He naturally could not salute me, and at the same time he did not wish to ignore me. He bore no ill-will to a man who, as he and all Berlin knew, had striven to the last for peace.

When in a body we left the Embassy, where the whole remaining staff—thirty men, seven women and two dogs—had been concentrated, on the Monday morning, a small crowd gathered outside and watched our luggage being put on to military lorries. It was an absolutely silent crowd, and if there was hatred or hostility in their hearts, they gave no single sign of it. There were doubtless a number of Gestapo agents among them in plain clothes, and yet the people were speechless, when a little vocal abuse of the "encirclers" and "warmongers" would probably have been gratifying to their masters. But the older people in Berlin had not been misled by Goebbels' propaganda: they knew full well that the Embassy had done its utmost to preserve the peace.

Once again there was hardly a soul to be seen in the streets all the way from the Wilhelmstrasse to the Charlottenburg station where the special train was awaiting us. The whole effect was one of apathy and unhappiness, or bewilderment. As Colonel Denis Daly . . . said to me, "This is a funny war." It was true: from the attitude of the German people no one would have guessed that we had declared war on them, or could feel that they wanted to fight us. The impression persisted right through Germany. In 1914 the blinds of the trains, provided for the British and French missions, had had to be kept drawn throughout the journey. This time they were drawn on only one or two occasions, when we stopped for a while at the larger stations, such as Hanover; but, as the conductor apologetically said, it was merely to save me from being inconvenienced by the curiosity of idle spectators. The older man in the street in Germany was stunned with horror at the idea of war. But, as one of them had said to me, "The others are too strong. What can we do? We are too small. We can do nothing." German youth may have been enthusiastic, but age certainly was not.

In Paris and the rest of France it was the same. None of the excitement and frenzied enthusiasm of 1914 could be detected— only the inevitable call-up, the crowded railroad stations full of troops, the tearful leavetakings, the black-outs, and the gas masks, scenes that were repeated in every town and city throughout most of Europe. There was a stoicism, a feeling that the job had to be done, but there wasn't much enthusiasm for it. Pierre Mendès-France remembers that he was upset, but hardly surprised since he had been convinced for a long time that war would break out and its impact would be worldwide. He arranged for one of his assistants to replace him as the mayor of Louviers, a town of 15,000 near Rouen, and then enlisted in the air force. "I immediately asked that I be assigned to a squadron as a flier," he recalls, adding that he was despatched to start his training at French bases in Syria and Lebanon.

In the British Empire and Commonwealth the news of war came without sensation. Special services were held in churches, and the aged militia of Canada and Australia were hastily mustered to guard "vital" bridges or buildings, but that was all. Australians and New Zealanders hardly expected an attack or bombardment, and consequently little public patriotism was

displayed. In Toronto a German exhibition was quickly dis-
mantled and the Royal Canadian Mounted Police began rounding up Nazis. French Canadians in Quebec, not unexpectedly,
were wary and sceptical of being involved in yet another bloody
European war, especially one which French-language newspapers
had been suggesting was none of Canada's business. Others were
quick to take commercial advantage. The Toronto *Star* of September 1, 1939 ran an ad which announced "In Peace or War . . .
Radio has become the universal channel of international communication." This accompanied a special offer for Rogers-
Majestic receivers—"$16.95 up."

But for most Canadians war brought only sadness and reflection—especially if they were themselves veterans. Architect Arthur
Erickson recalls his father's reaction:

> I was being driven across the newly opened Lion's Gate Bridge
> in Vancouver by my father when we heard of the Declaration
> of War. I remember, because I felt the weight of his concern for
> my destiny, because in the first war he had lost both legs above
> the knee and his life had been an unending struggle to rise
> above this handicap, live a normal life and bring up a family
> unburdened by his loss. I remember his resolve that evening to
> work to ensure that the new veterans would not suffer the
> humiliation and rejection that he had had to endure on his
> return from the First World War and I remember his urgent
> wish that it would end soon—for I was only fifteen.

Australian novelist Hal Porter was anxious to enlist, but his
flesh proved weak.

> One Friday in June 1939 I'm an accredited bachelor, the next
> Friday I'm married to Olivia, a woman I've known a week.
> The Bishop of Gippsland grants the Special Dispensation
> idiots marrying *tout d'un coup* require. We marry in St.
> John's Church of England, Bairnsdale, my boyhood country
> town.
>   I'm twenty-eight, immoderately healthy, perfect cannon
> fodder and, although able to keep myself in ungilded comfort
> have not enough also to keep, even in "amusing" Bohemian
> discomfort, the elegant and costly being I've recklessly acquired
> by marrying into a family of four glamorous sisters—a sort of
> Australian, pre-World War II version of the indestructible
> Gabors.

Extra money being needed, I elect to discard (temporarily, I promise myself) a snobbish resolve never to write deliberately for money. I go up to Melbourne, sign a contract to write for a wireless station twenty half-hour plays on famous assassinations, and set to work. Weeks pass. On September 1, 1939, after hours in the Melbourne Public Library working on Abraham Lincoln's assassination, I arrive very late, tired, and sober at the posh restaurant where the stinking-rich paramour of one of my sisters-in-law is celebrating something inglorious. The others, Olivia included, have reached a destination of champagne tipsiness it is too late for me to start for. I politely eat some turkey, sip a little *Moët et Chandon*, and am allowed to beg off. My youngest sister-in-law's fiancé unselfishly offers to drive me home to my flat and some midnight-oil-burning. At the restaurant the declaration of war news has caused no more than a ripple. In the car we off-handedly chatter of our intention to enlist. He does. I disqualify myself seconds after quitting his car: another one fells me. My value as cannon fodder drops to zero.

As a writer I resent the lack of war experiences. Thousands of men know something I never shall. Maddening that I'll never know whether the knowledge they have is worthless or priceless. Since I suspect it is priceless I can never not feel there is a hole in my nature.

Interestingly, in neutral America, New York City was placed on what was called a "war footing" by its colorful mayor, Fiorello LaGuardia, although in practical terms nothing happened. The streets were crowded and people stopped to gaze at the "Electric Bulletin" in Times Square giving the latest news of Poland and the invasion. Most Americans were grave, but hasty surveys revealed that they felt the United States should stay out of the war. At the World's Fair, business was brisk and the "Foreign Area" buzzed with activity. The Polish exhibit was thronged and many felt it was just as well that Germany was not represented. Canadians were reported to have stopped in large numbers at various public and police information booths throughout the city to ask how to get to trains bound for Montreal or Toronto so they might go home and join up.

Douglas Fairbanks, Jr. was with Hollywood's celebrated "British colony" when he heard the news.

My wife and I . . . had planned that weekend to join some friends in chartering a yacht to sail over to Catalina Island. Among these friends on the boat were Laurence Olivier, Vivien Leigh (she was not married to Olivier then) and her mother, David Niven, Robert Coote, and two or three other non-professional friends. The broadcast from London with Chamberlain's voice announcing the commencement of hostilities found not only us but everyone on every boat in the harbor and every house ashore silent, tense and grimly attentive. It was a moment which would defy the most articulate of descriptive talents. We all knew what to expect yet, for some reason, none of us were as fully prepared as we might have been when at last our worst apprehensions were confirmed. We just sat on the deck under the California sun in stunned silence, each one deep in his or her own thoughts. I venture to think that all those thoughts and emotions were pretty much the same. One of our number, I forget who, finally broke the silence by announcing that it was time for a drink. We then tried our best (we tried a bit too hard, I fear) to appear light-hearted, and we rather nervously made forced, silly jokes, which I suppose were a result of a controlled form of something a bit less than hysteria, but more than just ordinary shock. It wasn't long before we had all had more than our share of drink, and Olivier, who in those days looked like a younger version of Ronald Colman, decided he would be the harbor's and the yacht club's *Cassandra*, and began rowing around the anchored boats warning of the apocalypse to come. Eventually someone complained to the yacht club's Commodore that "Ronald Colman was drunk and insulting and must offer his apologies!" Unfortunately, poor Colman was in another boat, quietly minding his business (being, as usual, very unobtrusive and both shocked and embarrassed to find how he had been falsely accused of "shouting insults and proclamations.") Subsequently, we all found our common emotional refuge in the exchange of brave words and confident intentions. Within a week or so, Niven was off to Great Britain intending to rejoin his old regiment, and Olivier began taking a course in flying so that he could return immediately upon conclusion of his professional commitments and present himself to the Royal Navy as a qualified pilot, which is, indeed, what he did shortly after.

In the months following Germany's successful strike eastward it was only at sea and occasionally in the air that the war was hotly disputed. Neither England nor France struck at Germany during that time and western Europe slipped uncomfortably into the *sitzkrieg* (the "twilight war") or, as the British called it, "The Bore War." An Allied opportunity was allowed to slip away. By attacking Poland, Germany had left its "westwall" denuded of armor, aircraft, ammunition, fuel and first-rate personnel. By contrast, France alone had seventy divisions, more than three thousand tanks, and mastery of the air. But the uncertainty, fear, and timidity that had so paralyzed the democracies throughout the 1930s and had culminated in Munich continued to mar their judgment and reactions even after the war's declaration. In a way the "phoney war" was an extension of the appeasement policy— the Germans were free to conquer lands in the east as long as they left Western Europe alone. Some still hoped Hitler would be satisfied with his eastern gains and quit. It was the Führer's timetable, therefore, that took precedence.

The exiled German Kaiser wrote to his cousin Queen Mary, the Queen Mother, that Chamberlain "was inspired by Heaven and guided by God." It was the former Kaiser's first communication with a member of the British Royal Family since the end of the First World War.

American industrialist HENRY FORD refused to believe that war was imminent. On August 29, three days before Hitler invaded Poland, he told reporters that the European countries "don't dare have a war, and they know it. It's all a big bluff."

1. Wrecked destroyers USS *Cassin* and USS *Downes* in front of battleship USS *Pennsylvania*, Pearl Harbor, December 7, 1941 (*National Archives, Washington*).
2. D-Day plus 6. General Eisenhower (right) and other senior American officers inspect the landings, June 12, 1944 (*Library of Congress*).
3. Canadian troops landing with bicycles in anticipation of an easy dash inland, June 6, 1944 (*Public Archives of Canada*).

2

3

CHAPTER 5

The Course of the War

4

5

4. Hiroshima after the explosion (*Imperial War Museum*).
5. An atomic bomb of the "Little Boy" type dropped at Hiroshima (*Imperial War Museum*).
6. Mushroom cloud, 20,000 ft. over Japan (*Imperial War Museum*).

6

THE SECOND WORLD WAR had two phases: the bold, strategic victories scored in Europe by Nazi Germany and in Asia by Japan, and the slow, deliberate drive by the western democracies and the Soviet Union to push the aggressors back. It took mere months to accomplish the first; the second required years of dogged, bloody effort. Nothing exemplified the daring thrusts of the first phase better than the Japanese attack on Pearl Harbor in 1941, while all the internecine difficulties of the second were painfully demonstrated in the Allied assault on Normandy in 1944. The momentous decision to use nuclear weapons against Japan in 1945 could be defined as yet another phase, but the full implications of that action—apart from the appalling statistics of death and destruction—have not yet been fully realized. It may well be that the bomb has put an end to global war.

Like all conflicts, the Second World War had its ironies. Ostensibly hostilities erupted because England and France declared war on Germany for invading their ally Poland. Yet, six years later when the firing ceased and Germany admitted defeat, Poland was still not free. She was occupied by Soviet troops, the same armies that had fought on the Allied side. And in the east, the successful American offensive against Japan meant that the Chinese could throw off their oppressors; but unfortunately for American policy makers, the wrong Chinese—the communists— were the eventual victors. Five years later the United States, by now in firm alliance with those former arch-villains, the Japanese, was embroiled in another Asian war—in Korea this time—fighting the new enemy: Chinese communists. And, irony of ironies, only ten years after the war's end, a sovereign Germany—along with the other guarantors of Munich: Britain, France, Italy and the isolationist United States—was a member of the North Atlantic Treaty Organization (NATO), committed to defend Western Europe against the encroachments of Soviet Russia.

The Second World War was a total war, a conflagration into which every element of the society and economy of each of the belligerents (and of a good many other countries as well) was drawn—and had to be drawn—for a modern war like this one could only be conducted by states puffed up into superpowers.

But what really set the Second World War apart, certainly when compared to the inexorable grinding slog of the First World War, was ingenuity. More than anything else this was a war of technology, of science and industry used in a way that had never been seen before. And that made it everybody's war, the first great living-room war, in which bombing raids brought the front lines to the home front and the mass media took the home front to the front lines. Radio galvanized national sentiments and fears and brought outrage and urgency to the most remote part of the Australian outback or the tiniest American hamlet.

It was the first time that a war was fought more conclusively in the air rather than on the ground—from the blitzkrieg in Poland, through the Battle of Britain, Pearl Harbor, the saturation bombings of German cities, and the atomic drops on Hiroshima and Nagasaki. And behind it all, there was a secret war and a war of secrets in which deception and subterfuge were conducted on a massive scale. The Allies had the ULTRA secret, the body of intelligence they had derived from Enigma, the German decoding machine which they had secretly obtained before the war broke out. They exploited this advantage skillfully and at times ruthlessly. Germany and Japan, spurred by flagrant racial motives, were waging aggressive wars of expansion. The Allies fought for much more complex reasons, and as the war crested it became evident that Russian, British, and American strategic thinking was frequently divergent, as much motivated by preoccupations with the postwar world as with the world at war. While it raged, a basic commonality was maintained: the unconditional surrender of the Axis powers and of imperial Japan was the goal. To gain this end, every conceivable trick and technique would be employed. And once the war was won the winning of the peace would require even more cunning.

THE JAPANESE attack on Pearl Harbor on December 7, 1941 shouldn't have been a surprise—at least not to American military and political leaders. Japanese aggressive expansion had been in bloody evidence in Asia for more than ten years. True, the chief victim had been the Chinese, but both British and American business interests had suffered, and it seemed inevitable that a collision with either or both of the two western powers (or their allies) must occur—if not for moral reasons, then because of commercial ones. Besides, American intelligence had broken Japanese codes. By 1941 the Americans knew an attack was coming; the question was where.

JAPAN WAS an unusual society. Although nominally westernized, it retained much of its traditional society and culture, and despite a veneer of parliamentarianism, it was virtually a feudal state. Like Italy, Japan had ended the First World War on the side of the victorious Allies, and also like Italy, Japan would forge new loyalties over the next two decades. The war had greatly accelerated Japanese industrialization, and by its end, modern industry, increasingly controlled by the *Zaibatsu* (the great hierarchic family combines), existed side by side with traditional agriculturalism. Moreover, the Japanese had captured many of the Asiatic markets traditionally serviced by European colonial powers.

Like Britain, with whom it was frequently and favorably compared, Japan maintained a high standard of living by importing raw materials and exporting manufactured goods. The 1920s saw a tremendous increase in Japan's exports of raw silk to the United States and textiles to Britain and its empire. Unlike Britain, however, Japan didn't have that global empire. Its traditional foreign market was China, and when Chinese nationalists began erecting protective tariff walls in the 1920s to aid in "westernizing" their own country, the Japanese were worried. Then the Wall Street Crash of 1929 drastically cut American demand for silk and triggered an intense economic crisis in Japan. As a result, ultra-nationalist groups, highly critical of the moderate, liberal governments that had marked the 1920s, became popular. When Japan, at the London Naval Conference of 1930, accepted even further reductions in her fleet's strength than she had agreed to at the Washington Conference in 1922, these nationalists took to the streets denouncing the move as a national disgrace.

Circumstances and conditions were strikingly similar to those in another great victim of the Crash: Germany. Mass unemployment, social unrest, and a bleak economic horizon all contributed to propel militarists with their easy solutions to political influence and power. And the ready solutions were likewise similar: massive rearmament programs to swallow unemployment followed by aggressive expansion, if not commercially, then militarily.

Japan made its first expansionist move with the invasion of Manchuria in 1931. It was not only an attack on China, but an assault on the principle of collective security. Worse it was a territorial violation and a precedent that soon would embolden Germany and Italy to flout the policy also. Buoyed by their successes, the militarists consolidated their power in Japan and flaunted it abroad. In 1933 Japan stalked out of the League of Nations and in 1936 abandoned the Washington Treaty she had signed fourteen years before. At the same time, Japan declined to participate in any disarmament talks and willingly joined the Anti-Comintern Pact with Germany in November of 1936 in exchange for German recognition of the Japanese puppet regime in Manchuria.

In 1937 Japan presented the United States with an Asiatic equivalent of the Czechoslovakian question in Europe: she invaded China, seized the large peripheral cities and the main seacoast ports and forced both the government of Chiang Kai-shek and Mao Tse-tung's communists to flee into the countryside. A virtual reign of terror followed as the Japanese viciously strove to conquer huge, unwieldy China. Foreign observers, especially Americans who, as a nation, had had a running love affair with China for more than a century, were horrified as a full measure of modern industrial warfare was doled out including indiscriminate civilian bombing, rape, looting, torture and murder. Relations between Japan and America soured noticeably through 1938, and in 1939 the United States announced that it would not be renewing the long-standing Japanese-American commercial treaty of 1911.

What Japan needed most, not only in the struggle to subdue China, but also for domestic purposes, was oil. To attain it the Japanese seized the opportunities afforded by the war in Europe, and the consequent distraction of the European colonial powers.

Fuel for their war machinery, their industry and their commercial ambitions was in the oil-rich Dutch East Indies and the Malay Peninsula. In July 1941, after forcing a compromise with Vichy France, Japanese troops moved into Indo-China, opened the important port facilities of Camranh Bay for their invasion fleets and seized Saigon, the capital. They installed the usual puppet government, and cast covetous eyes towards the East Indies.

At first Prince Konoye, the moderate Japanese prime minister, tried negotiating for oil, with the free Dutch government, but the Dutch refused to deal with the aggressors and courageously effected oil embargoes. By way of response, the Japanese Imperial General Headquarters initiated plans to attack the Dutch East Indies from their newly acquired Vietnamese base. Then, on July 24, 1941, U.S. President Franklin Roosevelt demanded the withdrawal of all Japanese troops from Indochina. Two days later he froze all Japanese assets in the United States and then placed his own embargo on oil. In the meantime, amazingly, Japan had secured a non-aggression treaty with its old enemy, the Soviet Union.

In October 1941 the rigid imperialist and militarist General Hideki Tojo became Japanese prime minister. He was slight, buck-toothed and bespectacled. The very personification of the American image of the Japanese, he was nicknamed "The Razor." For Tojo and the tight knot of supporters who clung to him, the oil embargoes made war inevitable. Oil was the only way to ensure the survival of Japan and her putative empire—a massive swath of oceanic territories in the Western Pacific and South and Southeast Asia. Tojo had no intention of conquering or even invading the United States. Rather, he wanted to wage war as a popular crusade to drive all westerners from Asia. His strategy was to knock out the American fleet and then to destroy the smaller British, Dutch and Australian forces, and then with those nations wearying of what the Japanese were certain would be an unpopular struggle, drive a good bargain at the conference table.

But where to strike? For a naval power like Japan, the answer was obvious and, indeed, had always been so: hit the Americans in their chief Pacific bases. In fact, planning an attack on the American fleet's main base at Pearl Harbor had been a regular feature of the final examinations in Japanese military academies throughout the 1930s.

By the autumn of 1941 both sides needed time for war preparations so the oil negotiations were purposefully dragged out in Washington. In mid-November Admiral Isoroku Yamamoto, commander-in-chief of the Japanese fleet, began to collect his forces, and on the 26th he struck out into the stormy North Pacific with a fleet of six aircraft carriers, two battleships, three cruisers, nine destroyers, a squadron of midget submarines, eight oilers and a general supply vessel. The date of the projected attack was December 8, 1941—December 7, Pearl Harbor time. That morning, the Japanese fleet was 230 miles from its target, in the same position as the aggressors had used in American war games in 1932. As the men cheered, the Japanese carriers swung round into the wind and launched two full strikes of torpedo and dive-bombers. By 7:54 a.m. Hawaii time the rising sun emblems on the wings of the planes could be seen over a still slumbering Pearl Harbor.

In the space of two hours more than 350 carrier planes swept over the island skillfully splitting up so that the sorties and bombing raids came from every direction. There were 94 ships of the United States Navy in Pearl Harbor that morning. When the Japanese were finished, they had sunk or crippled 19, destroyed or damaged 349 aircraft, and killed more than 2,400 civilians and military personnel. Their prime targets were eight battleships. Of these, the *Arizona* was blown up, the *Oklahoma* capsized, the *California* and *West Virginia* sunk at their moorings, and all the others were damaged. The only bright spot for the Americans was the failure of the accompanying Japanese submarine attack. Five, possibly six Japanese midget ships were destroyed, and it was probably because of this poor performance that the Japanese never launched a concentrated submarine building program to compare with that of their Nazi allies.

The raid was devastating, but it was not the mortal blow that Japan had intended. The bombers failed to destroy the mammoth American oil storage depots in Hawaii and missed the four large Pacific Fleet aircraft carriers which were away from the harbor on maneuvers. Their survival would prove decisive and their escape underlined the limitations of the Japanese intelligence service.

What Pearl Harbor exposed was America's cocky and foolishly complacent attitude in the face of the concrete threat of war. Astonishingly, Admiral H.E. Kimmel, the U.S. commander of Pearl Harbor, had not even put the base on a war-footing. He knew the dangers. Nevertheless, men were allowed shore leave right up to the night before the attack, and no extra air reconnaissance or sea patrols were ordered. Indeed, among top American military leaders there seemed to be a defiant resistance even to the idea that Pearl Harbor could be a prime Japanese target. The Americans thought their base was invincible, and they assumed the Japanese thought so too. When U.S. Chief of Staff General George Marshall was told of the bombing raids, he was incredulous and suggested the reports must be wrong, surely it was Singapore that was under attack. Finally, Pearl Harbor revealed the destructive rivalries and inadequate liaison among the U.S. Armed Forces. At 4:50 a.m. on December 7, a Japanese midget submarine had been detected entering the harbor gates, but amazingly, no alarm was sounded. And most damning of all, at 7 a.m. Japanese planes had been spotted on radar by two privates who reported that a large number of aircraft—close to 140—were approaching the island. The army dismissed the report as a flight of navy planes, or perhaps a group of B-17s which were expected from the mainland, or more likely a mistake made by two inexperienced soldiers. A mistake had been made, all right, probably the biggest interservice foul-up of the entire war.

The Japanese plan had been carefully coordinated. At precisely 1:00 p.m. on December 7, Washington time, Japanese Ambassador Admiral Nomura was supposed to give U.S. Secretary of State Cordell Hull an official notice that negotiations between the two countries were at an end. The bombs were to start dropping twenty minutes later. But Admiral Nomura's staff didn't finish decoding, translating and transcribing the official note until Sunday, and consequently Nomura did not reach Hull's office until 2:21 p.m., a good hour late. Hull, well aware of the ongoing attack, glanced at the message proffered by the Japanese ambassador (who explained apologetically that it should have been delivered at 1:00 p.m.) and, trembling with anger, declared that in his "fifty years of public service" he had "never seen a document that was more crowded with infamous falsehoods and distortions." He curtly dismissed Nomura.

Thanks to a few sloppy and inept clerks the attack on Pearl Harbor violated the polite conventions of war among civilized countries, the etiquette that demanded a nation should give a proper warning and a declaration before unleashing military action against another. So it became a sneak attack, a diplomatic blunder that would change the course of the war. For Americans, the bombing of Pearl Harbor became a monumental symbol of Japanese treachery, as President Roosevelt put it, "a day of infamy," one that would meld the entire nation to one purpose: destroying the Japanese.

MOST AMERICANS heard about the attack on Pearl Harbor on their radios. A lot of them didn't even know where it was. Only one network, the Mutual Broadcasting System, broke into its regular broadcast—a football game—to deliver the flash; others waited for the news break. In the east that came at 2:30 p.m. Many who missed the bulletin learned of the crisis when they tuned in for the CBS presentation of the New York Philharmonic at three o'clock. Artur Rubinstein was the soloist that afternoon. He played the Brahms Second Piano Concerto with Artur Rodzinski conducting. At the end, the CBS announcer, Warren Sweeney, walked on stage and asked Rubinstein to read an announcement. But Rubinstein looked at the paper, blanched and shook his head. Although he wasn't officially a citizen yet, he felt American both emotionally and spiritually.

Instead Sweeney, himself, read the bulletin that would be the first general news of the Japanese attack. The audience was stunned and some people wept. Suddenly Artur Rodzinski turned to the orchestra and in a spontaneous patriotic gesture struck up "The Stars and Stripes Forever."

In Washington Margaret Truman, the vice-president's daughter, was nursing a cold:

> I stayed in the house and listened to the New York Philhar-
> monic, simultaneously telling myself I should be doing my
> homework. Suddenly there was a voice interrupting the lovely

music, announcing that Japanese planes had attacked some obscure, distant place known as Pearl Harbor. Since the Japanese had been attacking China for over three years, and Pearl Harbor sounded Chinese to me, I couldn't see what all the fuss was about. Mother wandered by, and I remarked crossly that the network had a heck of a nerve, interrupting good music to talk about a foreign war. . . .

My mother gasped and rushed for the telephone. The next thing I heard was her voice excitedly talking to my father in Missouri, telling him that the Japanese were attacking Hawaii.

Out in the Pennant Hotel in Columbia, Missouri, Dad put on his clothes and raced across the road to a private airport, where he begged the owner to get him to St. Louis as fast as possible. They flew in a small plane, and he arrived just in time to catch a night flight to Washington. It was quite a trip. Every time the plane landed, another congressman or a senator got on. Ordinary citizens were ruthlessly ejected, and pretty soon the plane was a congressional special. They arrived in Washington around dawn. With no sleep, Dad rushed to the Capitol. I soon followed him, thanks to a neat trick I pulled on my mother. I was still running a fever, but I fooled Mother into thinking it was gone by holding my mouth open after she inserted the thermometer. I was not going to let a cold keep me away from seeing history made. Mother gave me her entrance ticket and I zoomed to the special session of Congress. By the time I got there the only seat left was in the photographer's gallery. This gave me the same view that the rest of the nation later saw in the movie theaters, as President Roosevelt announced the day of infamy and called for war. I then followed the senators back to the Senate, where I heard my father vote for a declaration of war.

Dr. Benjamin Spock was also at home:

I was . . . doing desk work, while my wife and son went to a performance of *Dumbo*, when the radio announced the attack. I was horrified and yet excited by the magnitude of the event. Eventually my wife entered the apartment exclaiming, "You should have come along, the movie was great." I said, "While you were gone, the Japanese bombed Pearl Harbor." My wife replied, in an absent-minded tone, "You really should have gone with us."

In Dallas, 2,500 people were spending Sunday afternoon at the movies watching Gary Cooper in *Sergeant York*, the popular film biography of the great American hero of the First World War. When the news was announced heralding U.S. involvement in the Second at the film's end, the crowd broke into thunderous applause. Newspapers began turning out extra editions as the afternoon wore on, and the airwaves soon carried little else but war news.

People idly twisting the radio dial were in for a shock. Isaac Asimov was one of them.

> I was 21 years old. I had just finished a short-short science fiction story, "Time Pussy," and felt sufficiently relaxed to turn on the radio. I turned it on just in time to get the flash. I listened dumb-founded and ran to wake up my father. "Pappa, Pappa," I said, "we're at war." It was the only time I ever was sufficiently irreverent to disturb my father in his sleep. He did not complain.

As more and more people learned of the attack, the competition for news increased among the networks, and war rumors and speculation became rife. In the wake of such a blow to national security, many Americans began looking around fearfully and suspiciously. Who was loyal and who was not became a common, albeit cruel speculation.

Dave Brubeck, the jazz musician, was in his senior year at the College of the Pacific. He had turned twenty-one the day before.

> My song-writing brother was by now a fully-fledged composer studying with the great French composer, Darius Milhaud, and teaching in Concord High School. I had gone to his home to celebrate my coming of age with him and his new family. Howard (my brother) and I had gone to the service station to get gas for my return trip when the announcement came over the car radio. We looked at each other in total disbelief. We knew at that moment our lives were forever altered.
>
> I thought of my Japanese friends in school and the Nisei families we had known in Concord, and my heart went out to them, because I knew they were as American and as loyal as I, and I feared for them. I was right on both counts. The government acting in hysterical haste rounded up the Japanese, and interned them. Of course, they were never proven to be disloyal, and, in fact, many brave young men died in Nisei

divisions in Europe in order to redeem the family honor. I cannot understand how we could have allowed such an injustice to occur. Financial ruin and emotionally scarred lives have never been recompensed. It is a strain that most historians have been able to blot out, but not those who experienced it.

At the White House, President and Mrs. Roosevelt had been expecting a large party for lunch, but shortly before the meal Roosevelt called to cancel. Frank Knox, the secretary of the navy, had just telephoned him with the news. "No," Roosevelt is said to have gasped into the phone. Then, composing himself, he called Cordell Hull at the State Department who, even then, was waiting for the tardy Japanese ambassador. Earlier that bright, sunny day the president had complained of sinus trouble. All that was forgotten now as he ate a hasty meal at his desk with his advisor Harry Hopkins.

The White House Guard had been reinforced, a fact noted by the large, silent crowd that had gathered in Lafayette Park to watch the mansion. Eric Severeid, then a youthful CBS news correspondent worked late that night in the White House press room.

> Ed Morrow, on this night of all nights in a lifetime, was dining inside with the Roosevelts, they having declined to cancel the invitations despite the sudden events. He came into the office around midnight and said: "It's pretty bad." He looked in my direction and continued: "What did you think when you saw that crowd of people staring through the White House fence?"
> I replied: "They reminded me of the crowds around the Quai d'Orsay a couple of years ago." "That's what I was thinking," he replied; "the same look on their faces that they had on Downing Street."

Time magazine in an issue that had come off the presses the day of the bombing, had begun its feature on war threats stating that everything was ready. "From Rangoon to Honolulu, every man was at battle stations."

The veteran journalist Theodore H. White was the magazine's Far Eastern editor.

That Sunday afternoon I was writing a rehash of the tensions in Asia, shaped by my conviction that, no matter what the Japanese were saying in Washington, we would have to fight them, when the telephone rang. One of my office mates, James Aldridge, who later quit journalism to write novels, lifted the phone, let it drop, and yelled, "Jeezus Christ! The Japs are bombing Pearl Harbor; it's on the radio." We rushed to the news ticker, and it was hammering out a bulletin: *Flash . . . White House says Japs Attack Pearl Harbor. . . .*

We were gleeful; I most of all. In that first hour none of us knew how badly the American fleet had been damaged at Pearl Harbor. But it was the right war, a good war, and it had to be fought and won. This is the only conviction of mine that has lasted unchanged for thirty-five years: it was better for America to have fought that war and won than to have let the world be taken by those who killed and had no shame in killing. Or even worse, to have fought that war and lost.

The following week *Time* magazine tried to sum up the mood of America's 132 millions. What, it asked, would people say in the face of "the mightiest event of their time"? The magazine answered itself: "What they said—tens of thousands of them—was 'Why, the yellow bastards.'"

Newsman Howard K. Smith was working for CBS in Berlin. He was the last American to leave Germany legally before the Germans declared war on the Americans. He secured his exit visa on December 6, 1941, and that night took a train from Berlin to Berne in Switzerland.

I had a room in the Schweizer Hof, across from the station. In the hotel bar, I met a couple of newspapermen I had known in Berlin. They treated me to welcome whiskys, then we had dinner. I had a T-bone steak big as a ham and almost two inches thick, garnished with six different vegetables. Afterwards I had a bicarbonate of soda, and went to my room to be alone and think. I filled my pipe with good American tobacco I had bought, and turned out the light. I sat before the window, looking down on the streets outside and smoked a long time, until the telephone rang. It was the *Portier* downstairs whom I had asked to let me know if a Mr. Conger [another American correspondent] from Berlin should arrive in the next couple of days. He said he was only calling to tell me, because I might be interested to know that Mr. Conger was not coming, because ten minutes ago the Japanese, Germany's ally, had bombed Manila and Pearl Harbor, and no more Americans could get out of Germany. I asked the *Portier* to get Berlin on the phone to see if the lines were still open. They were, and I talked briefly to [correspondent Jack] Fleischer. Fleischer said the situation looked critical, but everybody was glad the waiting was over. They might get other brands of Blues, but they would never have the Berlin Blues again.

If Americans had given birth to the blues they were also responsible for another musical phenomenon. Josef Skvorecky, the Czech novelist, was and remains a great fan of American jazz. In 1941, the price for his addiction in German-occupied Czechoslovakia was high,

The news of the Japanese attack reached me in the store of old Mr. Marsik, both of whose pretty visiting nieces I unsuccessfully tried to seduce that fall; by mistake, thinking they were the same one. Mr. Marsik sold bicycles, motor bikes, hardware of all kinds, and he was also our local supplier of the breakable Brunswicks. I was just making up my mind whether to spend my last fifteen crowns (borrowed from Benne, our rich trumpet player) on a record bearing the legend: *I've Got A Guy. Chick Webb and His Orchestra. With a Vocal Chorus*, when Lexa came in with the joyous news. The Yanks were in the war at last. Freedom smelling of saxophones popped up from behind the horizon of our mountain valley, and I bought the record. Later on I couldn't keep the joy of listening to the girl who was the Vocal Chorus just by myself. I didn't know it was Ella Fitzgerald (they did not put singers' names on the labels in those times), and played the record publicly, over the amplifiers in my Father's cinema. An infuriated local Nazi came to the projection booth, confiscated Chick, and later accepted two bottles of cognac in exchange for my not being shipped out of our pleasant little town to less pleasant regions of the Reich, where my Father was shipped himself, a little later on.

Half a world away, Hoagy Carmichael, the American composer and lyricist, had witnessed a strange portent:

On December 6th I was playing tennis on the beach area of Santa Monica, California with two naval officers. After the game I told the two officers that a dear friend of mine had returned from Honolulu and told me that he had talked with reliable sources and was told that the defense of Hawaii, in general, was in a deplorable state even to the state that the main overseas wireless wave was Japanese. The officers poo-pooed the conversation but the tennis game was to be renewed the next day. In the middle of the afternoon of December 7th we all heard the news. I looked at the officers and they looked away. But my main story is that late in the afternoon the sun-set was one that is rarely seen in Los Angeles—perfect red streamers from the sun filling the western sky—a perfect Japanese flag. It was beautiful but terribly frightening.

There were touches of humor though. In Chicago a woman at a jammed newsstand wondered what all the fuss was about. "We're at war lady," came the reply. "Well, what do you know," she said, "Who with?" In New Orleans, the Chinese vice-consul declared solemnly, "As far as Japan is concerned, their goose is over-heated." And in New York City, the chief of civil defense, Mayor Fiorello La Guardia, rushed madly through the streets in a police car with its siren shrieking, all the while screaming, "CALM! CALM! CALM!"

ROOSEVELT'S POLICY had always been to assist Great Britain by all means short of war. In January 1941 he had introduced the Lend-Lease bill whereby Britain could buy or lease American materials and pay the bills later, and in the spring of that year he initiated American anti-submarine activity in the Atlantic to protect British convoys. Douglas Fairbanks, Jr. was part of the undeclared American commitment to the Allied cause in the North Atlantic.

I was then a *very* junior officer on a destroyer, rolling around as one of several protecting the agonizingly slow convoys. One of my several jobs aboard ship was Assistant Communications Officer and on that morning it was my turn to be at that particular job. I was locked in the communications decoding room, banging out on the machine various messages that were coming to both the U.S. and Royal Navy ships at sea—wherever they might be. Some of these messages, which came out of the machine like ticker tape, referred to our particular convoy, but most referred to countless other addresses. These last were torn off and thrown away into a big basket by my side. At one point, a message came through addressed to all U.S. and

Allied ships and shore establishments, from U.S. Naval Headquarters in Washington. It read "Air raid on Pearl Harbor. This is not a drill." I had never before heard of Pearl Harbor and had neither the knowledge nor the faintest interest in what this seemingly meaningless message meant, so down into the basket it went with all the other messages. It was several minutes, and many messages later, that I dimly began to sense that perhaps there was an importance in that message which escaped me, and that it was possibly advisable to show it to our Captain, just on the off-chance it might make some sense to him. It took me some moments of digging around in the big basket through all the tape that was looking like streamers before I could find that particular message. I rushed up to the bridge with it to ask the skipper whether it meant anything to him and whether it was important. I will never forget his howl of angry surprise at my stupidity, combined with the excitement of learning that we, the U.S. nation as a whole, were now properly, officially and legally in the war, and not just the navy having its own private war in the Atlantic as helpers of our potential allies. Blinker signals then went out from us to all the other merchant and navy ships in the convoy who then began tooting and hooting and blowing whistles. There was, as I remember, a feeling of great exultation and excitement, and although we had been actively in battle and at our "unofficial" war for many months, this particular moment made everything seem a bit different. Many men had tears in their eyes, but whether they were tears of excitement, sadness, homesickness, fear, apprehension or what, no one could tell. Probably a mixture of them all.

If Pearl Harbor stunned America, it relieved and gratified those who would become her allies. Prime Minister Winston Churchill was sitting at a table at Checkers with United States Ambassador J.C. Winant and land-lease administrator Averell Harriman on the evening of December 7, 1941.

I turned on my small wireless set shortly after the nine o'clock news had started. There were a number of items about the fighting on the Russian front and on the British front in Libya, at the end of which some few sentences were spoken regarding an attack by the Japanese on American shipping at Hawaii, and also Japanese attacks on British vessels in the Dutch East Indies. There followed a statement that after the news Mr. Somebody would make a commentary, and that the

Brains Trust programme would then begin, or something like this. I did not personally sustain any direct impression, but Averell said there was something about the Japanese attacking the Americans, and, in spite of being tired and resting, we all sat up. By now the butler, Sawyers, who had heard what had passed, came into the room, saying, "It's quite true. We heard it ourselves outside. The Japanese have attacked the Americans." There was a silence. At the Mansion House luncheon on November 11 I had said that if Japan attacked the United States a British declaration of war would follow "within the hour." I got up from the table and walked through the hall to the office, which was always at work. I asked for a call to the President. The Ambassador followed me out, and, imagining I was about to take some irrevocable step, said, "Don't you think you'd better get confirmation first?"

In two or three minutes Mr. Roosevelt came through. "Mr. President, what's this about Japan?" "It's quite true," he replied. "They have attacked us at Pearl Harbor. We are all in the same boat now."

Anthony Eden was foreign secretary in Winston Churchill's Cabinet. He was on his way to Russia to meet with Premier Stalin when he received a phone call from the prime minister with the news of Pearl Harbor. "I felt that whatever happened now, it was merely a question of time. Before, we had believed in the end but never seen the means, now both were clear."

The British historian and educator Sir Isaiah Berlin was working in New York, as an official of the British ministry of information. His job was to supply American journalists and other officials with facts about the British war effort.

On that Sunday I had lunch very late in a hotel in Lexington Avenue. I hurried back to my office in Rockefeller Center where I had some unfinished work to complete; on the way there, the taxi-driver informed me about Pearl Harbor. I cannot deny that after the initial shock, I felt exhilarated. . . . After this, there was no doubt about which side would win the war. I arrived in my office to find a colleague, an English-woman, writing to an American who had volunteered for the British airforce and was a prisoner-of-war in Germany, and just as I was about to share my sense of exultation with her, I saw that she was in tears. She felt for America; she had believed, with Roosevelt, that America could win the war without entering it, and the thought of the losses which America was bound to suffer upset her deeply. I did my best to persuade her that I shared her feelings, but this was not entirely sincere. I left her to see the head of my office, who was overjoyed, as I think most Englishmen living in America were.

For Australians the nature of the war changed entirely. No longer was it solely a European conflict, the product of their familial attachments, but rather a life or death struggle on their own door-step.

Sir Jack Brabham, the racing car driver, had just left school and started working and was "horrified that Japan would do such a thing."

> I had the sinking feeling that war was a lot closer to us than we had previously felt and started wondering how long it was going to drag on and whether I would be participating in it. I had already made up my mind that I would be an Air Force pilot.

Lady Casey, whose husband Richard had resigned from the Australian federal Parliament in Canberra to open Australia's first diplomatic post abroad in 1940, was in Washington.

> For all of us, American or not, there was an interval of numb incomprehension, like the pause after the inflicting of a wound when no pain can be felt. Then there rose in the United States a surge of rage with an aftermath of shame. The country was united in thought, consolidated into effort.
>
> An awful idea entered my head at this moment, but apparently it entered my head only. I feared that the President in declaring war on Japan might not also declare war on Germany.

Australian historian Manning Clark was teaching at a school near Geelong in Victoria.

> A week earlier the attaché to the Japanese embassy, then resident in Melbourne, had given a dinner at Menzies Hotel, for the men who had studied at Balliol College, Oxford. Towards the end of the dinner, when the room began to take on curious shapes, and the faces of the other intellectuals present began to register a warmth and a humanity for which they were not usually distinguished, the Japanese attaché, who, according to rumour was related vaguely to the Emperor,

told us solemnly: "Gentlemen, Japanese navy [pause] ... very strong." Then he giggled in drunken embarrassment. That night when saying farewell, the two of us discovered our eldest sons had been born in the same hospital in Oxford. So on Pearl Harbor day my wife and I were somewhat embarrassed to receive a huge parcel from the Japanese embassy. When we stripped off the elegant wrappings we found a pink nursery table and chairs for our son. On each item there was a white lamb. I believed then as I believe now he sent it out of the goodness of his heart. I should add that it lasted a long time, surviving in time the batterings of four young children, and our rather tempestuous life at Corio, Croydon and the early years at Canberra. Indeed those lambs lived with us all through those wild years until the calm down began. By then they were falling to pieces.

On that Sunday afternoon the Canadian diplomat Escott Reid was taking part in a discussion in the office of the under-secretary of state for external affairs in Ottawa.

The question under discussion was a warning which the governments of the British Commonwealth were about to present to Japan that a Japanese attack on Malaya, the Netherlands, East India or Thailand would mean war with the nations of the Commonwealth. We were not discussing the merits of the warning. We were discussing whether, as the British government had proposed, the British ambassador in Tokyo should present the warning on behalf of Canada. We agreed that that was not in accord with constitutional proprieties and that the Canadian chargé d'affairs in Tokyo should deliver a note to the Japanese foreign office associating Canada with the British representations. The only question which remained for decision was whether he should accompany the British ambassador or make a separate call immediately after mine.

In the midst of our deliberations we were interrupted by a telephone call from an officer of the department who was at home. He said that he had just heard over the radio that the Japanese had attacked Pearl Harbor. My recollection is that the under-secretary and the rest of us were incredulous and that we continued our discussion of the nice point of diplomatic protocol until we got through by telephone to the Canadian legation in Washington which confirmed that the attack had taken place.

I was greatly relieved by the news since it meant that the United States was now in the war. We had known for a week that a Japanese expeditionary force of fifty to seventy ships and about 30,000 men was moving south and we feared that this might result in war between Japan and the British Commonwealth with the United States still neutral.

Fears of a divided war effort plagued not only Lady Casey and Escott Reid. In Germany, Adolf Hitler was also distressed, at least in strategic terms, by his Japanese ally's decision to attack Pearl Harbor. He had hoped to persuade the Japanese not to attack the Americans, but instead to hit the Soviets at Vladivostok and thereby involve the Russians in a two-front war while keeping the Americans neutral. It wasn't a bad strategy, but as his advisors pointed out, it was in Germany's interest to have American military strength preoccupied in the Pacific. They argued that the American public might claim that America's fight was only in the Pacific arena and therefore insist that she abstain from the European war. In the tense days following Pearl Harbor Franklin Delano Roosevelt worried about how in the face of a decidedly isolationist Congress he could broaden American involvement to include a war against Germany as well as Japan. Adolf Hitler came to his rescue. Against all sane advice, the Führer declared war on the United States on December 11.

· D-DAY—JUNE 6, 1944 ·

ON SUNDAY, JUNE 4, 1944, in the town of Leatherhead in Surrey, Leonard Dawe, fifty-four, a quiet, unassuming school-teacher, returned home from walking his dog and discovered two counter-espionage agents waiting for him. The M.I.5 men had been investigating him for more than a month and they wanted to know why Dawe, the senior crossword compiler for London's *Daily Telegraph*, had been slipping highly secret code words into his puzzles. Only the week before, in two separate crosswords, Dawe (who prided himself on never using the same clue twice) had offered "Britannia and he hold to the same thing" and "But some big-wig like this has stolen some of it at times." The answers, which had been printed on succeeding days, were "Neptune" and "Overlord," the two key words for the projected and most confidential Allied invasion of Hitler's Europe. Poor, bewildered Dawe proclaimed his innocence, protested it was simply a fantastic coincidence, and finally the intelligence men seemed satisfied and went away.

Their concern was understandable. Operation Overlord had been years in the planning and its success depended on secrecy and meticulous organization, for the trick was not merely to get the troops across the channel to northern France, but to get them off the beaches before they were blasted to bits by German ground and air forces. Surprise was essential. Both the Allies and the Germans knew this. Only a few months before, in April, Field Marshall Erwin Rommel, commander-in-chief of Army Group B and architect of the hastily renovated German defense that was euphemistically called the Atlantic Wall, said to an aide: "The war will be won or lost on the beaches. We'll have only one chance to stop the enemy and that's while he's in the water ... struggling to get ashore." Then he added, "The first twenty-four hours of the invasion will be decisive." That first day—June 6, 1944, called by the Allies D-Day—was what the commotion was all about.

The operation was huge, for the Allies had assembled the world's largest armada, comprising 5,000 ships: 1,200 naval vessels including 6 battleships, 32 cruisers, 93 destroyers, 68 other escorts, 71 corvettes, and hundreds of smaller ships including precious minesweepers. In all some thirty-seven divisions—two million men—were scheduled to make the crossing in 4,000 transports. Their destination was Normandy, specifically five invasion beaches code-named UTAH, OMAHA, GOLD, JUNO, and SWORD located along forty miles of French coast from east of the Cotentin peninsula to the mouth of the Seine. A force of 7,500 aircraft had been amassed to provide air cover. On the other side, the Germans had fifty-eight divisions in Western Europe, twenty of which were highly mobile Panzers.

The invasion was as much engineered as planned. To speed up the landing operation the invaders were bringing their own artificial harbors called mulberries. And since the plan called for 14,000 vehicles to be landed on D-Day with a total of 95,000 by D plus 12, millions of gallons of fuel were required to get (and to keep) them moving. A submarine pipeline, code-named PLUTO, was stretched between the Isle of Wight and Cherbourg to maintain a flow of fuel. Among the other special contraptions were: landing ships which could cross oceans while carrying up to sixty tanks; landing craft tanks which were self-propelled barges able to carry three to five tanks and land them in three feet of water; the D.U.K.W., an amphibious truck which could be driven into the sea to float like a boat or roll on to dry land just like a truck; and a range of tanks, familiarly called "Hobart's Funnies" (after their inventor British Major-General Percy Hobart) which had been adapted to cope with water, sand, minefields and any number of other obstacles—natural or man-made.

Now, nearly forty years later, the course of this massive undertaking seems sure-footed, brilliant, ably accomplished and, given the weight of Allied strength, destined for victory. In many ways, events did move faultlessly and as planned, but the ambitious timetable established for D-Day lagged. The initial foothold was gained securely enough, but tough German resistance, particularly from two Panzer divisions, nailed down the Allied drive and kept it from its inland objectives. It took the Commonwealth Forces a month to secure Caen and its airport while the Americans needed as long to capture the port of Cherbourg and the Cotentin peninsula. Break-out from the beaches was hard won, and if the German forces had been able to exert more armor and air power, Allied success would have been doubtful. In the end, the Allies were lucky.

IN A SENSE the planning for Overlord had begun as the last of the scrappy survivors had been evacuated from Dunkirk in 1940. In those days of Allied retreats, the likelihood of a cross channel attack lay menacingly with Germany. However, the Battle of Britain, which raged for twelve weeks from July to October 1940, exploded all of Hitler's invasion strategies. The British downed 1,733 German aircraft, robbing Hitler of the air umbrella he required for an assault. On July 1, 1940, in the midst of the blackest period of the air battle, the British set up a new command called Combined Operations, partly as a morale booster, but also for the express purpose of masterminding the eventual reconquest of Europe.

In the meantime Hitler had invaded Russia in June 1941 and the Japanese had bombed Pearl Harbor six months later, precipitating the entry of the Soviet Union and the United States into the war, and shifting the brunt of the fighting away from Western Europe. Now that Britain no longer faced the threat of imminent invasion, and with the addition of two Allies to stem the Axis thrust, attention turned to another much more active front—in Russia itself—where the Soviets were being subjected to a savage, inexorable pounding.

Soviet Premier Josef Stalin demanded a second front immediately—an invasion of Europe—to relieve the pressure on his people. Anglo-American strategists divided over which route to follow. The British, recalling the costly tuition of Dunkirk and the more recent and disastrous Combined Operations Dieppe raid in August 1942 (in which 3,500 men were killed, taken prisoner, or went missing), argued that North Africa should be cleared of Axis strength before an invasion of Europe was attempted. The Americans were equally enthusiastic about striking in France, the European heart, threatening that if their arguments didn't hold sway, they might concentrate their forces on fighting Japan in the Pacific.

Although an Allied attack on northwest Europe in 1942 would have met less German resistance, Allied resources also would have been fewer, air superiority questionable, and furthermore, there simply would not have been enough landing craft to make an invasion feasible. Eventually the American planners were persuaded and the pressure for a second front was shifted to the Mediterranean, at least for the time being.

Russian pressures for a strike on Europe continued throughout 1943 even as the Allies cleared North Africa and began the hard-fought offensive through Sicily and up the Italian boot. In the meantime, largely because of ULTRA, the intelligence derived from intercepting German signals, the war at sea—the Battle of the Atlantic—had turned to the Allies favor and the war in the air—the strategic bombing of Germany—was hobbling German industrial ability and with it the effectiveness of the Luftwaffe.

The first plans for the invasion, or as the Americans preferred to call it, the liberation of Europe, were prepared under the direction of British General Sir Frederick Morgan, who conceived a first-day landing by three divisions. United States General Dwight D. Eisenhower and British General Sir Bernard Laud Montgomery later expanded this to five divisions, necessitating the assembling of more landing craft and a consequent delay in the operation. The logical landing site was the Pas de Calais. It had fine beaches and was only a twenty-mile run from Dover. Indeed, it was such an obvious choice that it was certain the Germans would be waiting. Finally, the Allies settled on Normandy. It was further away, but it had adequate beaches and fewer heavy German defenses to surmount. The idea was approved. On Christmas Eve, 1943, General Eisenhower was proclaimed supreme Allied commander; his deputy was Air Chief Marshal Sir Arthur Tedder and General Montgomery was named British commander in the field. The operation was given the name Overlord.

To facilitate the invasion, in late March 1944 the Allied bombing offensive concentrated on a systematic destruction of the communications links between Berlin and France, and photo reconnaissance of the Atlantic Wall was stepped up. Britain then was bursting with two million troops who were themselves eager for action. Now an elaborate guessing-game was devised for German intelligence: false tanks, phoney landing craft, inflatable aircraft, and other deceptions were deployed in southeast England to give rise to the idea that the blow would come at Calais. False radio traffic, intentional indiscretions around German sympathizers, and phoney military activity combined to hoodwink the enemy and to camouflage the preparations for the real attack. As well, the operation would coincide with Russian maneuvers in the east and intense partisan activity throughout occupied Europe.

Ironically, just as the First World War had a false Armistice, the Second had a bogus invasion. On Sunday, June 4, Allied Supreme Headquarters was stunned to learn that during the night a flash bulletin had come across on the Associated Press circuits announcing: "URGENT PRESS ASSOCIATED NYK FLASH EISENHOWER'S HQ ANNOUNCED ALLIED LANDINGS IN FRANCE." It was all a mistake. An AP teletype operator named Joan Ellis had been practicing on an idle machine to improve her speed, and somehow her practice tape had escaped the elaborate safeguards and censorship procedures and was broadcast to North and South America just before the nightly Russian communiqué. The error was caught and "killed" in only thirty seconds, but the damage had been done. Radio programming was interrupted, church bells rang out, men and women wept in the streets of Hot Springs, Arkansas, and in the polo grounds in New York a baseball game was halted for a minute's reflection. In his headquarters General Eisenhower was told about the "flash," but he merely grunted an acknowledgment. He had a real invasion to worry about.

June 1944 was a cold and rainy month, so miserable in fact that the Germans were persuaded that the long-dreaded invasion would have to be postponed. Indeed, on the morning of June 5, one day before D-Day, Field Marshal Rommel felt sanguine enough to embark on the long drive back to Germany from France to celebrate his wife's birthday. It proved to be one anniversary he should have observed belatedly.

That same morning, in a large country house near Portsmouth, General Eisenhower and his senior planners gathered to make the final decision about launching the strike. The weather was vicious—a constant drizzle driven by strong winds which whipped the channel into a savage froth. The chief meteorologist, Group Captain J.M. Stagg, was the most worried man in the room. In his opinion there was a 50/50 chance the weather would be fine on June 6. The invasion had been delayed once before, and now Eisenhower had to decide whether to postpone it again. It was not now or never, but it was certainly now or much later, and every delay increased the odds that the plans would be leaked to the Germans. "O.K., we'll go," Eisenhower decided finally. And so it was on.

Major General Richard Rohmer, former head of Canada's reserves, had, as he later put it, "The best seat in the house," on D-Day.

> That was probably the most enervating, euphoria-filled day of my now not short life. I was twenty-one, an old, experienced fighter/reconnaissance pilot, snugly strapped in my sleek, single-seater, camouflage-colored Mustang fighter, with broad black and white stripes painted around each wing near the point where it joined the fuselage. They were identification

marks so that the ships below us in the Channel on the way across and our troops on the beachhead would be able to identify us easily. I had painted the stripes on my aeroplane myself just the day before. When the order came to paint the stripes, everyone on my squadron knew that D-Day was at hand. This was the event we had been waiting for. All the training by the vast Allied Armies in the United Kingdom, all the air attacks on Germany and on the coastal radar sites and installations, the low-level photography of beaches that might be used for the invasion, the building of landing barges and ships, everything had been building up for one event—the invasion of Europe. 430 Squadron was keyed up and ready to go. Nothing could stop us.

At three in the morning . . . Flight Lieutenant Jack Taylor and I (we operated in pairs) were briefed by the wing-commander on our operation for the morning. Jack and I were to fly back and forth along the Canadian-British beach-head sector looking for enemy troop movements, spotting gun emplacements, watching for German tanks. If we found any targets we were to radio to Group Control Center. They would send in Spitfires and Typhoons to attack with rockets and bombs. Just before dawn we were airborne out of our base at Oldham, heading for the English Channel and our assigned location along the Normandy beach-head. As we crossed out over the coast at about 3,000 feet under a high overcast gray sky, there lay before us in the black water of the Channel hundreds of vessels, all churning through the heavy seas of that stormy day making south toward the coast of France. This was the largest armada of ships in the history of the world. Destroyers, troop ships, landing craft, patrol boats, vessels of every nature and kind, many trailing behind them protective balloons designed to impede air attacks.

As Taylor and I approached the beach-head just a few minutes before the first wave of troops was scheduled to hit the beaches, we could see ahead of us a wall of cloud rising up from the edge of the shore, towering several thousand feet above our assigned operation altitude of 3,000 feet. The problem was that the cloud base was only 500 feet. If we went that low we would be vulnerable to enemy ground fire and to the shells from our own battleships lying off shore, firing at gun emplacements and other targets immediately below us. Nevertheless, if we were to do our job we would have to get under that bank of cloud. There was no hesitation. In our wide battle formation we dropped down and crossed the beach to take up our station under the low cloud. No problem. As we turned over the mouth of the Orne River to fly west about two hundred yards inland from the beach we could see the first waves of landing craft approaching the shore, bobbing like corks in the heavy waves and the high winds of the D-Day storm. Beyond them out about a mile and parallel to the shore stood an apparently endless line of battleships, cruisers, destroyers, almost hidden behind the pall of smoke that constant firing had thrown up. The flashes of their guns firing directly at us through the black haze were like twinkling lights on a Christmas tree.

Below us as we sped westward the brown ground and sand were pockmarked from the demolition of the huge bombs that had been dropped on the beach-head during the night by hundreds of Royal Air Force and Canadian bombers. Now the enormous guns from the warships were engaged in pounding gun emplacements and fortifications. Their huge shells threw up clouds of dirt and debris below us as they smashed into their targets and the areas around them.

Inland, to the south of us, scattered over the green Normandy farm fields, we could see the huge Allied troop-carrying gliders that had been dropped in just a short time before. Some of them had landed intact. Others had crumpled as they crashed into the ground because of misjudged landings or enemy fire.

Coursing down the beach to our turn-around we kept careful watch for enemy fire coming at us, and particularly for enemy fighters that might emerge from the clouds to attempt to shoot us down. During our two and a half hours over the beach-head area no enemy aircraft appeared. Our overwhelming air superiority had obliterated much of the German airforce in France, and their bases.

At H-Hour just before 7:00 a.m. the first wave of landing craft hit the sands of the beach. The assault on Rommel's beach fortifications began before our very eyes. As the bow ramps of the heavily loaded craft dropped into the water we could see men and tanks spilling out into the turbulent water. It was an historic moment, the very beginning of the liberation of Europe. We were part of it, watching it from a vantage point that only a handful of other pilots had on that day at that moment.

Taylor and I stayed on station far too long, over two and a half hours, plotting the locations of bridges down, the state of enemy gun emplacements, the location of anti-aircraft weapons. We looked for German troop movements, but we had none to report. The Germans had gone underground in the face of the massive onslaught of bombs dropped during the night and the cascade of naval shells battering their position.

So entranced was I with the incredible sight below us and out to sea, while watching for other aircraft, I failed to observe that my fuel was running low. Suddenly I was shocked to see that my fuel gauges were reading almost empty and here we were a hundred miles from the south coast of England. After a hurried call to Taylor we turned and headed north, away from the beach-head, back out over the vast armada, still making its way across in unending lines from the beach-head to Great Britain's shores. At any moment I expected my engine to quit but I was quite prepared to bail out, happy in the knowledge that with that massive shipping below, I would certainly be rescued, rapidly fished out of the sea. If I had known how rough it was on the surface of the water I would have been less optimistic. Buoyed up by my excitement and enthusiasm for the beginning of this massive onslaught on Fortress Europe I was quite sure that not only the whole Allied Force was invincible but that I was too.

When we landed at an RAF airfield called Thorney Island on the edge of the south coast of England my engine was miraculously still running. When I had shut it down I jumped out of my aircraft and took the gas cap off the tank of the left wing and looked in. I could see no gasoline whatsoever.

We flew three more missions over the beach-head that day. During the last one in late evening we could clearly see that our troops had advanced inland a substantial distance from the open beaches that as privileged witnesses we had watched them cross that morning. As we flew back to England in the gathering dusk I was certain of two highly uncertain things—that I would survive and that Europe would be liberated. After all, I had seen the success of the beginning with my own eyes.

German radio was the first to broadcast news of the invasion— at seven o'clock on the morning of June 6. General Eisenhower cautiously held the official Allied release until he could be assured of announcing at least a partial success. Britons heard the news from radio bulletins, although a good many Londoners, having heard the drone of aircraft engines for nearly three hours the night before, had a good idea of what was happening. In the British

House of Commons, Prime Minister Winston Churchill impishly talked about the fall of Rome which had occurred two days before, and then, at noon, delivered the news everyone knew was coming. Cheers rang out all round and Churchill suggested, in yet another attempt to confuse the Nazis, that other landings were being considered.

In Washington, President Franklin Delano Roosevelt was asleep in a darkened White House when news of the assault came through. Later in the day he held a press conference cautioning against over-confidence which he feared would harm the war effort. "The war isn't over by any means," he said. "This operation isn't over. You don't just land on a beach and walk through— if you land successfully without breaking your leg—walk through to Berlin. And the quicker this country understands it the better."

In Germany Adolf Hitler was asleep in his retreat near Berchtesgaden. The architect Albert Speer, Hitler's Reichsminister for armaments and war production, was at the Führer's headquarters when one of the military adjutants told him the invasion had begun early that morning.

> "Has the Fuehrer been awakened?" I asked.
>
> He shook his head. "No, he receives the news after he has eaten breakfast."
>
> In recent days Hitler had kept on saying that the enemy would probably begin with a feigned attack in order to draw our troops away from the ultimate invasion site. So no one wanted to awaken Hitler and be ranted at for having judged the situation wrongly.
>
> At the situation conference in the *Berghof* salon a few hours later Hitler seemed more set than ever on his preconceived ideas that the enemy was only trying to mislead him. "Do you recall? Among the many reports we've received there was one that exactly predicted the landing site and the day and hour. That only confirms my opinion that this is not the real invasion yet."

For those in the war itself—whether as members of the armed forces, in government or in the media—the moment was climactic. Newsman Howard K. Smith was in occupied France.

> Impatient at being isolated in Switzerland as CBS correspondent covering underground movements in Nazi Europe, I had

crossed the border and joined the Maquis, the French Underground. I heard of D-Day on a radio in a small French border tavern among a troop of armed French guerrillas who all cheered the news. That night, we went out to a wild plateau and in the dark received a drop of arms, as pre-arranged, from a British bomber.

Donald Jack remembers that he was an "erk" in the Royal Air Force stationed at Bracknell, Berkshire, that morning when he heard the news broadcast over the camp tannoy system.

It was of more than immediate interest because we were due to land in Normandy on D+7 or so with RAF Tactical H.Q. Rear. I was overjoyed at the news and at the prospect of being in a battle if only as a radio operator. Not that I was at all a courageous person. One fellow aircraftsman, a swine called Standish, was always deliberately treading on my heels while we marched purposelessly about the countryside in columns of three, and he kept it up for days before I finally lost my cool and offered to wipe off his face. But all the same I was eager for danger in the field. In fact I'd volunteered for a commando outfit a year previously.... I was so delighted at the news that I cheeked a sergeant and ended up on jankers—trotting around that parade ground in full battle gear. And that's how I celebrated that momentous day.

In preparation for the invasion, the American soldier Dave Brubeck had been transferred from the army band to the infantry. All available manpower was enlisted to this supreme effort and musicians were reclassified as infantry replacement soldiers. Brubeck was trained as a sharp shooter and scout.

When I heard the news of the invasion, I must admit a feeling of both anxiety and relief. Anxious because I knew what it meant in loss of life and that the fate of the war in Europe was hanging in the balance, and relief to know that at least I was destined not to be in the first wave. I landed at Omaha Beach, on my way to Metz, ninety days after D-Day, and it did not take much imagination to recreate in my mind what had happened there. I was a fortunate soldier. My good luck continued, because after we were close to the front line, an Army truck with two Red Cross girls drove by the haystack where I was resting and asked if there was anyone in our group who could accompany them on piano. Naturally, I was quick to volunteer. We put on a show for the GI's that afternoon, and a colonel who heard me play decided to pull me out of the roster headed for the front line the next morning. He asked me to form a band, which I did, using as talent men who had been sent back from the front due to injuries or mental fatigue. We stayed up there close to but behind the battle lines, through the rest of the war in Europe.

Pierre Mendès France was in Algiers in charge of financial affairs in General de Gaulle's provisional government.

We were not certain at first whether this was merely another limited attack or whether it was the real thing. We had been waiting and hoping for this day for such a long time that all true French patriots, both at home and abroad, simply referred to it as "the landing."

Quite quickly we discovered that this was the decisive invasion which had been so anxiously awaited and which had taken so long to plan and get going.

From this point on we lived by our radios waiting for the hourly reports on how the invasion was progressing. Although we rejoiced at the first real successes, we were all very conscious of the terrible cost in human lives. . . .

I was getting ready to leave for the U.S. to take part in the Bretton Woods conference. It was symbolic that, at a time when the future depended on military operations, civilians from around the world were getting together to plan the financial and economic reconstruction of their occupied countries.

For many ordinary people, the news suggested that the war must be nearly over, or if not near the end, at least at its climax. In North America, newspapers had one word headlines: INVASION. Everyone knew what it meant. The feeling of climax had been heightened by the fall of Rome, now D-Day brought relief and fear, relief that "it was on" as the popular phrase put it and fear for those involved. The mood of the Allies at home was solemn. A few D-Day babies were celebrated, good bidding was recorded on the stock exchanges, and the Red Cross was flooded with eager blood donors. Otherwise, D-Day meant business as usual. *Time* magazine thought Americans had acted like—Americans, and told of a cab driver outside the White House who observed, "It may be D-Day but it looks just like any other morning to me."

Correspondents recorded a very different scene in Moscow, where they reported there was "dancing in the streets" and Moscow radio jubilantly called it the long-awaited, but without question, the "Victory Front."

Robert Fulford, the Canadian editor and writer, was a twelve-year-old boy still attending public school.

> As we filed into school another boy said to me "Have you heard about this big invasion of Europe?" I said yes. But it turned out several other kids around us hadn't heard about it. That was the first time I realized there were people in the world who didn't read newspapers or listen to news on the radio. My father was a newspaperman, and in the course of a day we usually had three or four newspapers in the house, and the radio on all the time.

Radio effectively supplanted all other news media. Portable recording equipment and an international pooling of resources and talent had provided listeners with coverage of the invasion only hours after it had occurred. It was estimated that radio audiences leapt 82 per cent. The Allies were well aware of the impact the news could have on a war-weary and occupied Europe. The BBC played a vital role in beaming broadcasts to occupied nations, thereby giving hope to the oppressed and encouraging resistance. But it wasn't only the Allies who were broadcasting propaganda that day. In Berlin, Dr. Joseph Goebbels, Hitler's propaganda minister, made the most imaginative use of the invasion story. He explained to the German people that the landings in Normandy were a carefully constructed German trap to lure the Allied forces to a spot where they could be annihilated. That evening, whether it was in Moscow, London, Washington or Berlin, victory was claimed on all sides.

Anne Frank, a young Dutch Jew in hiding with her family in occupied Amsterdam, wrote in her diary:

> "This is D-Day," came the announcement over the English news and quite rightly, "this is the day." The invasion has begun! . . .
>
> Great commotion in the "Secret Annexe"! Would the long-awaited liberation that has been talked of so much, but which still seems too wonderful, too much like a fairy tale,

ever come true? Could we be granted victory this year, in 1944? We don't know yet, but hope is revived within us; it gives us fresh courage, and makes us strong again. Since we must put up bravely with all the fears, privations, and sufferings, the great thing now is to remain calm and steadfast. Now more than ever we must clench our teeth and not cry out. France, Russia, Italy, and Germany, too, can all cry out and give vent to their misery, but we haven't the right to do that yet!

. . . [The] best part of the invasion is that I have the feeling that friends are approaching. We have been oppressed by those terrible Germans for so long, they have had their knives so at our throats, that the thought of friends and delivery fills us with confidence!

Now it doesn't concern the Jews any more; no, it concerns Holland and all occupied Europe. Perhaps . . . I may yet be able to go back to school in September or October.

But for Anne Frank the liberation came too late. She was discovered by the Nazis and subsequently died in the concentration camp at Belsen.

· HIROSHIMA—AUGUST 6, 1945 ·

BY MID 1942, six short months after Pearl Harbor, the Japanese had amassed a huge oceanic empire stretching northwards from the Gilbert Islands in the South Pacific to the Aleutians off the coast of Alaska. The British had been pushed out of Burma; Malaya, Indo-China, and the Dutch East Indies had all been occupied by the Japanese and Australia was threatened. Indeed, it had suffered its own version of Pearl Harbor with the devastating air attack on Darwin in February 1942. Effectively, the most the Allies could do against further Japanese aggression was to hold the line.

But then other factors came into play. As early as August 1940, Admiral Yamamoto, the strategist behind Pearl Harbor, had advised Prime Minister Prince Konoye, "In the first six to twelve months of a war with the United States and Great Britain I will run wild and win victory upon victory. But then, if the war continues after that, I have no expectation of success." Yamamoto's time was almost up. More important, the Japanese had failed to smash the American aircraft carriers at Pearl Harbor, which meant that the Americans had a floating base from which to launch aerial attacks. In April 1942 General James Doolittle and his carrier-based B-25s had been able to execute a daring raid on Tokyo itself. That did much to boost American morale and to demonstrate the vulnerability of the Japanese homeland.

The Pacific war would be won in the air. That was true even of the war at sea. All the major naval engagements were fought beyond the range of ship's guns, frequently with the enemy out of sight. The first great encounter was the Battle of the Coral Sea in which the Americans halted the Japanese advance on Port Moresby in Papua, across from Japanese-held territory in the Solomons. A month later, in June 1942, the decisive battle of Midway was a clear American victory thanks in part to their mastery of the Japanese codes. This battle, in which four Japanese carriers went to the bottom, showed conclusively that conventional naval vessels were obsolete. Japanese thrust and power were effectively broken; Midway was the turning point of the Pacific war, although it would be some time before this point became evident.

The initiative shifted from the Japanese to the Americans, but unlike the quick, decisive strikes of the Asian militarists, American strategists advocated a slow, deliberate advance on Japan by "leapfrogging" or "island-hopping." The strategy was to capture strategic islands or island chains, bypassing Japanese strong points, then to develop air strips and bases on the captured islands, and finally to employ air power to smash Japanese shipping and troop movements. Two parallel lines of advance were established, and after June 1943 the Japanese were thrown on the defensive. By October 1944 General Douglas MacArthur, the Allied supreme commander in the Pacific, who had been forced to retreat from Corregidor in 1942, was back in the Philippines. The naval battle of Leyte Gulf that same month effectively destroyed the remaining capital force of the Imperial Japanese Navy. In June 1944 Japan came under aerial attack from Allied bases in China and, with the capture of such air bases as Guam and Tinian in the Marianas chain, from the Pacific as well. The B-29 bomber became a frequent if uninvited visitor to the homeland of the Japanese Empire.

As the American advance continued and British troops pushed into Burma and Southeast Asia, Japanese resistance became near-fanatical. Three months of vicious hand-to-hand fighting were required to secure the island of Okinawa. American casualties soared to 50,000—a quarter of whom were killed. The Japanese simply refused to surrender, preferring suicide either by the ceremonial ritual of disembowelling themselves—*hara-kiri*— or more frequently by blowing themselves up with hand grenades held close to their chests. More than 100,000 died one way or another. These tactics and the squadrons of kamikaze suicide pilots eager to die a glorious death by diving into Allied warships suggested the type of reception that would await any invasion of the Japanese homeland. Even before the fall of Okinawa, Japan's principal cities became unceasing targets for massive American bombing raids, the Pacific equivalent of the saturation bombing that pounded Germany day and night. Incendiary bombs were a special horror, and on one night, March 9, 1945, 1,600 tons were loosed on Tokyo, killing an estimated 185,000 people and wiping out fifteen square miles of the city.

Still, Japanese militarist will was not broken, even though the emperor instructed a new prime minister, Admiral Kantaro Suzuki, to seek an honorable peace, one that hinged on the hope that a negotiated settlement could be reached through mediation by neutral countries, particularly the Soviet Union. Despite, however, the unprecedented personal intrusion of the emperor into public affairs, the militarists retained massive power and prestige in the exhausted nation. To the samurai of Japan, surrender, especially the unconditional surrender demanded by the Allies, would be humiliating beyond endurance. Japan, although shattered abroad, could still muster millions of troops and volunteers, plus six thousand aircraft for home defense.

Soviet Premier Josef Stalin was reluctant to aid in peace negotiations mainly because he had promised the other Allies at the Yalta Conference in February 1945 to declare war on Japan. This embittered the Japanese militarists even more and further entrenched their position. It therefore became increasingly apparent to the Americans that only some sort of great shock could force the Japanese to surrender.

Germany accepted an unconditional surrender in May 1945 and the European war finally ended. At the Potsdam Conference held in July 1945 Stalin formally announced his intention of declaring war on Japan in August. At the same conference a solemn pronouncement was issued urging Japanese leaders to surrender promptly or face the "utter devastation" of their homeland. It went unheeded. Militarist strength still prevailed in Japan, and even though the Japanese government showed a willingness to entertain the Potsdam declaration, the militarists did not.

An invasion of Japan had been on the books since 1944; indeed an attack was scheduled to begin November 1, 1945 against the southern island of Kyushu, to be followed in the spring of 1946 by a bigger invasion of the main island of Honshu. The scheme was called "Olympic Coronet" and the Allied casualties, projected on the fanatical Japanese defense of Okinawa, were expected to run upwards of a million men. Clearly Japanese losses would be many times higher. Russian participation on the mainland would aid the invasion, but Russian involvement in the Asian theater came with strings attached: they demanded "adequate compensations" in territory and occupation rights. Moreover, extensive Russian involvement would greatly disrupt the delicate Chinese situation. The cost would be astronomical in lives and concessions, and the assault wouldn't bring a quick peace.

Britain and the United States, however, held an ace: the atomic bomb. Surely the best kept secret of the war was the Manhattan project, their joint development of nuclear weapons. Physicists had known the theory for decades, at least as far back as the pioneering work of Ernest Rutherford in Canada and England. Experimentally, the atom had been split as early as 1932, under carefully controlled conditions in English laboratories, and by 1938 Otto Hahn in Berlin had duplicated the feat by splitting the nucleus of the uranium atom. The theory of nuclear fission had followed, and other scientists had experimented with the development of a controlled chain-reaction for industrial uses. A "fast" reaction could have military applications, but it had always been considered that the mass of uranium required for such an effort was far too vast to be carried aloft in the form of a bomb. Then it was shown that Uranium 235, if it could be isolated on a sufficient scale, might be adequate for the job. By 1942 an Anglo-American task force had been assembled. After $2 billion and years of experiments, they had provided a plutonium bomb for testing by the summer of 1945. It was first exploded in the New Mexican desert on July 16, 1945. The results were stupendous.

American President Franklin Delano Roosevelt had died in office in April 1945 and was succeeded by Harry S Truman. Truman suddenly found himself not only president of the United States and in charge of that country's massive war operation, but faced with the decision of whether to drop the bomb—a weapon so secret that as vice-president even he hadn't been apprised of its existence. Three months after his succession, at the Potsdam Conference, Truman and Churchill discussed the possibility of using the bomb against Japan. The two leaders agreed that its massive destructive force would inflict the almighty shock needed to bring the Japanese to their knees.

After Potsdam, Truman determined to use the bomb at the first opportunity. Secretly, a number of modified B-29s with specially trained crews were readied, and elements of the bomb found their clandestine way to the American base at Tinian in the Marianas.

Japan's skies were hazy during the first few days of August 1945. Then, on the night of the fifth, meteorological reports indicated that the weather the next day would be favorable for a visual drop. The orders were given, and at 2:27 a.m. on the morning of August 6, 1945, Colonel Paul Tibbets started the engines of the *Enola Gay*, the American B-29 bomber that a few hours later would deliver at Hiroshima the single most destructive weapon ever devised by man. *Enola Gay* was named after Tibbets' mother; its payload comprised a 4½ ton bomb called "Little Boy." "Little Boy" was not armed until the plane was aloft in case it crashed on take-off. Nobody wanted the entire island of Tinian to disappear. At 2:45 a.m. the *Enola Gay* and two observation planes stuffed with cameras and scientific instruments were airborne. Once their mission was completed, the world would never be the same.

THE JAPANESE CITY of Hiroshima was a flat sprawl occupying the delta of the Ota River; it had been sliced into six slender islands— not unlike a human hand—by the channels of the river, and the whole delta region was ringed by hills and small mountains. Hiroshima had been partially evacuated because of the threat of the American bombing raids, but the full force of the bombing missions had never struck the city. Its citizens, like those of Dresden, had become convinced they led charmed lives. And while more than 120,000 people had left, almost a quarter of a million remained.

The city that morning was peaceful. Early risers had observed an American weather plane some time before, but an all-clear signal reassured them that it had gone. Some had seen the approach of the *Enola Gay* and its escorts, but they assumed it was only a reconnaissance mission. The factories and offices of Hiroshima were hard at work that morning, much of it war work. Schools were filling, merchants were opening shops, and thousands of citizens were beginning another day with breakfast and a glimpse at the morning paper—just like in thousands of cities around the world.

Enola Gay began its bomb run at an altitude of about 32,000 feet precisely at 8:09 a.m. Six minutes later, "Little Boy" was released and the B-29, now almost five tons lighter, bounded into the air. Forty-three seconds passed. Then the bomb exploded at an altitude of 660 yards.

A gigantic, intense flash filled the sky. Some said it was pink, others blue, yellow or purple. It was followed by the eruption of a fireball a hundred yards wide which radiated a heat of 300,000°C and melted granite for 1,000 yards from the "hypocenter," the point of the bomb's impact. Instantly, eighty thousand people were killed—a good many of them simply vaporized. Thousands of others were burned so badly that they would spend months and years afterwards dying agonizing deaths. Two-thirds of the city's ninety thousand buildings were destroyed. Thousands of fires broke out, a thick cloud of smoke and dirt covered everything, but was soon replaced by a towering, fearsomely beautiful mushroom cloud. This cloud would become the symbol of the new age—the atomic age.

Below it, amidst the turmoil and debris, were those who came to be known as the *hibakushas*, the survivors of the blast. Blinded, crippled, demented, their seared flesh hanging in fetid shreds from their bodies, they stumbled into the rivers that divided the city, vainly sought hospitals and clinics, and attempted to escape by every and any means. The city had had two hundred doctors; only twenty could be found. Of 1,780 nurses, 1,654 had disappeared and only three of the city's fifty-five hospitals or clinics were functioning. Hiroshima had been incinerated.

Dr. Michihiko Hachiya was one of the *hibakushas*.

Clad in drawers and undershirt, I was sprawled on the living room floor exhausted because I had just spent a sleepless night on duty as an air warden in my hospital.

Suddenly, a strong flash of light startled me—and then another. So well does one recall little things that I remember vividly how a stone lantern in the garden became brilliantly lit and I debated whether this light was caused by a magnesium flare or sparks from a passing trolley.

Garden shadows disappeared. The view where a moment before all had been so bright and sunny was now dark and hazy. Through swirling dust I could barely discern a wooden column that had supported one corner of my house. It was leaning crazily and the roof sagged dangerously.

Moving instinctively, I tried to escape, but rubble and fallen timbers barred the way. By picking my way cautiously I managed to reach the *roka* and stepped down into my garden. A profound weakness overcame me, so I stopped to regain my strength. To my surprise I discovered that I was completely naked. How odd! Where were my drawers and undershirt?

What had happened?

All over the right side of my body I was cut and bleeding. A large splinter was protruding from a mangled wound in my thigh, and something warm trickled into my mouth. My cheek was torn, I discovered as I felt it gingerly, with the lower lip laid wide open. Embedded in my neck was a sizable fragment of glass which I matter-of-factly dislodged, and with the detachment of one stunned and shocked I studied it and my blood-stained hand.

Where was my wife?

Suddenly thoroughly alarmed, I began to yell for her: "Yaeko-san! Yaeko-san! Where are you?"

Blood began to spurt. Had my carotid artery been cut?

Would I bleed to death? Frightened and irrational, I called out again: "It's a five-hundred-ton bomb! Yaeko-san, where are you? A five-hundred-ton bomb has fallen!"

Yaeko-san, pale and frightened, her clothes torn and blood-stained, emerged from the ruins of our house holding her elbow. Seeing her, I was reassured. My own panic assuaged, I tried to reassure her. . . .

The shortest path to the street lay through the house next door so through the house we went—running, stumbling, falling, and then running again until in headlong flight we tripped over something and fell sprawling into the street. Getting to my feet, I discovered that I had tripped over a man's head.

"Excuse me! Excuse me, please!" I cried hysterically.

There was no answer. The man was dead. The head had belonged to a young officer whose body was crushed beneath a massive gate.

We stood in the street, uncertain and afraid, until a house across from us began to sway and then with a rending motion fell almost at our feet. Our own house began to sway, and in a minute it, too, collapsed in a cloud of dust. Other buildings caved in or toppled. Fires sprang up and whipped by a vicious wind began to spread.

It finally dawned on us that we could not stay there in the street, so we turned our steps towards the hospital. . . . We started out, but after twenty or thirty steps I had to stop. My breath became short, my heart pounded, and my legs gave way under me. An overpowering thirst seized me and I begged Yaeko-san to find me some water. But there was no water to be found. After a little my strength somewhat returned and we were able to go on.

I was still naked, and although I did not feel the least bit of shame, I was disturbed to realize that modesty had deserted me. On rounding a corner we came upon a soldier standing idly in the street. He had a towel draped across his shoulder, and I asked if he would give it to me to cover my nakedness. The soldier surrendered the towel quite willingly but said not a word. A little later I lost the towel, and Yaeko-san took off her apron and tied it around my loins. . . .

I paused to rest. Gradually things around me came into focus. There were the shadowy forms of people, some of whom looked like walking ghosts. Others moved as though in pain, like scarecrows, their arms held out from their bodies with forearms and hands dangling. These people puzzled me until I suddenly realized that they had been burned and were holding their arms out to prevent the painful friction of raw surfaces rubbing together. A naked woman carrying a naked baby came into view. I averted my gaze. Perhaps they had been in the bath. But then I saw a naked man, and it occurred to me that, like myself, some strange thing had deprived them of their clothes. An old woman lay near me with an expression of suffering on her face; but she made no sound. Indeed, one thing was common to everyone I saw—complete silence.

All who could were moving in the direction of the hospital. I joined in the dismal parade when my strength was somewhat recovered, and at last reached the gates of the Communications Bureau.

Familiar surroundings, familiar faces. There was Mr. Iguchi and Mr. Yoshihiro and my old friend, Mr. Sera, the head of the business office. They hastened to give me a hand, their expressions of pleasure changing to alarm when they saw that I was hurt. I was too happy to see them to share their concern.

No time was lost over greetings. They eased me onto a stretcher and carried me into the Communications Building, ignoring my protests that I could walk. Later, I learned that the hospital was so overrun that the Communications Bureau had to be used as an emergency hospital. The rooms and corridors were crowded with people, many of whom I recognized as neighbors. To me it seemed that the whole community was there. . . .

The hospital lay directly opposite with part of the roof and the third floor sunroom in plain view, and as I looked up, I witnessed a sight which made me forget my smarting wounds. Smoke was pouring out of the sunroom windows. The hospital was afire!

"Fire!" I shouted. "Fire! Fire! The hospital is on fire!"

The alarm was given and from all sides people took up the cry. The high-pitched voice of Mr. Sera, the business officer, rose above the others, and it seemed as if his was the first voice I had heard that day. The uncanny stillness was broken. Our little world was now in pandemonium. . . .

The sky became bright as flames from the hospital mounted. Soon the Bureau was threatened and Mr. Sera gave the order to evacuate. My stretcher was moved into a rear garden and placed beneath an old cherry tree. Other patients limped into the garden or were carried until soon the entire area became so crowded that only the very ill had room to lie down. No one talked, and the ominous silence was relieved only by a subdued rustle among so many people, restless, in pain, anxious, and afraid, waiting for something else to happen.

The sky filled with black smoke and glowing sparks. Flames rose and the heat set currents of air in motion. Updrafts became so violent that sheets of zinc roofing were hurled aloft and released, humming and twirling, in erratic flight. Pieces of flaming wood soared and fell like fiery swallows. While I was trying to beat out the flames, a hot ember seared my ankle. It was all I could do to keep from being burned alive.

The Bureau started to burn, and window after window became a square of flame until the whole structure was converted into a crackling, hissing inferno.

Scorching winds howled around us, whipping dust and ashes into our eyes and up our noses. Our mouths became dry, our throats raw and sore from the biting smoke pulled into our lungs. Coughing was uncontrollable. We would have moved back, but a group of wooden barracks behind us caught fire and began to burn like tinder.

The heat finally became too intense to endure, and we were left no choice but to abandon the garden. Those who could fled; those who could not perished. Had it not been for my devoted friends, I would have died, but again, they came to the rescue and carried my stretcher to the main gate on the other side of the Bureau. . . .

Fires sprang up on every side as violent winds fanned flames from one building to another. Soon, we were surrounded. The ground we held in front of the Communications Bureau became an oasis in a desert of fire. As the flames came closer the heat became more intense, and if someone in our group had not had the presence of mind to drench us with water from a fire hose, I doubt if anyone could have survived. . . .

Huge raindrops began to fall. Some thought a thunderstorm was beginning and would extinguish the fires. But these drops were capricious. A few fell and then a few more and that was all the rain we saw. . . .

The streets were deserted except for the dead. Some looked as if they had been frozen by death while in the full action of flight; others lay sprawled as though some giant had flung them to their death from a great height.

Hiroshima was no longer a city, but a burnt-over prairie. To the east and to the west everything was flattened. The distant mountains seemed nearer than I could ever remember. The hills of Ushita and the woods of Nigitsu loomed out of the haze and smoke like the nose and eyes on a face. How small Hiroshima was with its houses gone.

On board the *Enola Gay*, buffeted by the shock waves, and now heading back to Tinian, the crew was stunned. One later said succinctly that they had experienced "a peep into hell."

Aboard the cruiser USS *Augusta* which was carrying President Harry Truman home from Potsdam, the crew was crammed into the mess to hear the president announce that the bomb had been dropped on Hiroshima. They were ecstatic. On shore, civilians listening to radio reports seemed perplexed. Somehow, most believed, the war had been decisively shortened and now would quickly draw to a close.

Soon phone circuits were plugged all over North America with the excited chatter of people realizing that either loved ones wouldn't have to go after all or that they would be home soon. Isaac Asimov was working in a navy yard.

> . . . My draft status was in one of its many moments of uncertainty. My wife and I were getting ready to take the train to New York, where I meant to inquire if, and when, I might expect to be inducted. The radio was on (my wife was ironing; I was reading Durant's *Caesar and Christ*) and the announcement came. "Hmm," I said, "I wonder how that will affect my draft status?"—It didn't. I was inducted on November 1.

Canadian architect Arthur Erickson was on a troop ship in convoy from Bombay when the BBC overseas news announced the bombing.

> We had been at the usual evening pastime of playing Liar Dice in the officers mess, and vanquishing our rivals with gin and bitters. I can remember the joy of anticipating the war's end tempered with horror and awe over the event. But our relief was profound for we had doubts about our preparedness for our mission. Each one of us, of ten Canadians attached to the British Force 136, had been assigned to lead an "Indian Field Broadcasting Unit" consisting of a squad of Gurkhas, India radio technicians, and Canadian Nisei N.C.O. assistants and to penetrate or move close enough to enemy lines to persuade them over loudspeakers to surrender. It was a demoralization

tactic which, though sound in theory, proved to be fatal in execution. We met peace on our arrival in Malaya, and almost a year later on our return we learned that without exception every brave little broadcasting unit that had gone into action had been wiped out.

The war had ended months before for Donald Jack, still in service, and now stationed in Allied occupied Berlin.

Like so many of my generation I was enormously influenced by John Strachey's *The Theory and Practise of Socialism*, and in Berlin on August 6 I was a red-hot socialist and it showed even in my music criticisms for the *Berlin Air Line*, a Service newspaper I helped to establish, and for which we charged one mark per copy. Normally, this would have been a gross over-charge, but to the Allied serviceman who could sell a pack of cigarettes on the black market for 100 marks, this was nothing, so the paper flourished and we made a really embarrassing profit, something like 3,000 per cent. But it was part of my social consciousness that I wanted to do some good with all that loot, so we sponsored concerts at Gatow Airfield by the Berlin Philharmonic, and I am still proud of my contribution in keeping that orchestra together in the months following the Nazi collapse. (I even helped to get an English score to them, Britten's Soirées Musicales.)

I was writing a review of a concert conducted by Sergiu Celibidache when I heard the news over AFN Berlin (American Forces Network, located in Max Schmeling's mansion) that an entire city had been obliterated by a single bomb. I was hardened to bombing by then, and even the fire-bombing of Hamburg, which was, I now understand, even worse than Hiroshima, stoked feelings only of vengeful satisfaction at the time. But the thought of a city being wiped out by one bomb was almost unbearable. Thousands dead within seconds? Never before or since have I felt such rage and anguish, and when I talked about it with my friends my face was all screwed up because of these feelings, and it seemed to me in my emotional naivety to confirm everything that Strachey said about the self-destructive impulses of capitalism.

Wartime radio offered neither details nor reflections, and so most people eagerly awaited confirmation and more details of the bombing in the newspapers. Journalists scrambled for superlatives. The story of the bomb was not only the biggest of the war, but the most closely guarded.

That secrecy was certainly confirmed in Oak Ridge, Tennessee, one of the bomb's production sites. In thirty-five minutes 1,600 newspapers were sold at the phenomenal cost of $1 each. The buyers were plant workers, anxious to find out—at last— what they had been working on all this time.

Writers found it hard to convey the precise nature of the weapon. Texts explaining nuclear fission were, understandably, garbled in a good many newspapers. President Truman's speechwriters had played it safe in his official announcement by describing the bomb as "a harnessing of the basic power of the universe." It was easier to write abstractly of "the most destructive force of all time" or "the dawn of a new era," the "biggest event in the history of time" and one that was "stunning," "horrific," "cataclysmic," or merely "staggering." For once the adjectives were not exaggerations. London's *Daily Express* began its editorial, "The world has changed overnight." And even the BBC recognized the magnitude of the event, extending its nine o'clock news beyond the customary fifteen minutes.

In Italy *L'Osservatore Romano* recalled a prescient antecedent. Leonardo da Vinci had destroyed his plans for a submarine because he had feared that it would lead to the end of civilization. Perhaps the same should be done with the atomic bomb. The Montreal *Gazette*, puffed up with national pride, explained that Canadian uranium had been essential to the project and that it had been Lord Rutherford, while a physicist at McGill University, who had laid the foundation of modern nuclear physics.

A day later the paper had some second thoughts, and in an editorial recalled a statement from Robert Fulton, the inventor of the steamboat. In 1806 Fulton had been experimenting with torpedoes and was reported to have said, "I have no doubt war will be put to an end by being rendered so murderous." The *Gazette* concluded that "the murderous energies of the Atomic Bomb may either bring Fulton's prophecy to fulfilment or the world to destruction."

As time passed and the news of the horrible loss of life, the maiming and the effects of radiation sickness became generally known, not just editorial pages but letters columns appeared stuffed with fearful descriptions of the consequences of the act.

Church leaders were particularly quick to condemn. And then, too, there were strange bedfellows. John Foster Dulles, who later as U.S. secretary of state would routinely take the world to the brink of nuclear incineration, observed on behalf of the American Federal Council of Churches: "If we, a professedly Christian nation, feel morally free to use atomic energy in that way, men elsewhere will accept that verdict . . . the stage will be set for the sudden and final destruction of mankind."

The magnitude of the destruction caused many to ponder religious and philosophical questions about the very nature of existence. The British journalist Katharine Whitehorn was staying with some friends in a bungalow in Berkshire.

> The news came through in the evening, and I remember lying awake on my mattress thinking about it. Did this mean, if the world could be destroyed, that all the certainties and values in which I'd been reared went for nothing? How could this, that or the other—Beethoven, mountains, G.K. Chesterton, Housman's poems—be eternal, if the whole thing could go up in a puff of smoke? And by the time I went to sleep I had decided that if they *were* eternal, that they would be so whether the world continued to exist or not. The physical world could go and they would remain. Which is I suppose as near a definition of what I mean—or at any rate then meant—by believing in God as I could describe it. And it was Hiroshima that oddly gave me the conviction.

The military men who had fought the war also paused for reflection. T.H. White, a *Time* correspondent, describes the effect of the bomb on American General Douglas MacArthur:

> The news came on the armed forces radio while I was shaving, on a day of terminal madness and joy. My instinct was to hurry to my post in Chungking, but first I wanted to talk to MacArthur himself. He received me two days after the bomb dropped, the day after he himself had been briefed for the first time on the bomb and its nature by Karl Compton of MIT. After some pleasantries of reacquaintance, he got at once to the bomb, no longer roaring as he used to roar. "White," he said, "White, do you know what this means?" "What, sir?" I asked. It meant, he said, that all wars were over; wars were no longer matters of valor or judgment, but lay in the hands of scholars and scientists. "Men like me are obsolete," he said,

pacing back and forth. "There will be no more wars, White, no more wars."

Three days after Hiroshima, a second bomb, this time made of plutonium and named "Fat Man" after Winston Churchill, was dropped on the "westernized" city of Nagasaki. The blast itself was even greater, although the damage was slightly less because air raid precautions had been more thorough and there was no fire storm as in Hiroshima.

Japan was convinced by the shock treatment. And if she had needed further persuading, it came the following day when Russian troops attacked in force from Siberia and Outer Mongolia. On August 14, the world learned the news of the Japanese surrender. The Americans duly claimed credit in Washington, the Russians in Moscow.

The Second World War officially came to an end on the deck of the battleship USS *Missouri* in Tokyo Harbor on the morning of September 2, 1945. But the world still did not understand the consequences of the Hiroshima and Nagasaki blasts. In Japan itself people were aware of the terrible nature of the explosion and the horrors of the unexpected radiation, but they were used to fearsome calamities. The B-29 fire raids, measure for measure, had been more destructive.

Should such a powerful, conclusive weapon have been used against a civilian population? Was there no other way? Certainly the rigid inflexibility of the "unconditional surrender" policy was exposed in all its poverty. Some scientists had counseled against using the bomb; others had urged it as a ready end to the war. Military men and politicians alike had generally favored the bomb. For Truman and Churchill there had been no hesitation—not only would the bomb bring an end to war, but they were certain it would guarantee a satisfactory peace, especially since it was controlled by a British-American monopoly. And then, too, there was the psychological deterrent. Surely the very existence of a weapon of such destructive capability would make war unthinkable in the future.

Canadian General E.L.M. Burns was in charge of the Canadian section of the 21st Army Group Headquarters in a spa in occupied Germany, Bad Salzuflen.

In World War I, there had been some bombing of cities, but its scale was relatively so small that the determination of the warring governments was not affected. Between the world wars, air generals developed the theory that a sufficiently powerful air force bombing the enemy's cities and industries could inflict such death and destruction that his will to continue fighting would be overcome, and he would have to accept a dictated peace. From 1940 on, in the Second World War, there were air offensives; the German "blitzes" on London and other British cities, and the British bombing of Germany, as the only offensive means they could use at that time. But although vast destruction and heavy civilian casualties were inflicted, even when the United States joined in the British air offensive, it was never powerful enough to overcome the defenses and force surrender.

When Japan remained the only member of the Triple Alliance to continue fighting, the creation of the atom bomb made it possible to apply fully the theory of direct attack on the enemy's civilian population and industry to force surrender.

It was not long before scientists and politicians with broad vision perceived that, while the secret weapon had brought victory to its inventors, it would not long remain a secret. If atomic weapons were allowed to be developed without restraint, there would never be one all-powerful atom-armed nation, but a threat to all the nations which could have no limits. So one of the first problems to which the newly formed United Nations addressed itself in 1946 was how to make the world safe from war, and especially atomic war. Thirty-three years later the problem is not much closer to solution.

For ex-Reichsmarshal Hermann Göering, then awaiting trial at Nuremberg as a war criminal, the news brought only mild interest. "A mighty accomplishment," he said, adding, "I don't want anything to do with it. I am leaving this world." He committed suicide shortly afterwards, leaving others to try to sort out the implications and realities of the terrible world he had helped to bring about.

The *New York Times* on August 7, 1945 had written with convincing relevance for the future: "One consequence stands clear: civilization and humanity can now survive only if there is a revolution in mankind's political thinking." The statement still stands.

EDGAR RICE BURROUGHS, the creator of Tarzan, was having breakfast at a hotel on Waikiki Beach, a few miles from Pearl Harbor. Oblivious to the bombing raid, he went on, later that day, to play a game of tennis.

LUCILLE BALL and DEZI ARNAZ were in New York City and flew immediately to Los Angeles to be with their families. Within a week Cuba had declared war on Japan, and about a month later Arnaz received a commission as a lieutenant in the Cuban Army. He resigned and joined the U.S. Navy instead.

ERNEST HEMINGWAY covered the D-Day invasion as a war correspondent for *Colliers* magazine. He was reported anxious to move on to Paris to visit his old haunts.

When she heard about Hiroshima, anthropologist MARGARET MEAD tore up every page of the book she had almost finished. As she wrote in her autobiography, *Blackberry Winter, My Earlier Years,* "Every sentence was out of date. We had entered a new age."

DOUGLAS FAIRBANKS, JR. was on leave from the navy when his mother called him on the telephone to ask whether he had heard the radio that morning. "They've just dropped some new bomb on Japan," she said. "Just another block-buster, I expect," he answered. "The papers always have to write something sensational. Take no notice."

1

2

1. Protesting for Hungary's cause,
   Vienna, November 1, 1956 (*Miller
   Services*).
2. Soviet tanks guard a Budapest
   intersection during anti-Russian
   demonstrations (*United Press
   International*).
3. Hungarian refugees in neutral
   Austria arrive to board train for
   resettlement in Switzerland,
   December 1956 (*Miller Services*).
4. Aerial view of blocked ships in
   Suez Canal, November 26, 1956
   (*Radio Times/Hulton Picture
   Library*).
5. Unidentified Russian vessel sailing toward Cuba—and the American blockade (*Miller Services*).

3

CHAPTER 6

Cold War Confrontations

4

5

NOT SO LONG AGO the expression "Cold War" seemed an anachronism, a concept as out of touch with current thinking as flashy-finned Chryslers and ducktail haircuts. Yet in the wake of the Soviet Union's incursion into Afghanistan, America's boycott of the Moscow Olympics, Ronald Reagan's ascendancy to the White House, and American involvement in El Salvador, the Cold War seems to be with us once again. In truth it never ended; it merely thawed for a few years.

It was Winston Churchill's friend Bernard Baruch, the American financier and presidential advisor, who coined the term Cold War to encompass the political and diplomatic conflicts erupting between the United States and the Soviet Union after the Second World War. By the early 1950s the iron curtain had clanged firmly into place and the European continent had been roughly sliced in two: the western half, liberal and democratic and under the sway of the United States and the omnipotent Yankee dollar, and the eastern half, communist-influenced and Soviet-occupied. These divisive European developments had counterparts elsewhere as Soviet and communist ideologies spread into Asia, Africa, and later to Latin America.

The manicured niceties of centuries of European diplomacy became largely irrelevant as world affairs became checkered by sporadic confrontations between the superpowers. The West's fondest international wish was embodied in the concept of "containment," the idea that Soviet expansion must not be allowed to spread any further and that the West must encourage and even initiate internal divisions and revolt within Soviet-controlled regimes. The Soviet blockade of West Berlin in 1948 was checkmated by the heroic winter saga of the Berlin airlift, which gave an extra fillip to the development of the North Atlantic Treaty Organization (NATO), a unique effort which marked the end of the traditional American policy of "no-entangling alliances." A communist counterbalance, the Warsaw Pact was founded in 1955. Once more, as it had been in the decades before the outbreak of the First World War, the world was split into two armed camps. Only this time the arsenals had the capacity to be truly devastating.

Over the years the Cold War has manifested itself in many guises, including the spectacular technological race for outer space in which the Americans effected a grandstand performance in July 1969 when astronaut Neil Armstrong planted an American flag on the lunar surface and took his "one small step for man" and "giant step for mankind." But ruthless as that extraterrestrial competition was, it was the merest intramural scrimmage compared to the big-league showdowns of the interlocking Suez Crisis and Hungarian Revolution of 1956 and the Cuban Missile Crisis of 1962. The first marked an indirect collision of the two emergent superpowers while the second, heightened and perhaps even escalated in the western camp by television, was a fearful thirteen-day confrontation in which the world not only readied itself for war, but prepared for nuclear attacks with all their terrible aftermath. And certainly nothing has more ably demonstrated the reluctant and untidy demise of the old European hegemony and the emergence of its confident but equally shackled successors than the events of 1956 and 1962.

ON MARCH 9, 1953 Josef Vissarionovich Stalin died. His achievements had been as awesome as the country he had so ruthlessly and single-handedly governed: the industrialization of the primitive Russian economy, the successful prosecution of the largest war the world had known, and the spread of the communist movement. On the other hand, his inability to comprehend or cooperate with the West had spawned a world fraught with tension and produced in his own country a paranoid record of imprisonment, torture, slaughter and mass suffering probably unequaled in history. The Soviet regime had been no less harsh in dealing with its European satellites. Riots in East Berlin in June 1953 emphasized the vast difference between the economic well-being of western peoples and those under Soviet hegemony. That same year—1953—saw the end of the Korean War, the Soviets detonate an H-Bomb, and the inauguration of Republican General Dwight D. Eisenhower, succeeding Democrat Harry S Truman, as president of the United States.

By 1956 Nikita Khruschev's claim to the Soviet leadership had been substantiated, and at the Twentieth Soviet Party Congress in February of that year he solemnly denounced the excesses and brutality of the Stalin regime. The effects of this official softening, wrongly interpreted by some as genuine liberalism, ripped through the satellite countries, and the call for de-Stalinization soon became interpreted as de-Sovietization.

In June 1956 strikes and rioting erupted in Poznan, Poland, principally because of the high cost of living, but also because of an oppressive Soviet presence. Before it was over, fifty-three workers had been killed in the fighting. Then in mid-October, Wladyslaw Gomulka, a confirmed communist but a dedicated Polish nationalist, was elected first secretary of the Communist Party. He initiated a series of orderly reforms that temporized the tensions between Poland and the Soviet Union. They did not dispel them entirely, however, as further strikes in 1970 and the confrontations of 1980 and 1981 attest.

Polish reforms aroused democratic hopes in radical young Hungarians. On October 23, 1956 near the Polish embassy in Budapest, a huge crowd crushed around the statue of General Josef Bem, who in 1848 had helped Hungarians resist Hapsburg rule. Writers and students addressed the crowd, stridently calling for reform and democratization. Jittery police, recalling the Polish outbreaks a few months earlier and the vicious riots of 1953 in East Berlin, answered the crowd with tear-gas and mass arrests. Savage street-fighting broke out and spread throughout the city. Martial law was soon declared, and Soviet troops, tanks and aircraft were called in against the demonstrators. Nevertheless, riots quickly swept all of Hungary. At least in part they were spurred by a critical fuel shortage and a poor harvest, but it's also true that the foolhardy use of Soviet force triggered a smouldering Hungarian patriotism that lashed out fiercely and blindly at the Russians, and particularly at fellow Hungarians who were believed to have collaborated with the Russians.

Budapest was the explosive center. That first day students and workers attacked a huge statue of Stalin, ripped it from its pedestal, severed the head, and rolled it roughly down the street as thousands cheered. For ten days thereafter Hungarians struck at more than symbols in a clash in which three thousand died and thousands were imprisoned as patriots fought valiantly to wrestle Hungary free from Soviet domination.

For a time all went well. Former Premier Imre Nagy, a communist moderate, was restored to power by a worried Soviet leadership, and the Russian troops were withdrawn from the capital. In Moscow Premier Khruschev appeared to have accepted the Hungarian revolt as he had earlier accommodated Polish disgruntlement. Nagy assembled a new government, including non-Communist Party members, and then announced a series of liberal reforms. Within days the popular democrat and patriot Cardinal Josef Mindzenty, imprisoned since 1948, had been freed. But all of this liberalism exacerbated rather than dampened democratic fervor in students and workers. By Halloween Nagy had also allowed the reestablishment of forbidden political parties, and the next day he suggested that a free Hungary would withdraw from the Warsaw Pact and proclaim itself neutral— along the model of Austria.

This was too much for the Kremlin. Janos Kadar, one of Nagy's disgruntled minions, formed a counter government in eastern Hungary and called out for strong Soviet military support. He was not disappointed. Russian tanks and some 300,000 troops rolled into the country and into Budapest itself on November 4. Their orders were simple: "Conquer or exterminate."

Hungarian rebels looked frantically to the West for help but none was forthcoming, for the western democracies were pre-occupied by events in a more traditional sphere of influence: Suez.

THE SUEZ CANAL was scarcely a modern idea. The scheme to establish a waterway between the Mediterranean and the Red Sea was a dream some forty centuries old when the French engineer Ferdinand de Lesseps oversaw construction of the massive project from 1859 to its completion a decade later. Britain, wary of the repercussions of a French-controlled canal on her far-flung Asian and African empires, had been resolutely opposed to the project. But once the waterway had been completed, Britain wanted to ensure that its ships had safe passage to India and the other imperial interests in the Far East. In 1875, at the initiative of Prime Minister Benjamin Disraeli, Britain bought out the holdings of the bankrupt Egyptian Khedive and became the largest shareholder (40 per cent) in the Paris-headquartered Suez Canal Company.

In 1888 at Constantinople, a convention was signed by all the major European powers declaring the canal neutral and guaranteeing "free and open" passage to all nations "in time of war as in time of peace." (This right was denied to nations at war with Britain in each of the world wars and to Israel after 1948.) Britain was the guarantor of the convention, and British troops guarded the canal for the next three-quarters of a century. For much of this time as well, Britain was the virtual ruler of Egypt. Finally in 1954, wincing under the lash of anti-British rioting fomented by the rabid nationalism of General Mohammed Neguib and Colonel Gamal Abdel Nasser, Britain agreed to withdraw, a process that was completed by June 13, 1956. Six weeks later President Nasser nationalized the Suez Canal Company, touching off what became known as the Suez Crisis.

Nasser's rash action sprang from a number of motives—for one thing he was the ambitious leader of a pan-Arab movement whose prime purpose was the destruction of the Jewish state of Israel. When the British withdrew, the insulating buffer between Arab and Israeli was gone. As well, Nasser, like other emerging Third World leaders, was actively courting funds from rival world powers to finance local projects—in his case the construction of the Aswan High Dam, the instrument he hoped would facilitate industrialization and extend the arable lands of the Nile Valley. A joint Anglo-American loan seemed a certainty until the American secretary of state, John Foster Dulles, jealous of Soviet influence in Egypt, clumsily but dramatically withdrew the offer without even consulting his British allies. It was at this juncture, on July 26, 1956, that Nasser seized the canal, arguing that he would raise the necessary revenues from canal dues. As he put it, "I look at Americans and say may you choke to death on your fury." World reaction to this high-handed act was uniformly negative, but any attempts to placate the situation over the summer or negotiate a new deal were loudly declined by Egypt. Anyway, the Eisenhower administration was too preoccupied with winning the presidential election that coming November to intervene in the squabble and risk having it erupt as a campaign issue.

Britain and France were outraged by Nasser and determined to take decisive action. Not only had he embarrassed them politically and diplomatically, but he now controlled much of the flow of oil that their industries needed so vitally. As the summer faded the two waning European powers drew up "Operation Musketeer," a secret military plan for an assault on the canal that included a coordinated Israeli attack across the Sinai Desert. Israel felt boxed and threatened by an Egyptian blockage in the Gulf of Agaba which cut off trade from the southern Israeli port of Eilat. Something had to be done.

At the time the late Golda Meir was Israeli foreign minister and directly involved in plotting the Sinai Campaign.

> On 24 October, in total secrecy, we began to mobilize our reserves. The public—and, by the same token, I suppose, Egyptian intelligence—was given the impression that because Iraqi troops had ominously moved into Jordan (which had recently joined the unified Egyptian-Syrian command), we were preparing for an assault against that country, and our troops massing on the Jordanian border helped to lend authenticity to the rumour. A week before the Sinai Campaign was to start, a conference of Israeli ambassadors took place at the Foreign Ministry, partly so that I could meet with some of our more important representatives abroad before the UN General Assembly convened. They went back to their respective posts four days before the war broke out not knowing anything about it. Sharett, who had gone to India as soon as I took over at the ministry, was actually talking to Nehru when they got word that the Sinai Campaign had begun, and Nehru couldn't believe that his guest knew nothing about it. But total secrecy was vital.
>
> Every now and then during the last week or two before the campaign began, working at the Foreign Ministry or trying to get organized in the foreign minister's residence (to which I had moved in the summer), I found myself longing to talk to someone about what I knew was going to happen on 29 October. There is nothing lonelier or less natural for a human being than to have to keep a secret that affects the lives of every one around her, and one can only do it, I think, by an enormous, almost superhuman, effort. Wherever I went and whatever I did, I was never, for one instant, unaware of the fact that within a few days we would be at war. I had no doubt that we would be victorious, but however great our victory might be

there would still be great suffering and danger. I used to look at the young men in the Foreign Ministry or at the boy who delivered my newspapers or at the builders working across the street from my home and wonder what would happen to them when the war started. It was not at all a good feeling, but there was no other way for us to get rid of the *fedayeen* or force the Egyptians to understand that Israel was not expendable.

MEANWHILE THE NEWS of disturbances in Hungary clattered out on the western world's teletypes late in the evening of October 23, causing not the merest ripple of concern. France was agog with the climactic kidnapping of the Algerian rebel leader Ben Bella the day before, which Parisians confidently predicted would take the leadership—and the sting—out of the troubles that beset their wayward African departments. That same day a man who would soon figure prominently in events both in Hungary and in the Middle East, the British Prime Minister Sir Anthony Eden, was also in France to receive an honorary doctorate from the University of Caen. In the afternoon the French prime minister, socialist Guy Mollet, a key schemer in Operation Musketeer, angrily addressed the Chamber of Deputies on the calumnies of President Nasser and the impertinence of his Suez policies. At the same time Mollet's foreign minister, Christian Pineau, was across the Channel in England, conferring with his British counterpart, Selwyn Lloyd. The subject was Suez, and newspapers reported that the British position appeared to be hardening.

The next day—October 24—was different. Suddenly, as it became apparent that the Budapest demonstrations were more than a student scuffle, that lives had been lost, and that the communist regime was threatened, the international media took note and, in fact, for most of a week made Hungary a hot news story. But it was difficult to keep the focus sharp because the Hungarian government had imposed not only tight censorship but such rigid border controls that most western newsmen were still hopelessly scrambling to get into the country. A handful were already in Hungary or had somehow gained access to a source within the country, and slowly, after a couple of days, their dispatches began to filter out. They told of an entire nation convulsed in a desperate effort to cast off the shackles of an oppressive puppet regime, of a spontaneous, enthusiastic, and popular revolt against strong-arm tactics, an emotional outburst that had suddenly, almost impulsively, grown into revolution.

There were other sources of information as well. The British legation in Budapest was linked by its own radio to London and kept up a steady flow of reports—which was just as well since telephones and teletypes were either regularly tapped or, mysteriously, shut down. As the days passed, news increasingly came from radio broadcasts—not official radio, but from plucky "Free" stations, ham radios, which began broadcasting sporadically at first and then in a constant stream.

Western listeners and readers were heartened by the gutsy determination of the rebellious Hungarians. They were quickly dubbed "freedom fighters" by the press, although it was not at all clear exactly which freedom they espoused—communist or capitalist. It was enough that they were fighting the Soviets, and all the major newspapers of the English-speaking world editorialized about "History on the March" (*The Times*), "Heroic Martyrs" (The *New York Times*), or "Tyranny shaken" (The *Daily Telegraph*). Western leaders responded more cautiously. "The heart of America," said President Eisenhower as he campaigned for reelection, "goes out to the people of Hungary." But nothing else was offered. In London, Anthony Eden spoke of "sympathy and admiration," and later he pledged £10,000 to the International Red Cross for Hungarian Relief—but he gave nothing more substantial. It wasn't that the two great western democracies were indifferent; rather they were genuinely surprised by events in Hungary and confused as to what action they should take. Soviet intentions were unknown, and the Americans felt strongly that only the United Nations could be a safe and decisive forum for intervention. However, swift action could only be taken by the Security Council, and there the Russians could—and surely would—use their veto to prevent any assistance to their satellite, armed or diplomatic.

So western leadership did nothing, although public pressure mounted as news trickled out about the viciousness of the fighting, of the horrible massacre of children at Magyarovar, or of tanks indiscriminately firing into peaceful Budapest crowds. And then, quite suddenly and amazingly, the Russians were leaving. By

Sunday, October 28, jubilation swept Budapest. The people had won. *Daily Mail* correspondent Noel Barber was one of the few western correspondents in the city and in his book, *A Handful of Ashes*, records the scene at the Hotel Duna where he had a room.

> The hall porter grabbed my hand and shook it and literally crying tears of joy added, "Monsieur Barber! C'est la victoire! nous avons gagné!"
>
> The entrance hall was jammed with people jostling each other and shaking each other's hands. A man, with Franz Joseph moustaches curling almost to his ears—a man I had never seen before—came up and said in stilted, correct English: "I am glad you are here, sir, to see us. This is the proudest moment of our history."
>
> A knot of freedom fighters jumbled and bustled their way through the doors carrying a big flag—with the usual hole in the centre—and one stood on another's shoulders and nailed it high up on the wall in front of the reception desk. He fell off the other man and everybody roared with laughter. Somebody started the Hungarian national anthem and all joined in until the melody almost suffocated the hall.
>
> Everybody was shouting slogans I did not understand and all tried their phrase-book English on me:
>
> "Bloody Ruskies!" cried one.
>
> "We free!" shouted another.
>
> "Happy Budapest!"
>
> "Is war end!"
>
> "Ruskie mata!" . . .
>
> There was still no menu in the Duna restaurant—just a standard meal of soup and potatoes with a little goulash. There was still no bread. But at least the soup was hot, and there seemed to be two or three more pieces of meat than usual. . . .
>
> Somebody turned on a radio in the dining room. Nagy was about to broadcast. As he started to speak, the noise of the people talking, like the chatter of a thousand starlings, ceased in one breath. A big fat man at the next table, his napkin tucked under his chin, had a forkful of potatoes half way to his mouth. As Nagy's voice came over, firm and purposeful, the fork and the potatoes went back to the plate and shortly, the man started crying. . . .

Similar moving scenes were occurring all over the country. Strangers hugged each other in the streets, even as others moved among the rubble dusting lime on fresh-killed bodies, or searched beneath flag-draped coffins for a son or a father. During the next few heady days of Hungarian freedom, western writers and cameramen, along with their readers and listeners, celebrated the Hungarians' victory—and shared in their revenge. Television didn't yet have the easy, sophisticated coverage that videotape would bring to war, but stills were regularly shown on the news and there was an abundance of "experts" to interpret and confirm that the Russian empire was in decline. On the streets, however, crowds picketed United Nations headquarters in New York urging guarantees, and American longshoremen refused to unload Soviet ships until they were certain that the last Russian tank and soldier had left the country. A kind of euphoria drenched Budapest that weekend as Premier Imre Nagy desperately tried to hold his disparate government together. It all seemed too easy, too good to be true.

IT'S CERTAINLY UNLIKELY that many of the Hungarians who were dancing in the streets that weekend or beginning on Monday morning (the 29th) to clear the rubble from their shattered homes listened to western radio broadcasts telling of an Israeli strike, supported by French fighter aircraft across the Sinai Desert against Egypt. Operation Musketeer had been launched. On October 30, using the pretext that the canal was endangered, Britain and France sent ultimatums to both Egypt and Israel demanding they withdraw to ten miles from either side of the canal. Not all members of the French government were in agreement with this decisive action. Pierre Mendès-France remembers:

> The day before England and France sent their ultimatum to Nasser, I was told of the decision. I went to beg Guy Mollet to reconsider this step. At eleven that evening we had a rather heated and dramatic confrontation. He assured me that the Anglo-French initiative was the only way to solve the problems in the Mediterranean region (which for the French government meant Algeria). He was determined to carry on with the plan and had no doubt that a rapid military victory would be achieved.

The next day I attended the debate on this issue at the National Assembly. The halls were boiling over with fanatical discussions. Most members were convinced that the occupation of Egypt would end all arms shipments to Algerian nationalists and thereby resolve a colonial problem that had started to exasperate French public opinion. All were firmly convinced that the Anglo-French invasion would be successful.

When our caucus met, I argued vehemently with my colleagues who were part of the government and especially with Bourges-Mannoury, Minister of War, and with Maurice Faure, Undersecretary of State for foreign affairs. They did not doubt for a minute that the operation would be successful and that it would be underway immediately (in fact it took several days to get going). When the question came to a vote, the government received an overwhelming majority in a climate of general euphoria.

The Egyptians, naturally enough, were not anxious to withdraw from their own territory and absolutely refused the Anglo-French demands. On Halloween, October 31, therefore, two hundred RAF Canberras, Venoms and Valiants plus forty French Thunderstreaks were despatched to bomb Port Said and other Egyptian targets. An amphibious invasion was slated to follow-up the bombardment, but since it was scheduled to sail all the long way from Malta and Gibraltar, surprise was out of the question. In any event the plans were changed and rechanged. In the end it was, as one military historian phrased it with typical British understatement, "an appalling muddle."

Escott Reid was then Canadian high commissioner in New Delhi.

The attack angered me because it was a reversion to days which I had thought were ended, the days when wealthy, white European nations rode roughshod over poor coloured countries in Asia and Africa. My anger was the greater because the attack diverted attention from the aggression which the Soviet Union had launched against Hungary and I felt that if only the world's attention could be concentrated on Hungary, the Soviet Union might decide not to crush the Hungarian Revolution. . . .

That evening [October 31] I met the British Deputy High Commissioner at a diplomatic reception. I said to him that Britain by its aggression against Egypt without any consultation with its fellow members of the Commonwealth and the North Atlantic Alliance had seriously weakened both. He drew himself up and said, "I'm High Commissioner, I cannot accept such remarks from you." Later at the reception he took me aside and said, "Escott, I agree entirely with what you said but with other members of the British High Commission within earshot I had to say what I said." I replied, "I'm no good at quoting Latin but there is a Latin saying which keeps going through my head." "Yes," he said. "It has also been running through mine." "Quem Jupiter vult perdere dementat pruis." "Whom the gods would destroy, they first make mad."

News of the bombardment was a surprise to most people in the West—even to those at the top. President Eisenhower had been in the hospital for a routine check-up on October 29 when the Middle East erupted, and as British and French bombs were falling, he complained about his old Allies: "I just don't know what got into those people. It's the damndest business I ever saw supposedly intelligent people get themselves into." A lot of Americans felt the same way.

Now Suez and Hungary shared the front pages and the editorial columns, and *Time* called the ongoing events a "World Crisis." The inside pages, though, were crammed with the lavish bounty of the American Dream: ads for the new finned '57 model cars, reviews of Maria Callas at the Met (an "operatic volcano" said the *New York Times*), and notices for films like *Around the World in 80 Days, The Solid Gold Cadillac*, and *The King and I*. 1956 was a banner year in the "Fabulous Fifties," one in which America and the American dollar were loved around the world— but particularly by Americans themselves. It was the year that Elvis Presley and Rock 'n' Roll became a craze, of the fairy-tale marriage of actress Grace Kelly to Prince Rainier of Monaco, of the Olympic Games at Melbourne, and of W.H. Whyte's revealing portrait of American big business, *The Organization Man*. And for all Americans, overriding everything else that autumn, it was the year of presidential elections—slated, fatefully, for November 6. In the midst of all this, war or rumors of war and revolutions in far-off places, despite the searing headlines, took a definite second place.

Unlike either self-obsessed America or outwardly staunch France, Britain cleaved completely over Suez. A mix of euphoria and despair, the mood of the country reminded those with very long memories of the Boer War. More chillingly, others recalled Munich. Was this, outraged Britons argued wildly, the reward for years of White Man's Burden? The Empire was largely gone; little was left east of Suez but memories and emotions. The bombings and all the attendant braggadocio gave recalcitrant imperialists one last supercharged moment.

British newspapers were quick to take sides, the Tory press either beating the war drum, as with Lord Beaverbrook's imperialist *Daily Express*, or cautiously admitting to some anxiety, or "deep disquiet" as the *Times* put it. Labour and Liberal papers were adamantly opposed to the adventure. It was "Eden's War" and nobody else's said the popular *Daily Mirror*, and "Folly on the grand scale" as it was condemned in the *News Chronicle*. The respected *Manchester Guardian* claimed: "Millions of British people are deeply shocked by the aggressive policy of the government. Its action is a disaster of the first magnitude. It is wrong on every count—moral, military and political."

In the House of Commons the Labour Opposition Leader Hugh Gaitskell exploded in anger, pointing out that the "reckless and foolish" decision had been taken in direct violation of "the three principles that have governed British foreign policy for at least the last ten years—solidarity with the Commonwealth, the Anglo-American alliance, and adherence to the Charter of the United Nations." The question that was asked over and over was simple and direct: was Britain at war or not? But the government refused to give a straightforward answer.

Particularly dumbfounded were Commonwealth members, especially the old white Dominions, who couldn't understand why they had not at least been consulted. On November 1 the Canadian Prime Minister Louis St. Laurent sent a stiffly worded telegram to Sir Anthony Eden which read in part:

> Thank you for your message of yesterday, which reached me at five o'clock our time, in the afternoon. I understand, of course, that in view of the rapidity with which your government and that of France felt it was necessary to act, it could not be otherwise; but the first intimation I had of your government's intention to take certain grave steps in Egypt was from the press reports of your statement in the House of Commons.

I must add that without more information, and information different from that which we now have, about the action of Israel, we cannot come to the conclusion that the penetration of its troops into Egypt was justified or that the probable resistance of the Egyptians necessitated the decision of the UK and France to post forces in the canal zone. No doubt, however, your own information is much more complete than ours. We now await developments, and information concerning them, with most anxious interest.

Neither could the United States comprehend how Britain and France—but especially Britain—could have flaunted the Atlantic Alliance. American journalists speculated freely that weekend about the demise of the alliance and concluded that the "special relationship" between Britain and America lay in ruins. Eisenhower's reelection campaign, so carefully constructed to avoid controversy, became dominated by foreign affairs and America's role abroad.

In England two thousand protest meetings were estimated to have been held in the week after the bombings. Angry telegrams poured into Downing Street day after day, and the general post office reported a nine-hour delay in delivery because of the backlog. Every member of Parliament and a good number of civic officials received a small mountain of correspondence, most of it against Eden's strategy. Church groups were particularly adamant in condemning the interference and universities were not far behind.

In the meantime the invasion fleet of Operation Musketeer chugged slowly on. In the melee everyone had forgotten something else too—there were already Britons in Egypt, some thirteen thousand working at various jobs, not a few still connected with the operations of the canal. What about them? As for the canal itself—the ostensible object of the invasion—once the bombing had begun Nasser had arranged for forty-seven old and not-so-old canal company ships to be seized, filled with concrete, and sunk in the main channels. Whatever the outcome of the crisis the canal would be closed for some time. And that would cost Britain, the principal user, a good deal of money.

The serious Sunday newspapers were all against the government on November 4. *The Observer* expressed the general tenor:

"Not since 1783 has Britain made herself so universally disliked ...
Sir Anthony Eden must go." Testy crowds began to grow outside
Downing Street, and police cordons were strongly reinforced. The
Union Jack was burned in Edinburgh, thousands marched in
Oxford to condemn the affair, and throughout the world there
came a realization that there was probably worse yet to come.

Journalist and MP Douglas Jay remembered the mood of that
weekend:

> On Sunday 4 November I travelled to Taunton and back, for a
> public protest meeting which had been organized on the spur
> of the moment, but was attended by six hundred people. I
> spoke with a good deal of violence, because that was how I felt;
> and the meeting responded with an intensity of feeling which
> I had not met at any public meeting for years past. One of the
> strange manifestations of the Suez crisis was the series of
> instantly improvised, yet crowded, public meetings springing
> up in the most unlikely places. The dominant motive in my
> mind, which I believe the great majority of the Labour Party
> and many others shared, including high civil servants, was
> fear that the reputation of the country was being mutilated;
> and that the whole system of international security and the
> UN for which the war had been fought was now being
> endangered. Looking back with hindsight twenty years later, I
> am inclined to think the damage was even greater than most
> of us then feared.

The biggest protest that Sunday was in London. A huge
cheering, jeering crowd estimated at thirty thousand assembled in
Trafalgar Square, waved their red banners freely, and then,
numbers reduced somewhat, marched down Whitehall to Downing Street holding placards proclaiming "Law not War" and
"Eden Must Go." Paul Johnson, then assistant editor of *The New
Statesman*, was among them and recalled the event ten years later:

> The most important lesson of Suez, which I haven't seen
> drawn in any of the anniversary pieces, was the way in which
> it demonstrated America's complete undependability as an
> ally. I don't at all blame Dulles for his devious diplomacy: he
> was trying to avoid a war at all costs and the methods he used
> were perfectly legitimate. Nor could Eden reasonably expect
> US backing once the fighting started. What was indefensible
> was the way in which the US Treasury deliberately speculated

against sterling. The government was prepared to carry on despite the hostility of the UN, Soviet threats and deep divisions both at home and in the Commonwealth. But the risk of an enforced devaluation was unacceptable. It's a sobering thought for the present government that, if they should step out of line with Washington, they are even more vulnerable to financial chastisement than poor old Eden.

For many people of my generation, Suez was the most exciting time of our lives—the equivalent of the Spanish Civil War to our elders. The issues seemed absolutely clearcut: right on one side, wrong on the other. We lobbied MPs, stuck up posters, broke up cocktail parties with angry arguments. It was my first experience of public speaking—standing on a rickety chair outside factory gates and haranguing a sea of sullen faces. On Suez Sunday we all thronged to a monster rally in Trafalgar Square, where Nye Bevan made one of the most sparkling speeches of his life. Then the cry: "To Downing Street"—and the huge, uncontrollable surge into Whitehall. From being comfortably ensconced in the middle of the mob, I suddenly found myself mysteriously in the front rank, with mounted police advancing purposefully towards us. I remember thinking: "I'm glad they're not French cops." Then a few minutes of complete confusion, in which I lost my umbrella and a button from my coat. Some of us reassembled at the Ritz for tea, where a kind waiter took my coat away to have the button sewn on. We honestly believed we were helping to influence history and would have been dumbfounded to know that our task was being accomplished far more effectively by a few hard-faced bankers in Washington.

Despite the seemingly ubiquitous demonstrations against the government, public opinion polls later reported that most Britons were understandably frustrated by Nasser's unlawful seizure and supported Eden's efforts. Among them was Sir Alec Guinness who was acting in Feydean's farce *Hotel Paradiso* at the Winter Gardens Theatre.

> Walking down The Strand, after performing in the theatre, I recall a ragged and hysterical little group squealing, "Hands off Suez!" They angered me quite measurably, as did the official American attitude. I consider that for once my crystal ball was all too clear and vivid.

At the time the reverse seemed true. Because those who protested had the ear of the media, their impact was enormous. Opinion too appeared split along party lines, although it is more likely, since the Tory party survived the debacle with ease, that the country divided on class lines. Lost in the barrage of liberal sentiment was the fact that a good many prominent figures supported the government's position—Sir Winston Churchill for one, and the ordinary working man for another. Chester Cooper, American liaison between British and U.S. intelligence in London, had a unique perspective. He remembers a conversation with a London cab driver. Cooper asked the man what he thought of the bombing and British belligerence. "Well, guv'nor," came the reply, "I'm with the PM all the way. No bloke can fight a cold war in a hot climate."

THE TWIN CLIMAXES of the Hungarian and Suez affairs occurred within hours of one another. The Russians returned to Hungary on Sunday, November 4, and it was an indication of the international confusion that some Siberian soldiers stared at the Danube and asked the locals whether it was the Suez Canal. The following day, November 5, was Guy Fawkes' Day, and in England Gamal Abdel Nasser proved a popular substitute for poor Guy and was roasted throughout the country. Meanwhile in Egypt the English and French parachute assault preceding the poky seaborne invasion hit Port Said. Certainly November 5 was a day to remember that year.

Sir Anthony Eden:

> At 8 a.m. on the 5th, some six hundred British parachutists had begun their jump on Gamil airfield to the west of the town, which itself lies on the west bank of the canal entrance. At the same time five hundred French parachutists dropped to the south of Port Said near the waterworks, which they seized, together with an important bridge over the interior basin. Gamil airfield was quickly secured and the British parachute battalion advanced eastwards into the town itself. Continuous support was given by aircraft from the carrier force. At 1.45 p.m. a reinforcing drop of a hundred men with vehicles and heavy equipment was made at Gamil airfield. A further

four hundred and sixty French parachutists were dropped on the southern outskirts of Port Fuad, on the east bank of the canal, which they proceeded to occupy. Resistance was offered by the Egyptians during the morning, but at 3 p.m. the local Egyptian commander offered to discuss surrender terms on behalf of the Governor of Port Said. At 3.30 a cease-fire was ordered, while negotiations went forward. About an hour later I gave this news to the House, which was then noisily cross-examining the Foreign Secretary. I am not sure that I was wise to do so. The effect in the House was instantaneous, the Government's supporters rising to their feet to cheer and wave their order papers and the Opposition being temporarily subdued. By this announcement I told the world of the cease-fire, thus alerting those who would not welcome it and giving them an opportunity of working against it.

At seven o'clock in the evening a further signal arrived stating that the Egyptians had agreed to our terms. Their forces in Port Said had begun to lay down their arms, and their police were co-operating with us in the town. I was immensely relieved. It seemed that our operations had succeeded instantly and at remarkably small cost. An hour and a half later came a very different message. The Governor of Port Said reported that he could not now agree to the terms and that fighting must resume.

Who had caused him to reverse his decision? It is hard to believe that the Governor would have negotiated a cease-fire and then have proceeded to actual surrender without the knowledge of his Government. Nasser must have known during those five hours what was going on in Port Said. I am convinced that this reversal of action was prompted from further afield. We may never be able to prove it, but what is certain and significant is that loudspeaker vans toured Port Said announcing that Russian help was on the way, that London and Paris had been bombed and that the third world war had started. At this moment a menacing letter from Bulganin had been despatched to me, the first word I had received from him since our decision to intervene. Encouraged by the attitude of the United States and the United Nations, the Russians had taken their decision. The Soviet Consul became suddenly active in Port Said, stimulating resistance and promising help. The Russian hat was now in the ring.

Canadian General E.L.M. Burns has a slightly different perspective on the day's events:

It was some years before the full story of the French-British-Israeli collusion was revealed. The intention was to disguise the object of the invasion, which was really the overthrow of the Nasser regime, and recovery of control of the Suez Canal. The immediate result was to bring the Soviet Union into the politico-military conflict unequivocally on the side of the Arabs.

The danger to world peace became clear when Bulganin, prime minister of the Soviet Union, sent notes to Britain, France and Israel, warning that the USSR was prepared to resort to force if necessary to halt aggression against Egypt. A simultaneous note to President Eisenhower suggested that the USSR and the USA should unite forces to halt Anglo-French aggression. President Eisenhower rejected this suggestion summarily.

The history of the conflict in the Middle East since the hostilities of 1956 shows the continued involvement of the superpowers. The Soviet Union has supplied modern arms and training in their use to the Arab countries, as well as political support. There have been ups and downs in the Soviet-Arab relationships, of course. Britain and France, once leading western influences in the Middle East, have now very little weight there, because of their alliance with Israel in 1956. The United States stands as the provider and protector of Israel.

With the superpowers on opposite sides in the Middle East conflict, when oil from that area is vital to the west, the situation is seen by most observers as a potential detonator of a third World War. The peace treaty between Egypt and Israel on 26 March 1979, important as it is, has not brought unqualified peace.

Immediately, as in any war zone, the normal flow of news was curtailed. Press censorship in Egypt was heavy, and information from Hungary now came only fitfully over Radio Free Hungary since all the telephone and teletype lines had been severed. In New York the Russians used their veto in the United Nations Security Council to prevent Hungary being discussed and forced the debate to be shifted to the slower moving General Assembly. On the 6th, Hungarian Premier Imre Nagy was seized by the Russians and whisked away to imprisonment, interrogation and—eventually—execution. As thousands of refugees began their desperate dash to the border, the slow drama of the inevitable Russian triumph was caught best by the free radio stations, so vigorous a week before in their broadcasts in French, German and English and now lapsing into silence, one by one.

Radio Free Rákóczi—November 6:

Peoples of the World: Hear the call for help of a small nation! . . . We have seen atrocities committed under the command: "Down with Fascism!" We are no Fascists. We will prove this to an independent international committee, but we cannot prove it to those who reply to us with phosphorus bombs. Help, for with the slogans of helping democracy they are taking away the last possibility for a democracy. This is Radio Rákóczi, Hungary. We have read an appeal. Radio Free Europe, Munich! Radio Free Europe, Munich! Answer! Have you received our transmission? . . .

Urgent flash. Attention, attention!
We desperately need guns, ammunition and food parachuted in . . . Attention, attention. Munich. Munich. Take immediate action . . . We urgently need medicine, bandages, arms, food and ammunition. Drop them for us by parachute. Attention, attention! Take immediate action! Attention, attention! Take immediate action! The Soviet troops called on us to lay down arms. We will not comply with this call. If necessary we will keep on fighting for the freedom of Hungary against the foreign occupiers to our last drop of blood.

And then on November 7:

Must we appeal once again? Do you love liberty? . . . So do we. Do you have wives and children? . . . So have we. We have wounded . . . who have given their blood for the sacred cause of liberty but we have no bandages . . . no medicine . . . And what shall we give to our children who are asking for bread? . . . The last piece of bread has been eaten. In the name of all that is dear to you . . . we ask you to help. . . . Those who have died for liberty . . . accuse you who are able to help and who have not helped. The UN is able to stop further bloodshed . . . Or shall we lose faith in the [world's] conscience and decency . . . when we are fighting for world freedom? . . .

And later that same day:

We are asking for immediate armed help. . . . Please forward this appeal to President Eisenhower. . . . We are fighting against overwhelming odds. Possibly our radio will soon be annihilated. We shall continue to fight a partisan war. We ask for urgent . . . help, we ask for armed help for Hungary. Attention, Attention! We ask you to forward the above call for help to President Eisenhower. . . . We ask for immediate intervention, we ask for immediate intervention, we ask for immediate intervention. Continue to listen to our broadcasts. As soon as we have time to come from the firing line . . . we will continue. . . .

For Suez too November 6 was the final day. American, Soviet and Commonwealth pressures, including a disastrous run on the pound, finally forced Eden to cave in and accept a United Nations peace-keeping force based on a Canadian initiative proposed by future Prime Minister Lester B. Pearson. The order for a general ceasefire commencing at sunset went out to the British troops. At first the French were all for carrying on by themselves, but finally they agreed to quit. British troops at the front were stunned and the French, particularly the officers, were enraged. Once again the army had been betrayed by its allies and by the politicians.

And finally on that jammed November day, the Americans, pleased to be kept out of a war, were nonetheless wary enough to return a successful general to the presidency. Eisenhower beat Adlai Stevenson by a landslide.

Anti-British demonstrations rocked Ceylon (now Sri Lanka), and in Karachi, in Pakistan, ten thousand students demonstrated against British actions. In Dacca an enraged mob set fire to the British Information Office shouting "Down with Britain." In Latin America there were sharp, angry confrontations at British and French missions, and in Havana, Cuba, demonstrators vented their frustrations by attacking the local Renault dealer.

Reaction to the vicious Russian assault on Hungary was as predictable as it was futile. In Montevideo a crowd shouting "Viva Hungria" burnt the Russian consulate to the ground; tear gas was needed to disperse a Buenos Aires mob chanting "Murderers" in front of the Soviet embassy. Candlelit services were held throughout Europe and America for the dead, and plans were hatched to help the living—if and when they managed to get themselves out of the country.

In Canada and the United States a "Legion of Freedom" was promoted, and one thousand men were reported to have signed up to fight in Hungary. Some said it was reminiscent of the Spanish Civil War only with the characters playing different roles. Elsewhere, in normally quiet Luxembourg, the Soviet ambassador and his wife were forced to barricade themselves in the embassy basement as angry students mobbed the building and then set it on fire. Brussels saw mounted police charge an incensed crowd of protestors in front of the Soviet embassy, and in Rotterdam and other ports stevedores refused to touch Russian ships. In a more straightforward way in The Hague, bakeries refused to deliver bread to the Soviet embassy.

Eventually, on November 8, the United Nations General Assembly demanded the withdrawal of Soviet troops from Hungary. And two fruitless weeks later, on November 21, the UN made a formal motion of censure against the U.S.S.R. But by then the moment and the opportunity had passed.

By November 7 all military operations in Suez had halted and a UN Emergency Force had been hastily marshaled to police the canal. An exhausted Eden, fueled by pep pills, tried to pick up the pieces, arguing that with the UN keeping the Arab and Israeli forces apart the Anglo-French requirements had been met. It was an unconvincing argument. The reckoning showed that Nasser still ruled the canal, Britain's moral prestige had sunk to a new low, and world attention had been diverted from the brutal Soviet moves in Hungary. A shattered Eden, his health broken, resigned shortly afterwards. It was, Nasser later said, "the Curse of the Pharaohs."

Labour MP Douglas Jay had a much more Freudian analysis of Eden, as he wrote in his memoirs:

> How did Eden come to make such a colossal miscalculation, and how did the British Cabinet system fail to stop him? Part of the answer, I believe, was the persistence of that perennial political fault: fighting the last battle and avoiding the mistake made last time. Just as Baldwin and Chamberlain thought they were avoiding the mistakes made at Versailles; Eden when faced with Nasser, and John Foster Dulles when faced with North Vietnam, both imagined they were avoiding the mistakes made against Hitler, and so made equal and opposite blunders. Partly responsible also, no doubt, was Eden's personal character. One observer, an ex-civil servant,

in conversation with me, predicted trouble from the start "because we are in the hands of that dangerous phenomenon, a weak man who wants to prove he is strong." Watching Eden myself in all his Commons appearances, at each stage of the long Suez tragedy, I was convinced that there was truth in this: that we were in the presence of a civilized but irresolute man, with a streak of hysteria, who was conscious that he was no Churchill, but anxious to prove to the Conservative Party that he could act like one. For Eden the tragedy was bitter. If he had never become Prime Minister, he would have preserved his once great reputation. As W.N. Ewer remarked to me when it was all over, never were the words more true: *"Capax imperii nisi imperasset"* (Capable of ruling if he had not ruled).

IN THE FINAL ANALYSIS Suez proved that Britain and France were no longer major powers. Within a remarkably short span both countries had discarded their empires, the British effecting their withdrawal much more decorously than France's continually bloody exits from Asia and Algeria. The retreat from Algeria, by no means a popular move, threw France into the moral and intellectual quandary Britain had faced over Suez. France, after all, had been waging war since 1945 on behalf of its sagging empire. Part of the French enthusiasm for Suez had been to halt Egyptian aid to Algerian rebels. In 1958 the Fourth French Republic, threatened by a possible revolt by the Algerian Army, collapsed and Charles de Gaulle was called upon to save his country once more. He saved the country, ironically by discarding the empire and instituting a kind of imperial rule at home. One thing was certain: the future for Britain and France no longer lay overseas. Whatever future there was rested firmly in Europe.

Hungary and Suez demonstrated too that the western alliance was divided and the United States was the merest novice in world affairs, calmly pursuing foreign policy in terms of domestic affairs. As Professor Adam Ulam, a student of the period, remarked, the merest mention of the word "imperialism" was enough to cause Washington to abandon her closest allies. The legacy of Suez was shown in a lack of confidence and cooperation in NATO and, more importantly, as a kind of psychological paralysis on behalf of the whole alliance. Britain and the United States soon patched it up, but France has gone her separate way ever since. As for the Soviets, their bluster appeared confident, but in the end their brutality not only offended the West, but alienated them from the many Afro-Asian nations they had hoped to woo. Besides, the primary dilemma of the communist society had been laid bare—as it would be exposed in Czechoslovakia in 1968 and Poland in the 1980s. How was it possible to reconcile a society rigidly based on dogmatic Marxist rules with an evident human need for freedom—especially freedom of speech and freedom of thought? In a way the Soviets too were acting out domestic policy abroad. A quick decisive suppression of political agitation in the satellites was an effective way, or so the Soviets thought, of discouraging similar dislocation at home.

· THE CUBAN MISSILE CRISIS—OCTOBER 22-28, 1962 ·

AFTER A DOZEN or more years of sparring in central Europe, the Hungarian revolt, Suez, the U-2 spy plane incident, and the erection of the Berlin Wall, it is more than a little anomalous that the most significant clash between East and West occurred in a sleepy, sub-tropical island, ninety miles off the United States coast, in a place noted, when it was noted at all, for the superiority of its cigars.

Cuba had been a virtual U.S. protectorate since American forces had wrested it from Spain's crumbling empire in 1898. However, few would argue that the American presence was oppressive, and most would contend the opposite, particularly if they limited their inspection to that cosmopolitan tourist playground, Havana. A glance at the poverty and ignorance of the peasants in the countryside—most of whom were illiterate—drew a radically different picture of Cuban life, but few foreigners ventured outside the capital.

The head of government was Fulgencio Batista, an erratic, right-wing militarist who had ruled the island intermittently since the mid-thirties. Batista's government had always been sordid and corrupt, but in 1952 he suspended the constitution and imposed a one-party dictatorship. This latest abuse sparked Fidel

Castro, the son of a sugar planter and himself a lawyer, to stage an armed revolt. For six years Castro persisted in his rebellion against the ruthless and naked oppression of Batista's regime.

More than a little romantic, Castro and his bearded band attacked Batista's forces from the relative safety of the Sierra Maestra, a mountainous region in Cuba's Oriente province. Castro's courage and tenacity captured the enthusiasm and admiration of both western papparozzi and Cubans alike, and as the attempts to capture him grew more bloody, vicious and futile, Batista's own support within the Cuban Army dwindled. On New Year's Day, 1959 a victorious but surprised Fidel Castro rode triumphantly into Havana as Batista fled to the Dominican Republic.

Once in power Castro initiated a series of striking social and economic reforms. Large estates were seized and the land divided up among the peasants. Collectives were organized and a massive housing program undertaken. Although, at least at the outset, his government was hardly different from many of those he had condemned, Castro almost immediately became a hero to Latin America. Like so many other Caribbean adventurers, he ruled without an elected assembly, preferring to declaim his programs and his fervid anti-Americanism in tedious, lengthy tirades. Nevertheless, the crowds erupted in enthusiastic approval of his social and political dicta.

The United States did not echo the cheers. In fact when John F. Kennedy came to the presidency early in 1961, he inherited from the Eisenhower administration a shaky proscription to erase the Castro government. It culminated in April of that year in the "Bay of Pigs" invasion, a clumsy, amateurish Central Intelligence Agency operation in which 1,500 Cuban exiles were landed for the express purpose of fomenting a counter-revolution to topple Castro. There was no spontaneity and no overthrow and hardly any landing. Worse, Castro now turned actively to the U.S.S.R. for aid and succor. By early 1962 he was claiming that he was and always had been a communist. And he was arguing that the Bay of Pigs fiasco had been merely a feint and that a real American invasion of Cuba would very shortly become a reality.

Was it the fear, real or imagined, of an American invasion

that prompted the Soviets to install nuclear missiles in Cuba? And, if not, what was the reason? In retrospect, it is now clear that, far from protecting the Cubans, the Soviets used them as mere pawns in a scenario so daring and so chilling that even the most far-fetched political thriller is tame by comparison.

By placing the missiles, Khruschev was engaging in a high-risk ploy to secure advantages elsewhere. As far as a strike on the United States was concerned, these Intermediate Range Missiles were irrelevant. Although Soviet strength was not as formidable as analysts at the time thought, Soviet Inter-Continental Ballistic Missiles (ICBMs) were already satisfactorily deployed to hit every major American target—at least on a first strike basis.

No, Khruschev was playing for bigger stakes. He wanted a resolution of problems that had plagued the Soviets for years: the schizophrenic Berlin settlement and the threat that West Germany and China would develop nuclear capabilities. Specifically, Khruschev wanted the U.S. and the U.S.S.R. to adopt a joint nuclear non-proliferation treaty, and he schemed that the Russian missiles in Cuba could be used as a masterly lever in persuading the United States—probably through a confrontation at the United Nations—to negotiate a global settlement. It was a bold, but foolhardy move, but then Khruschev was known to be a gambler.

The Soviets began installing rockets in Cuba in September 1962, although it is unlikely that the Cubans even knew what kind of rockets were being emplaced. Certainly the locals had no control over them—it was a Russian show from beginning to end. The Soviets had helped the Cuban sugar-based economy with massive high-priced orders and subsidies, and now the Cubans were being asked to pay the bill, with the result that for two long weeks that autumn millions of lives hung in the balance. But the Soviets alone were not responsible for the super-charged tensions.

ON OCTOBER 16, as a result of aerial photographs from high flying U.S. U-2 planes, President Kennedy learned definitely that Soviet missiles were being installed throughout Cuba. For the next six days, while the American nation and the world remained ignorant, a powerful drama was being enacted behind the scenes in Washington. Kennedy was under the gun, for American technicians had concluded that in ten days time the missile sites would be operational.

Various alternatives were discussed by Kennedy and his advisors on the Executive Committee or "ExComm" as it was called. The hawks, led by former Secretary of State Dean Acheson and backed by the joint chiefs of staff, advocated a surprise air attack on the missile bases. The doves, led by Secretary of Defense Robert McNamara and the president's brother Robert, wanted a naval blockade followed by negotiations at the United Nations between the U.S.S.R. and the United States. The air strike found some favor, although at one point Robert Kennedy, who was against what he felt was Pearl Harbor in reverse, passed a note to the president saying, "I now know how Tojo felt when he was planning Pearl Harbor."

By the second day of discussions the air strike was discarded. The costs and the risks were too high. An airstrike would result in the deaths of probably 25,000 Cubans and many Soviets and almost certainly would provoke a war with the U.S.S.R. Besides, there was no guarantee that a conventional air strike would obliterate all the missile sites. Other schemes were considered—a private initiative to the Kremlin, a UN announcement, a general invasion of Cuba—but support for the blockade idea grew. To be called clinically a "quarantine," the blockade was particularly favored by Robert Kennedy, who argued that "surprise raids are not in the American tradition."

Through Friday, October 19, the private debate continued and the tension built, even while publicly the president went about his normal business—on this occasion campaigning for congressional elections in Chicago. But this was the day he determined to break the secrecy and tell the world what was going on in a televised address. Additionally, he decided to seek an endorsement for the blockade from the Organization of American States (OAS). The following day, back in Washington, Kennedy gave a final nod to the blockade proposal. In the Caribbean, 180 American ships were quietly put on the move and the Strategic Air Command placed on full alert. By Sunday, October 21, the secret—American style—was known to the press, but general agreements were maintained to keep quiet at least until after the president's speech scheduled for 7:00 p.m. the next evening.

Monday, October 22. Unlike Eden over Suez, Kennedy and his staff spent the day informing allies and enemies alike of their intentions. The world that night was posed. The president's press secretary had already announced that Kennedy's message would be "of the greatest urgency." Without any question, it was. Gone was the crinkly Kennedy smile, replaced by a sober, fatigued and grim expression, one made more serious still by his grave tone. Intentionally and internationally—on air—to millions throughout the United States and the world he made a statement that might easily have unleashed a nuclear holocaust:

> Good evening, my fellow citizens. This government, as promised, has maintained the closest surveillance of the Soviet military build-up on the island of Cuba. Within the past week unmistakable evidence has established the fact that a series of offensive missile sites is now in preparation on that imprisoned island. The purposes of these bases can be none other than to provide a nuclear strike capability against the Western Hemisphere.

Then he sketched in the background of the crisis before revealing the steps to be taken—"immediately":

> First: To halt this offensive build-up, a strict quarantine on all offensive military equipment under shipment to Cuba is being initiated. All ships of any kind bound for Cuba from whatever nation or port will, if found to contain cargoes of offensive weapons, be turned back. This quarantine will be extended, if needed, to other types of cargo and carriers. We are not at this time, however, denying the necessities of life as the Soviets attempted to do in their Berlin blockade of 1948.
>
> Second: I have directed the continued and increased close surveillance of Cuba and its military build-up. . . .
>
> Third: It shall be the policy of this nation to regard any nuclear missile launched from Cuba against any nation in the Western Hemisphere as an attack by the Soviet Union on the United States, requiring full retaliatory response upon the Soviet Union.
>
> Fourth: As a necessary military precaution I have reinforced our base at Guantanamo, evacuated today the depend-

ents of our personnel there, and ordered additional military units to be on a standby alert basis.

Fifth: We are calling tonight for an immediate meeting of the Organ of Consultation, under the Organization of American States, to consider this threat to hemispheric security and to invoke articles six and eight of the Rio Treaty in support of all necessary action. The United Nations Charter allows for regional security arrangements—and the nations of this Hemisphere decided long ago against the military presence of outside powers. Our other allies around the world have also been alerted.

Sixth: Under the Charter of the United Nations, we are asking tonight that an emergency meeting of the Security Council be convoked without delay to take action against this latest Soviet threat to world peace. Our resolution will call for the prompt dismantling and withdrawal of all offensive weapons in Cuba, under the supervision of United Nations observers, before the quarantine can be lifted.

Seventh and finally: I call upon Chairman Khruschev to halt and eliminate this clandestine, reckless, and provocative threat to world peace and to stable relations between our two nations. I call upon him further to abandon this course of world domination and to join in an historic effort to end the perilous arms race and transform the history of man. He has an opportunity now to move the world back from the abyss of destruction—by returning to his Government's own words that it had no need to station missiles outside its own territory, and withdrawing these weapons from Cuba—by refraining from any action which will widen or deepen the present crisis—and then by participating in a search for peaceful and permanent solutions.

Some Americans were roused to a fighting pitch by the address. In New York's Madison Square Garden, a meeting of nearly ten thousand Conservative Party Members booed and jeered, shouting "Fight! Fight! Fight!," and demanded an immediate invasion of the island. More frequently the news was received with grim determination, and it wasn't uncommon for entire families to respond by dropping to their knees to pray. Later men and women recalled feeling a barely controlled panic. The president, whom Premier Khruschev had bullied and humiliated at the Summit Conference in Vienna in 1961 and who had been blistered in the abortive Bay of Pigs invasion, was now calling bluffs.

People everywhere feared swift Russian retaliation. Harold Macmillan, then British prime minister, later recalled the days that followed Kennedy's announcement as "the week of most strain I ever remember in my life." One woman, steeped in the holocaust novels of Nevil Shute, like the then popular *On the Beach*, determined that when the end came she would gather her family around so they could all commit suicide together. Another recalled her father calmly, but determinedly, offering to shoot her best friend, the little boy next door, if his own father could not. As a measure of the hysteria, spectacular sunsets were interpreted as mushroom clouds and flocks of birds identified as Russian Iluyshin bombers. One man remembered his mother fixing him with a stare and declaring, "Thank God he's too young to fight." Whole families spent a frantic, apprehensive night in their basements.

Sir Isaiah Berlin was a visiting professor at Harvard at the time, and he recalls both the scene and his reaction to it:

I listened to the news on the radio in the company of a large number of students gathered in one of the public rooms in Lowell House. Again, I was out of harmony with the prevailing mood. The students, and one or two professors, were in the depths of gloom: war seemed to them inevitable, and with it the use of nuclear weapons and unimaginable horrors. There was total silence at the end of the broadcast and the company broke up into little depressed groups, talking in low voices. I was convinced that the Soviet Union would not risk a global war, that all this was feinting and shadow-boxing, that there was basically nothing to fear except some act of a madman in power, and that neither Kennedy nor Khruschev were in the least degree mad, nor were their henchmen. I went out to dinner with a French chemist and two or three American historians, and tried to persuade them that there was no reason for anxiety, let alone despair—that the only problem was how to allow the Russians not to lose too much face, how to provide them with some possibility of dignified retreat. I learnt afterwards that my assessment was totally wrong, that the fate of mankind hung by a thread, that the possibility of global war was higher than anyone in authority in the United States wished to conjecture. I remained in my fool's paradise for the remaining four days, viewed by others as a little deranged, as indeed I must have seemed. My friends seemed worried about my mental balance. There is something more acutely embarrassing about optimism, whether well-founded or baseless, in a society of convinced and rational pessimists, than the opposite—to be oppressed by anxiety in the midst of the happy and cheerful. I have never forgotten what it feels like to be conscious of being the only man with sight among the blind. The fact that I was totally mistaken, and that it was my companions who remained utterly sane while I was happily wandering in darkness, does not alter the queer, unsettling sensation. I ought to add that I was dining with Mr. and Mrs. Joseph Alsop at a farewell dinner for Mr. Charles Bohlen, who had been appointed U.S. Ambassador to Paris, a dinner attended by the President and Mrs. Kennedy. That was the day on which the photographs of the Russian missile bases on Cuba had been shown to the President. He behaved with complete sangfroid, talked about politics and the public news of the day in an (apparently) light-hearted way during dinner, and more seriously when the ladies left, and went into the garden where he told Charles Bohlen, and him alone, about the critical situation. But as none of the rest of us knew what had happened, that did not affect our mood. The crisis, so far as the public was concerned, broke only after I had returned to Harvard.

Elsewhere in Cambridge, Massachusetts, that night the mood was summarized in a two line scrawl posted on a student notice board:

TOMORROW'S WEATHER FORECAST
20,000 degrees and cloudy

Tuesday, October 23. Many awoke—if they had slept—to find all was quiet in Berlin, Washington and Moscow. American Secretary of State Dean Rusk discovered his under-secretary George Ball asleep on the couch in his office and woke him observing cheerily, "We have won a considerable victory. You and I are both alive." Shortly afterwards, in Moscow, the American ambassador received a note from Premier Khruschev. It accused the United States of "piracy." Washington interpreted this as stalling and took some comfort from the fact that the note had not included even the merest suggestion of an armed response. For the Kennedy government the rest of the day passed in receiving pledges of support from most allied nations. UN Ambassador Adlai Stevenson reported that the American action, if not exactly applauded in the Security Council, had won majority support. Of particular importance that day was a meeting of the Organization of American States. They too were behind the Americans, approving the action 18-0 with one abstention: Uruguay. Later that evening, a satisfied President Kennedy put his signature to the quarantine document; it would take effect at ten o'clock the next morning.

Now everything was in the open. The crisis was at its height, and millions of people tensed as the naval blockade formed a steel collar around Cuba. On the Atlantic, twenty-five Soviet ships moved inexorably toward the island, showing no signs of delaying their voyages. In Cuba itself, work on the rocket launchers continued at a frenzied pace. And everyone who had access to a television set or radio knew what was going on. A tense agony gripped the United States and the world, a world completely belted now by the electronic media, a world in which every possible nuance was instantly debated or probed by commentators or experts anxious to opine whether they would live a day, a week or a month.

Few conversations touched on anything but Cuba, few classrooms followed lesson plans, few families pondered anything but the possible consequences of the president's speech. All day newspaper headlines solemnly reported Kennedy's somber message of the previous evening. Editorialists showed remarkable variety. The English papers, even the Conservative ones, were openly skeptical. The world had been shoved to the edge of war; in fact the communist *Daily Worker* called the planned blockade "an act of war." In Japan, where nuclear devastation had been seen first hand, Kennedy's actions were regretted. In India they were openly condemned, the major theme being that America, like Britain during Suez, had violated international law with this self-imposed blockade—and moral law with its offensive saber-rattling. Closer to home in Canada—the potential battlefield of any nuclear duel between the United States and the U.S.S.R.—there was empathy for the president's position but worry that he had somehow set the world on an inexorable collision course.

Everywhere throughout the world, but particularly in the United States, ordinary lives seemed extraordinary that day.

People walked the streets holding transistor radios to their ears and clustered around newspaper offices in curious crowds reminiscent of old movies. Children were sent to school with thermoses and blankets—just in case.

University campuses were bristling with debate. At the University of Michigan graduate student Tom Hayden, president of the fledgling Students for a Democratic Society (SDS), organized an anti-Kennedy demonstration. On other campuses fist-fights broke out between blockade supporters and what were called "peaceniks." Elementary and high schools began to take emergency measures. Parents near schools were asked to stay home; their children would be sent back at the first sign of an attack—those who lived further away would barricade themselves in the school shelter or basement. Emergency drills were practiced and children were shown how to use safety equipment. Municipalities tested air-raid sirens and dusted off Civil Defense manuals. The Red Cross and hospitals began hoarding blood. Large and small cities started issuing lists of designated key buildings and subways to use as potential shelters.

Food stores were swamped and then stripped bare of tinned goods, dried foods, bottled drinks and other non-perishables. Los Angeles was reported effectively to have run out of food. "They're nuts," observed one California grocer about his customers. "One lady's working four shopping carts at once. Another lady bought twelve packages of detergent. What's she going to do, wash up after the bomb?"

A year before, there had been a mild interest in building private fall-out shelters. One dealer reported his inquiries ran one to two every month. On the morning of October 23 he received dozens of calls. Slogans began to appear chalked on buildings or pasted on hoardings—"Better Dead than Red" and "We Back Jack" seemed to be the most prolific. Slogans and signs were in clear evidence in the hands of the crowds who milled around U.S. embassies and consulates as well. "Cuba Sí, Yanqui No" became entrenched in the language, but there were others too: "Remember Neville" and "Millionaire Kennedy wants Cuba for his Friends." If some remembered Munich, others recalled an autumn day six years before in Budapest—some signs declared "Remember

Hungary" with portraits of Khruschev that were none too flattering.

In Cuba itself the newspaper *Revolucion*, in an extra edition, set the theme: LA NACION EN PIE DE GUERRA (The Nation is on the Brink of War). Banners were hung proclaiming "patria o muerte" or "Venceremos" and, curiously, in English at Havana's airport, "Cuba—Liberated Territory of the Americas." A poor agricultural nation of six million was facing the world's richest, most powerful country, thirty times its size in population alone. Nevertheless Cuba remained calm and quiet that day and for most of the ensuing week. On the evening of the 23rd Fidel Castro made an eighty-minute television address—a mere bulletin by his standards—exhorting Cubans to fight the invaders off. Some hoarding was reported of food, fuel and cigarettes, but government strictures ensured there would be no run on supplies.

Wednesday, October 24. The Americans expected their naval blockade would intercept Russian vessels before noon. They were ready, if necessary, to sink them. This, wrote Robert Kennedy was "the time of gravest concern for the President." He had "initiated the course of events, but he no longer had control over them." Anxious minutes passed in the Cabinet room, and then at 10:25 a.m. a messenger arrived with the news that some of the Russian ships had "stopped dead in the water." For a moment so did everything. Dean Rusk got off another *bon mot*, one that would become the most famous comment of the crisis: "We're eyeball to eyeball and I think the other fellow just blinked." Later it was learned that not all the vessels had turned back. The collision was postponed until the next day.

Now advice poured in from all quarters. UN Secretary General U Thant sent duplicate letters to Kennedy and Khruschev asking for a three-week voluntary suspension of the quarantine and of all arms shipments to Cuba in order to allow "the parties concerned to meet and discuss." Khruschev agreed, and Kennedy showed polite interest but was adamant that he would not talk until the Russians had agreed to remove their missiles.

Philosopher Bertrand Russell, ninety years old, blamed Kennedy directly for the crisis. He had already issued a statement:

Statement re: CUBA CRISIS

YOU ARE TO DIE   Not in the course of nature, but within a few weeks, and not you alone, but your family, your friends, and all the inhabitants of Britain, together with many hundreds of millions of innocent people elsewhere.

WHY?   Because rich Americans dislike the Government that Cubans prefer, and have used part of their wealth to spread lies about it.

WHAT CAN YOU DO?   You can go out into the streets and into the market place, proclaiming: "Do not yield to ferocious and insane murderers. Do not imagine that it is your duty to die when your Prime Minister and the President of the United States tell you to do so. Remember rather your duty to your family, your friends, your country, the world you live in, and that future world which, if you so choose, may be glorious, happy, and free."

AND REMEMBER: CONFORMITY MEANS DEATH
ONLY PROTEST
GIVES A HOPE OF LIFE
BERTRAND RUSSELL
23rd October, 1962

Now he telegraphed Kennedy to say that the president had taken "desperate action" for which there was "no reasonable justification." Kennedy responded by pointing out that Lord Russell's attention "might well be directed to the burglars rather than to those who have caught the burglars."

Public opinion, the pollsters have said, remained with the president and with America, although in Britain a large demonstration—the first of many—was held in Grosvenor Square opposite the massive new American embassy. There were also protests in Asia, Africa, both Western and (predictably) Eastern Europe and in Canada. Generally, people still expected either an attack or at least some kind of siege. Students sandbagged their school in Jacksonville, Florida, the stock market took wild swings in all the major markets, stores soon ran short of flashlights,

campstoves, radios, water purification pills, sleeping bags, phar-
maceuticals, and there was a run on nine hundred cans of
pemmican in Washington. Opinion swung like the stock market.
A sign in Atlanta declared "Peace in the world or the world in
pieces." Eddie Rickenbacker, the American World War I flying
ace, announced, "We should give the Cubans 24 hours to move
away from their missile sites and airports . . . and then bomb them
out of existence."

The fear of an end to the world brought personal decisions
too. Gore Vidal remembers:

> I had agreed to write the film *The Cardinal* for Otto
> Preminger. I had finished a first draft; he was being difficult.
> As I walked down 5th Avenue (one of the most beautiful
> autumn days that I remember), I thought to myself: the world
> is about to be blown up and here I am writing a screenplay for
> what will be a very bad movie. I rang Otto and quit the film.

And there was a lighter side. In Toronto, journalist and
editor Robert Fulford recalls:

> When something like the Cuban missile crisis happens, my
> instinct is to get all possible newspapers and fill myself up
> with details, as if knowing about it can make it right. This is a
> legacy of the crazy idea you hear in school that well-informed
> citizens make for a good democracy.
>
> Kennedy announced the blockade of Cuba—which was
> the real beginning of the crisis—on a Monday night, giving a
> speech that lasted, I think, from 7:30 to 8 p.m. I watched the
> speech and then walked across the room to turn off the TV. My
> ankle turned under me. I continued to walk on it, but at three
> in the morning it was aching so much the pain woke me up. I
> took some codeine, lasted through to seven o'clock, then went
> to a hospital. I also found an old cane that a previous owner of
> our house left behind. At the hospital my sprain was bandaged,
> and I made my way to the *Maclean's* office, using the cane
> with great lumbering clumsiness—I'd never had one before or
> since. I paused, leaning on my cane, at Ken Lefolii's office. He
> looked up from a manuscript and said: "I've never seen a man
> declare himself a non-combatant so early in a war."

And in New York, where the *New York Times* had received
fifteen thousand calls in only nine hours the day before, the movie
pages showed that there's always somebody who can turn a situa-

tion—any situation—to advantage. Wednesday the 24th was advertised as the "World Premier" of a film called *We'll Bury You* —"the true incredible story of the Red Terror" with "the most infamous cast of characters ever assembled." Business, apparently, was brisk.

Thursday, October 25. Early in the morning the Russian tanker *Bucharest,* bound for Cuba, approached the U.S. barrier, identified itself and its cargo, and was permitted to pass, although American warships shadowed it. Later, in the UN Security Council, Soviet Ambassador Valerian Zorin, in front of the dinnertime American TV cameras, accused the United States of trumping up the whole missile story. Where was the evidence, he asked? American Ambassador Adlai Stevenson, known in some circles as "Superdove," treated him to a savage tongue-lashing, quite out of character and certainly undiplomatic. Dramatically playing the TV prosecutor, he asked Zorin to deny that the Soviets had placed missiles in Cuba—and then pushed—"Don't wait for the translation. Yes or No." The Russian was trapped and tried to stall, but Stevenson pressed even harder. "You are in the Court of world opinion right now and you can answer yes or no." Again Zorin stalled and Stevenson exploded: "I am prepared to wait for my answer until hell freezes over if that's your decision. And I am also prepared to present the evidence in this room." And with that, Stevenson had aides come forward with easels and blown-up photos of the missile sites. The "Court of world opinion" was moved by this blazing show, and to buttress its case that bold action had been necessary to keep world peace, the Americans distributed thousands of copies of the photos.

Friday, October 26. The Americans stopped and searched an old freighter, leased under Russian charter. The *Marucla,* ironically, had been built as a liberty ship in Baltimore during the Second World War. And there was another irony: the ship that stopped it was the U.S. destroyer *Joseph P. Kennedy, Jr.,* named after the president's elder brother, killed in the same war. The *Marucla,* after a few tense moments, was searched and cleared. Then in Washington the state department learned, through a circuitous route, that the Soviets—in exchange for certain pledges— might agree to a de-escalation. To confirm this, a lengthy letter came over the teletype later that evening from Citizen Khruschev. He admitted for the first time that there were Russian missiles in Cuba, and agreed to remove them and not to ship any more if Kennedy would guarantee not to attack Cuba. A wave of optimism swept Kennedy and his advisors—although none of it was yet transmitted to a tense world.

Saturday, October 27. As Kennedy and the "Ex Comm," his most trusted counselors, grappled with Khruschev's proposals, a new message arrived from Moscow. It was firm, forceful and showed the touches of many hands. Its message boiled down simply: before the U.S.S.R. would remove the missiles from Cuba, the United States also had to agree to remove its Turkish air and. rocket bases. Once more the unseeing, unhearing masses beyond the walls of the Cabinet room and the Kremlin shifted nearer to extinction.

For a while the "Ex Comm" paraded frightening scenarios, and then the president's brother Robert offered a way out of the dilemma. Ignore Khruschev's second letter and answer only the first, he suggested. It was done, and the president announced to the world that he had accepted the Russian conditions. Then Robert Kennedy secretly told the Russian ambassador that if Moscow did not accept these conditions, if they did not remove the bases, then the Americans would do it for them. He also declared that it was on the books for the Turkish bases to be phased out. Now the question became whether the Russians would accept this diplomatic unorthodoxy.

Sunday, October 28. According to the Roman Catholic calendar, this date is the Feast of St. Jude Thaddeus, patron saint of the impossible. The answer to the American ultimatum was broadcast over Radio Moscow—in short, the Russians capitulated. The Soviet Union would "dismantle the arms which you described as offensive," and "crate and return them to the Soviet Union." The Russians were leaving Cuba. Some listeners recalled that on another October 28, six years before, they had also left Budapest—for a time. Could they be trusted? Kennedy had confidence, and it was further agreed that the United Nations should oversee the removal. Relief was universal—but it was less a celebration than a deep, almost audible, global sigh. One notable quarter, however, was infuriated. Fidel Castro, angry at having been used, vehemently refused to permit the UN entry for supervision of the Russian exit. In his fury he was reported to have kicked in a wall and broken a mirror. A few days later he angrily remarked that Khruschev had no "cojones" (balls).

THE LINGERING QUESTION was why the Russians had collapsed. The answer certainly was not that they were afraid of the blockade. Rather, it was the knowledge, gained through their intelligence network, that should the blockade fail the Americans in all likelihood would attack Cuba—first with an air strike, and then with an invasion. Cuba meant that much to the United States. Only a pawn in a larger Russian game, Cuba, for the Soviets, was not worth the real risk of nuclear war. So they pulled out the missiles—but they didn't leave Cuba entirely. It would remain a Marxist thorn in the new world. Of course, Soviet global policy was in ruins—no agreement would be forthcoming on the German question, and the Chinese would soon take their own nuclear path.

Within a year a limited test-ban treaty was signed, but not the comprehensive package Khruschev wanted; within two years, in any case, the principal figures in the confrontation were both gone, one dead from an assassin, the other ousted from power.

It is generally considered that Kennedy acted throughout the crisis with masterly firmness, authority and restraint, and much of his substantial reputation emanates from those thirteen terrible and tense days. The Russian adventure took the world to the brink without question, and that was irresponsible; but did Kennedy himself contribute to the dangers of nuclear war by his uncompromising response? Without doubt Kennedy had to take some action once the missiles had been detected. Moreover, he had been bullied by Khruschev more than once, and he had to show decisive leadership if he were to retain the confidence of his electorate. Nevertheless, no other event, since the Second World War, including Suez and Hungary, has thrown the world into such a spin of fear and paralysis. Television particularly heightened and escalated that fear. Cynics might speculate that the medium was used perfectly by Kennedy and with theatrical precision: the fearful first announcement, the "Perry Mason" courtroom scene of Stevenson baiting Zorin, the visual exhibits of the missile photographs, and all of it enacted against a backdrop of ships on a collision course at sea.

Universal television and radio made Kennedy appear the strong man and his advisors the wisest of counsels at a time when the United States was preparing for congressional elections. But it also brought high-level tensions and fears to ordinary people throughout the world. Was this necessary? No announcement in war or peace could compare with the Cuban coverage or had ever engaged the hopes and fears of so many people so dramatically and simultaneously. This was not the uncertainty of appeasement or the creaking of old colonial gunboats as in 1956. This was the Cold war made into a "cool" TV drama—but this time it wasn't fiction that would be happily resolved in time for the commercial at the end of the hour. It was also a gross simplification of complex issues. Moreover the confrontation techniques sidestepped and helped to detour traditional diplomatic channels like the United Nations. Why didn't Kennedy take his photographs to the United Nations and demand an impartial investigation, or through the United Nations arrange a summit with the Russians? The route that Kennedy chose, the blunt ultimatum, and the escalation of tension through the use of the media, especially TV, was as dangerous as the folly the Russians had engaged in—and, regretfully, it was probably a precedent.

On October 22 President KENNEDY vetoed Bill No. HR 8938, legislation that would have doubled the duty on bicycles imported into America.

NANETTE FABRAY opened in *Mr President* at the St. James Theater in New York the evening of October 22. Reviewers praised her performance as a "song and dance first lady."

1

1. Jacqueline Kennedy and daughter Caroline kneeling at President
   Kennedy's casket, Capitol Rotunda, November 24, 1963 (*United
   Press International*).
2. John F. Kennedy Jr. salutes as the casket of his father is carried
   from St. Matthew's Cathedral (*United Press International*).

CHAPTER 7

The Assassination of John F. Kennedy

NOVEMBER 22, 1963

PROBABLY NO EVENT in living memory has had a more wrenching impact than the assassination of John F. Kennedy on November 22, 1963. Much of the explanation lies in the times themselves. Popular myth suggests the 1960s were buoyant years if not of peace, certainly of prosperity and promise. Nothing symbolized that idealized vision more than the rich, handsome, young American president, John F. Kennedy. His untimely death, early in the decade, became not only a symbol of broken promises, but a harbinger of the violence and disorder that was to follow. Then, too, there was the manner of his death: the vicious, cowardly shooting of a popular and attractive young man. No small part of the public's response can be traced to the mass media, for it was the media which presented us with that devastating and graphic death scene of Kennedy—his skull smashed and his blood and brains splattered—lying cradled in his wife's arms as his limousine raced fruitlessly to a hospital.

As a politician John F. Kennedy owed much to mass communications. He might have been a rather ordinary American "patrician" dabbling in politics but for one important factor: publicity. His father's money and a well-oiled political machine had fixed him in the public eye and propelled him from election as a junior congressman in 1947 all the way to the presidency. That's not to suggest that Kennedy was without talent. He possessed more than his share of ability, charm and determination, but he had no monopoly on those qualities. His advantage was that he was able to exploit them through careful, determined organization and exposure.

He was a good candidate by any measure: well educated (at Harvard and the London School of Economics), well connected (politically through his father, the former ambassador to the Court of St. James and socially through his wife, the former Jacqueline Lee Bouvier) and, of course, he was a war-hero. Although these qualities are not always a guarantee of political success, he was capable and intelligent. As well, he was a clear and persuasive writer who at one time (before his older brother Joe's death in the war made him the new focus of his father's political ambitions) had considered becoming a journalist. And equally, if not even more important in the cash and carry world of politics, his father was one of the richest men in America.

As a politician Kennedy had the knack, not only of exploiting his familial and financial advantages, but of turning potential drawbacks into assets. He argued, for example, that his Catholicism should be regarded not as a liability but as a draw among the urban Catholics who had thronged to America's cities. The painful back injury he had sustained during the war while effecting the now famous PT boat rescue in the South Pacific threw him into a piteous round of agonizing operations in 1954. He used his convalescence to write a powerful collection of brief, stirring accounts about American politicians of boldness and conviction. Aptly titled *Profiles in Courage*, it became a bestseller and won Kennedy a Pulitzer Prize in 1957. More importantly, it gave Kennedy an intellectual stature and transformed him from a mere politician into a political philosopher.

Even Kennedy's abortive candidacy for the vice-presidential spot on the Democratic ballot in 1956 was turned to effect. His party's team of Adlai Stevenson and Estes Kefauver went down to decisive defeat against the "dream" ticket of President Dwight D. Eisenhower and his running-mate, Richard Nixon. When Kennedy came back four years later for a try at the presidential nomination, he was masterfully organized. Not only had he stumped the countryside in the gruelling primaries, but he had built a crack "commando" team led by his brother Robert which he unleashed on the convention floor to sway uncommitted delegates and entice defectors away from other candidates' camps. Despite a movement to draft Adlai Stevenson for a third try at the White House, Kennedy won the nomination handily.

Still, nobody thought the ensuing presidential election would be an easy victory. Richard Nixon, the Republican candidate, was bolstered by the prestige and recognition concomitant with the vice-presidency while, despite his best efforts, Kennedy was not yet either a national or an international figure. The innovative television debates during the campaign changed all that.

Anyone listening to the debates on radio would have concluded that each candidate spoke well and might even have given the edge to Nixon because of his greater experience and knowledge of foreign affairs. On television, however, Kennedy was the clear winner. Nixon had used a pasty face-cream to camouflage his heavy beard, with the result that he looked thoroughly sinister. By comparison, Kennedy was a natural. He radiated assurance, confidence and healthy good looks. Moreover, unlike Nixon, he had no obligation to defend Eisenhower's Republican administration. While Nixon mouthed familiar bromides about America's prosperity and strength abroad, Kennedy argued that circumstances—both domestically and internationally—were perilous and that a "supreme National effort" would be needed to "get the country moving again."

For many Americans, citizens of a confused and uncertain nation, one which had just stumbled through a barrage of cold war threats and incidents, Kennedy was the man to give the country that needed push. Nevertheless, the results of the 1960 presidential election were close. Kennedy's popular vote margin was only 119,000 out of some 68 million votes, although he led the Electoral College race 303 to 219.

JFK WAS FORTY-THREE when he came to America's highest office, the youngest man ever and the first Roman Catholic. In his inaugural address he resurrected an old American rallying cry and made it his own: he talked of a "new frontier" that would rejuvenate America, and over the following thousand days of his office, he sought to institute a vigorous extension of civil rights and a progressive social reform program. Congress was not so easily persuaded, despite Kennedy's growing popularity and spirited, eloquent appeals. In the end it was Vice-President Lyndon Johnson's wily political experience that saw much of Kennedy's legislation enacted.

His record was better in foreign affairs. His unwavering stand during the 1962 confrontation with the Soviet Union over missile bases in Cuba won the United States international respect, as did his 1963 initiative to establish a nuclear Test-Ban Treaty. Kennedy was the quintessential "man with a mission" and nothing exemplified this purpose and energy more than the Peace Corps, that unique combination of idealism, rhetoric, naivete and slog, or the Alliance for Progress, that euphemistic cooperative agreement with South American nations.

At home, as the baby "boomies" began to take their places in the universities and the colleges, Kennedy and his family became a focus for youth. He, his wife and their children were seen everywhere—on magazine covers, in newspapers, on posters and, of course, on television. Kennedy became a symbol of everything that was good about America, of peace and hope, of a new world as well as a new frontier. At a time when the rest of the western world desperately needed inspired leadership, the media made him everybody's president. It was television as much as foreign policy that allowed him to proclaim to a tumultous crowd of Germans in June 1963, "Ich bin ein Berliner."

Of course Kennedy made mistakes. Many of his domestic policies were soon fragmented and lost in the quagmire of congressional procedures. His commitments abroad were not always sagacious—he furthered American involvement in Viet Nam, and it is quite likely that his policies greatly contributed to the American disaster there a decade later. But it is very difficult to offer any real assessment of the Kennedy years or of JFK himself. His brutal death has transformed him into a mythical figure and, besides, most of the programs in his truncated administration were too raw to be evaluated. What might have happened in Viet Nam or anywhere else can only be surmised.

One thing was certain. John F. Kennedy was a politician, and the job of politicians is to get and then to stay elected. That was why he and his wife went to Dallas in November 1963. The next year's presidential election loomed and a lot of handshaking and buttressing had to be done to secure a full Texas commitment to the Kennedy/Johnson banner. The trip had been more successful than expected. Large, boisterous crowds had turned out in San Antonio and Houston. And in Fort Worth on the morning of November 22, 1963 people had waited more than an hour in drizzling rain to see the Kennedys. Despite the enthusiasm, Kennedy determined to keep to the schedule and go on to Dallas that same day.

John Kennedy was well aware of the dangers inherent in his highly visible position. He knew his American history: eighty-two attempts had been made on Lincoln's life before John Wilkes Booth succeeded, Garfield and McKinley were both assassinated, and each of the Roosevelts had been shot at. Prophetically, in Fort Worth that morning, Kennedy had observed to his wife and an aide that despite the best efforts of the Secret Service, "If anybody really wanted to shoot the President of the United States, it's not a very hard job. All that one has to do is to get in a high building some day with a telescopic rifle, and there is nothing anybody can do." Two and one-half hours later, he became the victim of his own prophecy.

The basic facts of the killing are clear. At 1:30 p.m. on November 22, 1963 as the presidential motorcade drove through the streets of Dallas, President John F. Kennedy was shot three times by Lee Harvey Oswald, a twenty-four-year-old ex-marine. Oswald, an employee of the Texas School Book Depository, fired his cheap Italian mail-order rifle from a sixth floor window in that building, gunning down Kennedy and wounding John Connally, the governor of Texas. Two days later in a Dallas police station, in full view of television cameras, Oswald was himself fatally shot, while under arrest, by Jack Ruby, a local night club owner. It is more than a little ironic that the murderer of politics first television star was himself the victim of television's first "live" murder.

THE DISTINGUISHED American journalist Theodore H. White has written, "The moments of history that crease the memory are rare, but come more frequently in our time than a hundred years ago because communications are instant. A triad of memories marks my generation: the strike at Pearl Harbor; the death of Franklin Roosevelt; the killing of John F. Kennedy. Each of us could write his own history of our time if we could but recall not *where* we were, which all remember, but what we *thought* when those incidents changed our world."

As far as Kennedy's death is concerned, White's remarks apply not only to his generation of Americans, but to most of the world. Americans, of course, were hardest hit; on that November day and the days that followed, the very face of America was numb. To reveal a cross-section of American life is to see an entire nation in shock.

In New York the stock market slumped before it closed its doors, and people spoke of a "frantic calm" descending upon the city. At the United Nations the flags of all 111 countries were taken down and replaced by the UN flag, which was then lowered to half mast. The bright lights of Broadway dimmed, and hundreds of its imitators throughout the country followed suit as inner city cores became ghost towns. Social life came to a virtual halt everywhere. Cinemas, theaters, concert halls, museums and art galleries shut down. Desperate efforts to confirm the news forced whole telephone exchanges to "blacken out." On streetcars, buses and subways people spoke openly to complete strangers of their shock and anger, and in department stores shoppers dropped to their knees to pray. The State of Texas itself was roundly cursed throughout the country.

In Washington, the late John McCormack was eating lunch in the restaurant of the House of Representatives when two newspapermen came over to his table first to report the rumor of JFK's murder and then, ten minutes later, to confirm it. McCormack, who as speaker of the House was next in line of succession after the vice-president, was "shocked beyond expression." On a plane coming back from Egypt where he had taped an interview with President Nasser, journalist Howard K. Smith was called into the cockpit by the pilot. He listened to the radio and felt like a "broken reed." The syndicated columnist Ann Landers was in the city room of the Chicago *Sun Times* when one of the reporters announced the news coming over the AP wire. The reporter didn't know yet whether the gunshot wounds were fatal, and Landers remembers everybody grabbing phones hoping to "get the beat from special sources."

At the United Nations Abba Eban, the acting Israeli foreign minister, was hit "hard and strong" and later told the official Israeli memorial meeting that the "world is darker than it was a week ago." In New Orleans Otto Preminger was holding a press conference for his new film, *The Cardinal*, when a publicist carrying a portable television set interrupted. The press conference ended abruptly and Preminger watched the set until Kennedy's death was announced. Then he canceled his plans for the afternoon and in his grief—for "I had known Jack Kennedy for seventeen years as a young vigorous, bright, and charming man"—walked aimlessly through the streets.

In Hollywood Stanley Holloway was making the film of *My Fair Lady* when the news began buzzing around the set. He and choreographer Hermes Pan dashed to the parking lot and turned on the radio in Pan's car to learn that it was "too true and fatal." The photographer Cecil Beaton, who was visiting the film capital, wrote in his diary, "My blood turned to pale liquid; I felt I was rushing through space down a lift shaft."

For those close to the fallen president the day was even more traumatic. Historian Arthur M.Schlesinger, Jr. was a presidential advisor to the Kennedy administration. On that Friday morning he was in New York for a luncheon with Katharine Graham, the editors of *Newsweek*, and John Kenneth Galbraith, who had come down from Cambridge for the occasion. Schlesinger recalls they were having pre-lunch drinks when,

> a young man in shirtsleeves entered the room and said, a little tentatively, "I am sorry to break in, but I think you should know that the President has been shot in the head in Texas." For a flash one thought this was some sort of ghastly office joke. Then we knew it could not be and huddled desperately around the nearest television. Everything was confused and appalling. The minutes dragged along. Incomprehensible bulletins came from the hospital. Suddenly an insane surge of conviction flowed through me: I felt that the man who had survived the Solomon Islands and so much illness and agony, who so loved life, embodied it, enhanced it, could not possibly die now. He would escape the shadow as he had before. Almost immediately we received the irrevocable word.
>
> In a few moments Galbraith and I were on Katharine Graham's plane bound for Washington. It was the saddest journey of one's life. Bitterness, shame, anguish, disbelief, emptiness mingled inextricably in one's mind.

In Washington Schlesinger and some White House colleagues went to Andrews Air Force Base to await the arrival of Air Force One bringing Kennedy's body and his blood-soaked widow back from Texas.

> A small crowd was waiting in the dusk, McNamara, stunned and silent, Harriman, haggard and suddenly looking very old,

desolation everywhere. We watched incredulously as the casket was carefully lifted out of the plane and taken to the Naval Hospital at Bethesda. Later I went to my house in Georgetown. My weeping daughter Christina said, "Daddy, what has happened to our country? If this is the kind of country we have, I don't want to live here any more." The older children were already on their way back from college to Washington.

Still later I went back to the White House to await the last return. Around four in the morning the casket, wrapped in a flag, was brought from the Naval Hospital and placed on a stand in the East Room. Tapers were lit around the bier, and a priest said a few words. Then Jacqueline approached the bier, knelt for a moment and buried her head in the flag. Soon she walked away. The rest of us waited for a little while in the great hall. We were beyond consolation, but we clung to the comradeship he had given us. Finally, just before daybreak, we bleakly dispersed into the mild night.

George E. Reedy, who served as Vice-President Lyndon Johnson's press secretary, was in Washington.

I got a call to come to the White House. Walter Jenkins was already there. And the two of us were in a rather embarrassing position. Because with [Lyndon] Johnson down in Dallas, they more or less regarded me and Walter as the two who were in control, and neither one of us wanted to be in control.

The major thing was still the grief of all the Kennedy people. And I can remember Arthur Schlesinger walking up to me and just saying, "George, this is terrible." And then bursting into tears. They were bringing every decision to us. Very minor ones, very petty ones that really they should have made themselves. And we were trying to tell them that. Such things as having a forklift out at the airport to bring the coffin out of the plane. We got the whole feeling that the Kennedy people here were trying to transfer power. And of course neither Walter nor I wanted to be in that position. In the first place, the President wasn't here. And we didn't want to be the people laughing at the funeral feast. I can recall that when the plane finally arrived and we got into a helicopter, I sat next to Ted Sorensen, and he said, "George, I wish that goddamn State of Texas had never been invented." I knew the man was overwrought. It was a foolish reaction. It could have happened in Arizona or Boston or anyplace else. I just didn't comment.

Manning Clark, the Australian historian, was touring in the United States. At Richmond, Virginia, he and his party stopped to buy gasoline.

> We offered a lift to two students who were hitching rides to New York. Not long after we set off . . . one of the students said: "Our President was assassinated today." I thought he must be kidding me, and took no notice. So, to my relief, he and indeed all of us lapsed into the stupors of long distance travelers, till out of the corner of my right eye, I saw the huge black drapes in front of a Howard Johnson and an electric sign bearing the words "Our deepest sympathy." And I knew what he had said was true: they had killed John Kennedy. In the excitement of the moment I must have driven very erratically because within minutes a policeman was telling me to "Pull over, driver." So there we all were once again in a decisive moment of the twentieth century, not meditating on what the event had meant for humanity, or doing any of those things which the Prayer Book once told me were "meet and right." Instead I was having a petty battle of wits with a traffic cop, and caught up in the excitement, the exhilaration of winning an argument. I knew that in the presence of death there were always mourners and mockers. But this time it seemed that no event was stranger than the follies of the human heart. Thinking about the historical significance of the assassination had to wait its turn.

Lyricist Sammy Cahn, who with James Van Heusen had written "High Hopes," the song which had become Kennedy's campaign theme, was on a TWA plane flying from New York to Los Angeles. On the plane he met an old friend, Mortimer Hall, who also had worked hard to elect Kennedy.

> It wasn't long before our conversation turned to the new president and his family and how we both felt he was doing as a president. One word led to another and we suddenly found that we were both a little disenchanted because while we kept reading about all the people who were being asked to the White House for one occasion or another, neither I nor Hall had been asked. The point being that during almost all the five and half hour flight from New York to Los Angeles we both spoke constantly of JFK.
> Arriving in Los Angeles, I remember vividly being met by Harold, the ever faithful house-man who worked for me and

my then wife. We exchanged, I thought, a rather restrained greeting. Now that I think back, everything while we waited for our luggage was strange and almost still-life. After about ten minutes Harold said, "Isn't it terrible?" I asked, "Isn't what terrible?" He said, "Haven't you heard?" "Heard what?" I asked. He then almost whispered the horrendous news. It started for me and the world, I guess the most agonizing and anguished week of my life.

I, like the world, was glued to my TV set, went without food, without rest and without any of the normal things we take for granted. Looking back now to use TV parlance the whole world went into "still-frame" so to speak.

To this day whenever I hear the song "High Hopes" I am not only reminded of one of the most incredible young men I have ever known but of that flight from New York to Los Angeles!

Composer Hoagy Carmichael was practicing golf at a country club in the Palm Springs area.

Someone shouted "President Kennedy has been shot." I was shocked, of course, but more so when some woman came running out of the club house shouting. "Well, I hope they got him good." And at that moment I remember losing a good bit of my faith in humanity.

Richard Nixon had flown to Dallas on November 20 to attend a board meeting of the Pepsi-Cola Company, and returned to New York early on the morning of November 22. As he rode into the city from the airport, he heard on his taxi driver's radio that President Kennedy had been killed. Later in the day Nixon called FBI Chief J. Edgar Hoover in Washington.

He came right on the line and without wasting words I asked, "What happened? Was it one of the right-wing nuts?"

"No," he replied, "it was a Communist." Months later Hoover told me that Oswald's wife had disclosed that Oswald had been planning to kill me when I visited Dallas and that only with great difficulty had she managed to keep him in the house to prevent him from doing so.

I never felt the "there but for the grace of God go I" reaction to Kennedy's death that many people seemed to imagine I would. After eight years as Vice President I had become fatalistic about the danger of assassination. I knew that given the number of people who, for whatever reasons, want to kill a President, it takes a combination of luck and the law of averages to keep him alive: I did not think of Kennedy and myself as interchangeable: I did not think that if I had won in 1960 it would have been I rather than he riding through Dealey Plaza in Dallas at that time, on that day.

The global reaction was less personal than that of Americans, but it was no less moving. In London Big Ben tolled mournfully once a minute for an hour, a ritual generally reserved for deaths in the British Royal Family. A crowd of more than a thousand people quickly formed before the American embassy in Grosvenor Square, and over the next few days thousands and thousands signed the embassy's condolence book. As in the United States the world stopped short. At the Old Vic, Sir Laurence Olivier halted a performance to ask the audience to stand while the orchestra played "The Star-Spangled Banner." Stan Kenton, the jazz musician, was in mid performance when he saw his American bus driver and road manager crying in the wings. Rather than conclude the show with the usual theme song, his band, too, played "The Star-Spangled Banner." Later the Westminster Abbey choir sang "The Battle Hymn of the Republic," and the huge church was packed to hear a eulogy delivered by the Archdeacon.

Sir Isaiah Berlin was reminded—as were so many others—of the death of Franklin Roosevelt.

On November 22, 1963 I arrived at Sussex University, in England, to deliver a lecture on Machiavelli. I dined with my hosts and was walking towards the lecture hall when someone said to me, "Isn't this terrible?" I thought, idiotically, he meant that it was a terrible thing to have to go in to lecture, since he knew, as all my friends do, the agonies I suffer before talking in public, whatever the occasion. I therefore said, "Yes, I do feel awful, but I suppose I must go through with it." A few yards later someone else said to me, "This is appalling news." I realised something had happened, and was told that President Kennedy had been assassinated. I found it impossible to continue walking—the last time on which this had happened to me (in an even greater degree) was when I read about the death of President Roosevelt in 1945: then I was dictating a telegram in the British Embassy, in which I served during the war, and my assistant came in with a torn-off length of teletype tape—I said testily, "I cannot look at anything while I am typing, please, please do not interrupt, I shall be finished in half-an-hour." He said, "I think that you had better look at this." When I saw that Roosevelt had died in Warm Springs, I behaved like someone paralysed, for some time. I wished to speak to no one: the world in which I had believed seemed to me to have caved-in. I realised that my feelings for Roosevelt and all he stood for were stronger than those for any other form of life at that moment—my admiration for Winston Churchill was second to that of no one, I knew he had saved our lives, but my sympathies were liberal and Roosevelt was my leader—as he was of the Americans I had come to know [and] with whom I had developed warm, intimate feelings of friendship; our hopes for a vast increase in justice, enlightenment, liberty and happiness seemed dead; he was the protector of our liberty and civilization. I continued in this state of torpor for days. I have no doubt this was unrealistic—Roosevelt's continued rule would not have achieved these things, and his successor, in some respects, did more for their realization than the great President himself. But I had no such thoughts at the time. Night had come—we must do our best and wait for the dawn of some unknown new day.

I did not feel so violently when I heard of the death of Kennedy, but he too, with all his obvious faults, was a liberator and a hero, on the right side on all the public issues that mattered. I begged to be allowed an interval of a quarter-of-an-hour or so before beginning my lecture. This was granted. I drank two glasses of cold water, came to and delivered my lecture in a perfectly normal manner.

These two deaths clearly made a difference to subsequent events, and not for the better, and were among the darkest moments of my life. I do not think that the death of any public figure alive today, apart from the feelings it might evoke if one knew them personally, as friends, would have a similar effect upon me. I suspect this is true of many millions of people alive today.

The actress Susan Clark was in London doing her first play, Jean Anouilh's *Poor Bitos*, in the West End's Arts Theatre.

It was a tiny theater equivalent to off Broadway. The dressing rooms were up many steps and very small. The women all shared one room. Across the hall, one of the younger actors had a small transistor radio. He frequently pulled practical jokes of a somewhat bizarre nature.

We were all extremely nervous. We wanted the play to be a success; we wanted the play to have good notices and to run for a long time, and our future was going to be decided, if not that night, within a week.

As we dressed in our eighteenth-century costumes and heavy pompadour wigs a very ashen-faced actor appeared at our door telling us that President Kennedy had been shot. At first we thought he was teasing but realized even he would not make up such a hideous story. We all gathered into his tiny cubicle and pushed up the volume of his transistor as high as it would go to catch the live broadcast from Dallas, Texas.

The first news that we could understand was only that President Kennedy had been shot but was still alive. We were all in shock, couldn't believe what we had heard. We were then summoned to take our places for the first act curtain, and the play went on and each intermission—there were two—we all crowded into the same actor's dressing room, he being the only one with a radio.

At the end of the performance that evening, after our curtain calls, the manager of the theater came on stage and asked for a minute of silence for the late President Kennedy, saying that he had been assassinated in Dallas, Texas.

Some of the news had been on the street when a few of the audience wandered out to have a cigarette or across the street to have a quick drink in the local pub, but most of them were in shock at the announcement.

We slowly undressed and quietly left the theater. The West End was totally dark—a tribute by the British to the American President. We all went home feeling a sense of loss and a horror of what had happened to a man we never met and had little knowledge of. It was the waste of a young life and the ugliness of the violence in a so-called civilized country that numbed us.

Douglas Fairbanks, Jr. was also in London, on a brief business trip.

I . . . was planning to take my eldest daughter, who lives there, to dinner and the theater. She telephoned me to ask if I'd heard the news on the radio or TV, which I had not. When she told me, I was so shocked I couldn't answer or make a sound of any kind for some time. I couldn't really absorb the news fully or come to grips with it. Somehow it seemed too shocking to be true. After ringing my wife in New York in the hope of learning that it was all some dreadful mistake and that it was just an unsubstantiated rumor, I then sat down, my head in a confused whirl. Shortly after, one of the London papers rang me up and asked would I prepare an article for the next day's evening edition, which would summarize the feelings of an American in London. . . . As I had known President Kennedy and most of his family for a great many years, I felt that I was reasonably well qualified to write just such an article and I sat down immediately, pleased to be given this opportunity to express myself about this awful tragedy. However, each time I began writing I felt that what I was about to say was being better said by others, especially those writers professionally accustomed to meeting newspaper deadlines. The paper kept sending a messenger around the next morning, every half-hour (naturally my plans for that evening had been canceled in the meantime) and every so often the paper's editor would ring me to ask if I was ready yet with my "obituary" article. I'd had so many false starts that I became panicky until, finally, at the very last half-hour, I managed to write something which proved at least acceptable but which, alas, arrived so late that it barely made the very last edition of the paper and hardly anyone ever saw it.

In West Berlin people lighted candles in darkened windows, and 25,000 students marched on city hall to be addressed by Mayor Willy Brandt. "I know how many are weeping tonight," he told them. "We Berliners are poorer . . . we all have lost one of the best." Further east in Poland there was spontaneous mass mourning and church bells tolled for fifteen minutes on the night of the funeral. In Yugoslavia the national flag was flown at half-mast, and schools were instructed to devote one full hour to a discussion of the president's policies and significance. President Tito himself broadcast a statement and went in person to the American embassy to sign the condolence book. Similarly, in Moscow a shaken, tearful Nikita Khruschev was the first to sign the book. Soviet radio played dirges while the television network carried the funeral, including the service in the church.

In Puerto Rico Pablo Casals mused that he had seen many great and terrible events in his lifetime—the Dreyfus case, the assassination of Gandhi—"but in recent history—and I am thinking of my own lifetime—there has never been a tragedy that has brought so much sadness and grief to as many people as this."

Premier Fidel Castro of Cuba greeted the news that Kennedy had been wounded with the remark, "Then he's re-elected." Later when he realized Kennedy was dead, Castro's mood changed. "Everything is changed. . . . I'll tell you one thing: at least Kennedy was an enemy to whom we had become accustomed."

In Cambodia Prince Sihanouk ordered court mourning. In Indonesia flags flew at half-mast. People cried in the streets of New Delhi. In Algiers a weeping President Ben Bella telephoned the American ambassador and said, "I can't believe it. Believe me, I'd rather it happen to me than to him." A group of natives in N'zerekore, Guinea, presented a sum of money to their American pastor to buy, according to the custom of the Guerze people, a rush mat in which to bury President Kennedy.

In Italy the Roman newspaper *Il Giorno* paraded the simple headline "Addio, John, Addio." The sentiment was not shared in Peking, where the *Daily Worker* ran a cartoon entitled "Kennedy Biting the Dust" showing the dead president lying in a pool of blood, his necktie marked with dollar signs.

In Kampala Ugandans crowded the residence of the American ambassador. In Mali President Keita came to the embassy with an honor guard to deliver a eulogy. In the Sudan a Bisharine tribesman told an American lawyer it was terrible that Kennedy's son was so young: "It will be a long time before he can be the true leader."

Journalist David Lancashire, at the time a correspondent with Associated Press, had a "spooky" premonition of the assassination.

> It was mid-afternoon in Cairo, where my wife and I were living aboard a houseboat on the Nile, and when she woke up from a siesta she said, "I've just had a very disturbing dream." My wife, Dedee, dreams only about people she knows, but this time, she said, "it was a stranger. A group of women in black robes came walking down the deck of the boat carrying a body, and when they turned, wailing, to go up the companionway, I saw that the body was President Kennedy's."
>
> "It's just the heat," I said. A couple of hours later she went ashore to meet a friend at the airport and I was alone on the paddlewheeler *Saphir* when the office telephoned to tell me John F. Kennedy had been shot.

Novelist Anthony Burgess also had a prophetic dream.

On the night of November 21 I was in bed in a hotel in Tenerife, reading, for the benefit of my rusty Spanish, a paperback copy of *El Cid*. I was greatly struck by the description of El Mayo Cid parting from his beloved wife Jimenes—"the parting was as painful as the parting of the flesh from the nail." I went to sleep on that and had a dream which I consider prophetic. A vast crowd was welcoming a young political leader whom they hailed as "The Kid! The Kid!" He was assassinated. I clearly saw his wife, whose name I did not know, though I knew it began, like Jimenes, with a J. She tried to protect her husband but failed. I woke up sweating and in great fright.

I flew back to England and, once at home, turned on the television set. There was no program on either channel. I wondered why and then thought of my dream. The Kid, El Cid, was K, Kennedy. Jimenes was Jacqueline. I knew what had happened. This knowledge was confirmed two hours later when a news bulletin came on the screen. I received a telephone call from America telling me that Aldous Huxley also was dead. I thought: "Poor Aldous. His death will make no headlines."

And from Gore Vidal:

I was at the Fiametta cinema in Rome, watching *David and Lisa* (in English). During the intermission, Jerome Courtland, a film actor, came down the aisle and said, "Kennedy's been shot." I left the cinema and walked over to Via Veneto where extra editions were beginning to appear. As I read the news, I could think of nothing but a dream that I had had two years earlier . . . a Technicolor dream. Jackie is dressed in pink, and weeping, and saying to me, "What am I going to do now?"

Writer Frederick Forsyth was the correspondent for Reuters International News Agency in East Berlin, covering East Germany, Czechoslovakia and Hungary.

It was a one-man bureau and consequently very hard work, but fascinating since this was just after the building of the Berlin Wall and Berlin was still thought to be the flashpoint (if any) for war.

On that particular night I had crossed Checkpoint Charlie into West Berlin for a break among the bright lights and frantic gaiety of that lively but slightly hysterical half of the Divided City. I was dining at a small restaurant called The

Paris Café on the Kantstrasse with a young lady. It was a perfectly ordinary evening until, at about 8:30 a voice cut into the background music coming through the wallspeakers with a spoken announcement. I don't know why I heard it, for nobody else in the restaurant did. Perhaps it was the unnaturalness of a pop record being cut off in mid-beat, but I listened to the announcement above the clatter of knives on plates, the clink of glasses and the chatter of a busy eating house. It was the announcement—the first I had heard—that President Kennedy had not only been shot, but was dead. One other person in the restaurant, a German woman several tables away, caught the last two words . . . *"Kennedy tot."* She screamed and the restaurant went silent in bewilderment. The spoken message from the wall was then repeated. This time the silence was not bewilderment, but of stunned horror.

Before it was over there was a mingling of screams from the women, shouts from the men and the crash of cutlery falling to the floor as people jumped to their feet and knocked the tables over. One woman near me burst into hysterical tears; the girl I was dining with reached across the table, grabbed my arm and whispered "Does this mean war." I said that I didn't think that it did, but it certainly meant my departure from Reuters unless I got the hell back to my job East of the Wall and started filing some copy. I shovelled some money on to the table, put the girl in a taxi and took my own car back through Checkpoint Charlie. The East German border guards were transformed; instead of ordering those in transit about the guardhouse, they were subdued, pale, badly frightened and eager also to know if this meant war. Back in my office I found most of the East German government spokesmen were also back in theirs, which helped, since I could prepare reaction stories for the rest of the night. It was dawn before I got to bed and by then the enormity of what had happened had begun to sink in. I couldn't sleep so I spent the day propped on the bed, staring out through the windows at the roofs and spires of one very frightened city.

Actress Deborah Kerr was in Puerto Vallarta filming *The Night of the Iguana.* She recorded that mournful weekend in her diary:

November 22, Friday. I came very gaily down to the beach this afternoon at 4:30, only to be told of the assassination of the President. The complete flood of disbelief—horror and shock—left me with a thumping heart and a knotted stomach.

It seemed very hard to go through the usual "Buenas Tardes" greetings to all the boat-boys, who were obviously unaware of the tragedy as yet, and our silence sailing across to the location must have seemed strange. Ava Gardner was in the bar as I came up the hill from the Jetty, and we looked at each other without speaking. I fell into a chair beside her and ordered a drink. Everyone around us was the same . . . silent, stunned and bruised.

Somehow, we got to work—and somehow we "carried on." But, unbearable tears flooded my eyes and throat when Jaime Contreras, our first assistant, called everyone to order and asked director John Huston for a minute's silence for John Fitzgerald Kennedy.

November 23-24, Saturday-Sunday. The weekend was spent sleeping and desperately trying to get news on our short wave radio. Richard [Burton] and Elizabeth [Taylor] came to dinner on Saturday evening, and although all of us were tired and had intended to go to bed early to try to get back on to a day-time schedule, we sat up until 3:30 debating the details of the whole incredible happening. Sunday brought us the further incredible and bizarre news of Oswald's murder. I began to feel we were all living in a lunatic asylum, and I felt that NOTHING would ever be the same again.

In Canada, schools and shops closed quickly and remained shut throughout the weekend. Theaters and sports events were canceled. The streets were subdued. One Toronto newspaper said it for all the non-American press: He was the "least foreign of all the world's leaders."

Robert Fulford, the Canadian journalist, says he often thinks of the phrase "the geography of memory" because he sometimes connects places with events in history.

On Bloor Street [in Toronto] there is a Hungarian restaurant called L'Europe—not a good one. Every time I pass it, which must be six or eight times a year, I think of John Kennedy, because I was in that restaurant on November 22, 1963, about the time Kennedy was killed, having lunch. I probably can't remember any other day or weekend of that year, but I can see myself sitting there (not knowing it was happening) then going back to the office where a secretary said "Mr. Kennedy's been shot," then going into the managing editor's office where there was a radio, then hearing the announcer say that a priest had just come out of the hospital and said Kennedy was dead, then phoning my wife: "Have you heard?" "Yes." Sobbing at both ends of the phone. "I don't believe it yet." "Neither do I." Then talking in the office, then off to the CBC to record a radio talk show for use on Sunday morning on which I think I said, "It was during what I suppose will now be known as the Kennedy era," then home for the long ghastly weekend of television. I could draw a picture—if I could in fact draw—of where I was as I saw Oswald being shot: in my dining room, at our old black dining room table. I even know what kind of shoes I was wearing (brown suede) and the kind of beer I drank to anesthetize the occasion (Labatt's 50). Of all those events you list, the death of Kennedy was the most important to people like me because it meant the abrupt end of a great surge of hope through the West—and also (though we didn't know it at the moment) it meant the end of *our* America (neither of those perceptions necessarily have anything to do with the truth of legislation, foreign policy, etc.). Anyway, my point about L'Europe is this: I can go to *Washington* for a weekend without thinking of Kennedy, I imagine I could go to Boston without thinking of him, but I can't go past L'Europe without thinking of him and how much he meant to people like me, liberals in all countries who were young when he was elected.

Poet and novelist Margaret Atwood recalls:

I was sitting in front of a typewriter at Canadian Facts, a market research company in Toronto. I was probably working on my first novel, the one that never got published, as I had a very understanding boss there who knew I could do the job in half the time scheduled for it; so I did the job in the morning and worked on the novel in the afternoon. Someone came into the office and said that they had just heard on the radio that Kennedy had been shot. I did not believe it. I thought it was a radio hoax, like Orson Welles' *The War of the Worlds*. I thought it was in dubious taste to make a joke like this. I kept on typing. Later in the day, it became evident that the reports had been genuine. Like most people, I was stunned. This was the first in what turned out to be a long line of assassinations, but nobody was ready for the first one. I thought of my friends in the United States and how devastated they would be. . . . I can't remember what I did for the rest of the day. I know that it took Kennedy a while to actually die, so I probably waited around, listening to reports and expecting he would recover. I simply could not believe that anyone would actually shoot a President. My own belief at that time certainly measures where we have all been since.

Kennedy's death soon captured the professional interest of the academic community. Pioneer studies were conducted of the whole communications process during the crisis, of how the mass media reported the events and analyzed them, and of the public's reaction during the next three days. A university of Chicago study showed the average television set was tuned to Kennedy coverage for 31.6 hours that weekend and that almost three-quarters of all Americans saw the funeral ceremony and procession. It is impossible to calculate the global coverage precisely, but it ran into the hundreds of millions of viewers. Television allowed viewers to go through the mourning process—from shock to horror to grief and finally catharsis—even though they were hundreds, even thousands of miles away. Mass emotions had never been focused so intensely before, nor analyzed so minutely.

One survey asked 1,300 people what other experiences they were reminded of when they heard of the Kennedy assassination. Most responded that they had never before had a similar experience; of those who could compare the event, most referred to the death of someone near to them, a quarter mentioned, like Sir Isaiah Berlin and Theodore White, the death of Franklin Delano Roosevelt in 1945. Eight per cent remembered Pearl Harbor; like Dallas, it happened suddenly, without warning, and it leveled a massive blow both to America's national security and sense of pride. But this time there was no external enemy like the Japanese against whom to focus hatred and revenge. One lone American— a social misfit to be sure—not a foreign and diabolical power had committed the crime.

As for the comparison between FDR's death and Kennedy's, FDR was an old and obviously sick man, one who had had a full and productive career, not a young man in his prime brimming with promise and potential. True, FDR's death late in the war created intense anxiety, as Americans, indeed all the Allies, mourned the loss not only of a leader but of a reassuring, capable father figure. But his death was not unexpected and it was the result of illness, not violence. FDR died at the height of radio's influence, and while it was extensively reported, the impact was diffused amidst a welter of war reports. No day in the Second World War, unlike that Friday in Dallas, could be described as a slow news day.

It is interesting to compare reactions as well between the Kennedy murder and later presidential assassination attempts—especially that of the attempt on President Ronald Reagan's life on March 30, 1981. Since that November day in Dallas more than 200,000 Americans have been murdered; indeed, on an average day 62 Americans are shot dead. When Ronald Reagan was wounded, people were shocked—but no one was really surprised. America had become a society where violent crime was so common that much of the population had become inured to it.

What is most remarkable about Kennedy's death is that it did not itself spark further violence or revenge at the time—other than the murder of Lee Harvey Oswald by Jack Ruby. Much of the explanation for the quietude of those grieving days lies in the inherent faith Americans have in their institutions and in themselves as a regenerative people. Another factor was the confident control shown by Lyndon Baines Johnson as he assumed the presidency. And then, too, mass communications played an important role.

What Americans needed to retain their faith in those institutions and to be certain of Johnson as their leader was a constant and uninterrupted flow of information. The mass media provided that service. Indeed, the coverage as so extensive that rumors and scares were simply drowned in the information flow. Dallas and its aftermath demonstrated, as would the Watergate scandal, the value of a free press in a democratic society. But the fact that most people watched television rather than read newspapers or listened to radios is the key to most researchers studying reaction to the Kennedy assassination.

Radio could have ignited passions; television, even at the supreme hot point of Oswald's "live" death, cooled them down. If as president John Kennedy lived through television, he also died through it and received a kind of retributive justice with the impromptu execution of Oswald, his killer. The funeral was also a media event, simultaneously a ritual and a catharsis for all who watched and mourned. Watching the funeral on television was like being there, and it allowed viewers to grieve and to exorcise their sorrow and their rage. Once the funeral was over, Americans could face the world again, subdued, but certain that their institutions were intact and that they were governed by good men.

Veteran broadcaster David Brinkley probably described television's vigil best in an article he wrote for *TV Guide* on the fifteenth anniversary of Kennedy's death:

> I thought then, as [Chet] Huntley and I and all of us on all the networks stayed with it to the last, day and night, that we helped the American people get through a sad and scary time by showing and telling everything there was, by preventing the spread of the frightening rumors always set afloat in times of public stress, by showing the swearing-in of the new president and showing the people that, even in a time so horrible, orderly government continued, and by giving the new President Johnson the means to speak reassuring words to a people who desperately needed them. I thought—and think—it was the most useful single service in television's history.

Coverage of the Kennedy assassination and funeral could well be television's finest hour; it might also be the apogee of mass media's impact. Certain theorists, like Alvin Toffler in his recent study *The Third Wave*, believe we are on a transitional edge between the industrial age—the era of mass communications, standardization and syncopation—and a new multi-choice age, a world of infinite variety in which decentralized individualism will be the norm.

Toffler argues that the breakdown of our creaking, industrial society is evident in the riots, revolutions, social and personal anxieties, and political dissent that surround us. As part of the process the communications industry is actively "de-massifying," as can be readily seen in the enormous drops in newspaper circulation, the recent decline in television viewing and the disappearance, or radical alteration, of such magazines as *Life* or *The Saturday Evening Post.* In the two decades since Kennedy's death the old mass forms have been replaced everywhere by more diversified media—media catering to individual tastes and idiosyncracies. The proliferation of new specialty magazines, the burgeoning of FM radio stations and the advent of cable TV all suggest that the monolithic media are on their way out.

If this is true, if uniformity and consensus are disappearing, then surely the day of simultaneous mass media news impact is waning as well, and if that is so, then our tired wired-up world might indeed have experienced its most complete news assault with the Kennedy killing and its painful, if cathartic, aftermath.

Our view is that there is some distance to travel before we reach Toffler's electronic nirvana. In the meantime competition for news coverage will be fierce. The monolithic media will not willingly contribute to their own demise and replacement by individuals. And they are very powerful. Four news services—Associated Press, United Press International, Reuters and Agence-France Presse—select or distribute almost 90 per cent of the international news printed or broadcast around the world. To capture our wavering attention, intense competition with attendant gimmickry and slickness is likely to typify news broadcasts of the very near future. The results will be an intensification of our present mass information bombardment. And for many it will be very difficult to sort out—in the vortex of words and visuals—what is important and what is not. That's ominous, because whether we are in Toffler's technological world or our own aging and decrepit one, the great danger is—and the Missile Crisis of 1962 points this out—that the news can always be manipulated, by presidents or prime ministers, by news agencies or government departments, for good or ill. The concern is not with technology itself, but with who controls the technology. The same is obviously true of media. In the final analysis the problems of the future, like the past, are mainly political.

NORMAN MAILER said, "For a time we felt the country was ours. Now it's theirs again."

Appendix

A Miscellany of Memories: From the Sinking of the *Titanic* to the Fall of the Shah.

Many of the people who responded to our questionnaire commented on events other than our key dates. We have collected some of these contributions and arranged them chronologically.

The Sinking of the Titanic

APRIL 15, 1912

Lowell Thomas, author and broadcaster:

When the *Titanic* hit that iceberg, I was editing a daily newspaper in a great gold mining camp, high up in the Rocky Mountains at a place that claimed to be the world's greatest gold camp—the Cripple Creek District. The name of the paper was the *Victor Daily Record*. Yes, indeed, the *Titanic* disaster was an important story to us even out there in the heart of the continent. After all, it was one of the most dramatic events of that era.

Stanley Holloway, actor and comedian:

I was appearing at the Old Tivoli Music Hall in the Strand in London in a musical sketch. Harry Lauder was top of the bill and all the men shared one small dressing-room. I well remember coming out into the Strand and seeing the news posters—FAMOUS LINER SUNK.

The Russian Revolution

1917

Sir Isaiah Berlin, historian:

In February 1917 I was not yet eight years old, and my impressions were, as you may imagine, visual rather than sociological. I remember being woken by my parents and standing on the balcony of our sixth floor flat in what was then called Petrograd gazing at the large crowds below holding banners which were inscribed with words like "Land and Liberty," "Down with Autocracy," "Down with the Tsar's Government," "All Power to the Duma" and the like. Troops were walking rather than marching towards them in formation, and the soldiers then seemed peacefully to mingle with the crowds. All this seemed to me most fascinating and I could not be torn from it. Later in the day, when I was taken for a walk, I did see a horrifying spectacle—a policeman, evidently loyal to the Tsarist Government, who, it was said, had been sniping at the demonstrators from a roof-top, being dragged by a mob to some awful end: the man looked pale and terrified and was feebly struggling with his captors. This image has remained with me and infected me with a permanent horror of any kind of violence.

The General Strike

MAY 3-12, 1926

Barbara Cartland, romantic novelist:

In the summer of 1925 the Government subsidy to the coal industry came to an end, the owners decided to reduce wages and enforce longer hours, and a threatened coal strike was only averted by the appointment of a commissioner to investigate conditions. The attitude of the Miners' Union and the T.U.C. was supported by many other unions and there was a general feeling all over the country that Labour should show its strength.

The Government immediately began to form an Organisation for the Maintenance of Supplies, and registered a large number of volunteers, but the Labour Party, with an extraordinary contradictory mixture of pacifism and over-confidence, made no arrangements. On May 3rd 1926, a General Strike came into effect and public transport ceased abruptly in a strange, almost eerie, silence. But non-union workers were determined, with that obstinacy which is a British characteristic, to get to their jobs. My brother Ronald was one of them. He was then working in the city and a friend called for him on his motor bicycle and, perched on the carrier, he set off gaily. Crossing Westminster Bridge a car laden with people swerved unpleasantly near them. Instinctively he drew in his long legs and a spoke of the wheel severed his heel from his foot. He was carried into Westminster Hospital and came home about an hour later. He was to be in agony for some weeks and on crutches for months.

For ten days there were no parties, no dances, no invitations of any sort—my men friends were working and working hard. All the "Berkeley boys"—so-called because the Berkeley Restaurant was one of the most fashionable dancing places at the moment and the same crowd danced there every night—had jobs in the O.M.S. Tight-waisted young men who latterly had been violently attacked in the Press as being "anaemic, bloodless, effeminate and effete" were all doing their bit now they were needed. The best dancer I knew was a special constable in the East End and he got a knock on the back of the head which necessitated six stitches. Another, criticized for his wealthy indolence, drove his car on a regular London to Manchester run with only about four hours' rest and sleep between the laps.

People of all ages were anxious to help. My mother offered to put up a young actor, Brian Buchel, who was driving a bus and couldn't get home at night. He would sometimes come in for dinner so tired that we had to keep him awake while he ate. After the first forty-eight hours there was little violence except near the docks. One day I accompanied Brian on his bus, sitting beside him in front and being given an immensely heavy truncheon to hold which I was ordered to use in case of trouble.

The bus was very old and very rickety. Our route was Cromwell Road, Hammersmith Broadway, and on to Richmond. In Hammersmith we broke down. Brian was doing his best to coax the engine back to life when a man came up and said—"Having trouble, sonny?"

Brian said he was.

"'Ere, let's have a look."

He cured the ailment, whatever it was, cranked up the engine and as we expressed our thanks remarked—"Be driving one meself again in a day or two."

When we got to Richmond and our last passenger descended we decided that "Tea for Two"—the song of the moment—had been very well earned. Accordingly we drove the bus with great difficulty and much coaxing up the hill to the Star and Garter Hotel. Parking it in the drive, Brian said airily to the attendant, "Mind my car, please," and, joined by our conductor, we sought our tea on the lawn.

Another time during the strike I was sent with a message by the local headquarters to whom I had offered my services to the Old Harrow Road. It was a cold, wet day and a white-faced young Jew, wearing his special constable armlet over a very thin overcoat, directed me to my destination—which was the Vicarage.

"Everything all right down here?" I asked.

"It's like a morgue," he answered. "I shall be glad when my beat's finished and I can get off to work."

"What do you do?" I enquired.

"Pianist in a dance band," he replied.

Lindbergh's Flight

MAY 21, 1927

Dave Brubeck, musician:

I was six years old and living in the then small California town of Concord when the news of "Lindy's" flight first reached us. The feat was later reinforced by the newsreels at the "movie house" owned by my uncle. My interest in aviation was keener than most boys' of that age, because a man, Vance Rundel, had built his own plane and lived a block from our house. He flew the mail route from Reno to San Francisco/Oakland, and landed at a small dirt airfield near Concord, because there was less fog in the Diablo hills than on the Bay side of the range. He flew with the aid of a simple compass, and had many daring stories to tell, which helped all of us youngsters appreciate just how great Lindbergh's achievement really was. It registered with greater impact than the first man on the moon because it was impressed more vividly in my mind as *one* man pitted against the forces of nature.

Outbreak of the Spanish Civil War

JULY 18, 1936

Joseph Losey, film director:

I was driving with my wife to our summer place in Vermont. It was a warm and beautiful day. The top of the convertible was down. The birds were singing. The radio announced the horrible event. Both my wife and I realized that for us this was the end of a postwar 1918 period and the beginning of the prewar 1939 period that would change all our lives.

The Battle of Britain

JULY 10 - SEPTEMBER 15, 1940

Christina Foyle, bookseller:

On September 15th 1940, when the Battle of Britain was at its height, I was having tea with Elinor Glyn, the famous author of the naughty novel *Three Weeks*. This intrepid lady, well into her eighties, lived throughout the Blitz in her elegant flat in Mayfair. Although so old, she was quite lovely, with clear green eyes and red gold hair. She always had with her a beautiful ginger Persian cat, even taking it to restaurants. At tea that day was Clarence Hatry, the financier, who had served a prison sentence for fraud, and had become so interested in books during his time as librarian in the prison, Wormwood Scrubs, that he had bought the famous Piccadilly Bookshop, Hatchards, on his release.

During tea news came to us that the great book wholesalers, Simpkin Marshall, had been entirely destroyed by fire bombs. Simpkins was one of the oldest booksellers in London and I was numbed by shock. Elinor Glyn received the news calmly, and Clarence Hatry just remarked, "My dear Christina, you must learn to bear the troubles of your competitors with fortitude."

I felt how much the elderly can teach the young in turbulent times.

Lovat Dickson, author and publisher:

On a Saturday afternoon at the beginning of September, the first massive daylight raid on the docks of London began, but where we were sitting in the garden, in the West End of London, perhaps ten miles away, we were only half-conscious that something unusual was happening. There had been thumps at intervals just before noon. We had not been shaken by these; the only odd thing had been that a beautiful sunny morning had clouded over unexpectedly. The dark increased until at three in the afternoon it seemed more like dusk. That was all we noticed.

We had decided to take a walk in Richmond Park. We left the car at Robin Hood Gate and started off towards the rise at the slow pace that I found maddeningly frustrating. Charles and Ashley lost no time in falling into argument. Ashley was a dramatist, and an exceedingly earnest one. Charles had been principal dramatic critic of *The Times*, and earnestness was something he assumed only when on public display as a writer or lecturer on a theme that called for it. Off duty, he was all for fun. He loved teasing Ashley, and he was engaged in this sport as we made our somewhat laboured way up the rise towards the crest of the slope crowned by a ring of trees. I remember the moment with sharp clarity because as we breasted the rise we were all laughing and what we saw made our smiles die.

Plumes of black smoke rose into the sky. "Good God, what's that?" asked Charles. "It looks as if London is on fire. It must be the Hun. He must be bombing the docks."

Those black clouds were petrol tanks going up. I had seen the dockland, and I knew what this meant. What shocked me at this moment was that I should be standing here on the crest of a hill overlooking London, laughing with my companions, while these bombs fell amongst those thin, flaky, odorous dwellings, and crushed the walls and ground into their stale old mortar the thin, starved and bent lives that had warmed them and had made them homes. I felt ashamed, angry not with the Germans, but with myself for having moved without any sense of direction through these last few years, for standing here on a hill-top, helpless when I might have been doing something to help. Help what, and whom and how? By shouldering arms, by putting my self-satisfied little head at the service of the Ministry of Information, by carrying on until I got the summons? It was too much. I could not find the answer, and it was here that my punishment began.

V-E Day

MAY 7, 1945

Heinrich Böll, novelist:
On May 1, 1945, wet, melting snow lay on the tents in the American P.O.W. camp in Attichy, near Reims. An American soldier went through the alleys of the camp with a megaphone and announced, "Hitler is dead! Hitler is dead! Hitler is dead!" I no longer remember

whether this politically and historically important piece of world news impressed us particularly. There were plenty of rumors flying and a joke made the rounds about a German soldier who was asked by a high-ranking American officer about what he would do if war were to break out between the Western allies and the Soviet Union. His answer: "I'd go to the church and pray for victory!"

We were hungry and waited for the next ration of soup, bread or coffee. The coffee was strong and very sweet, and some of us ate the coffee grounds—and for a few that had very bad side effects. Cigarettes were more difficult to come by than heroin is today. Top price: 120 marks, or a whole day's rations—and that for hand-rolled, not tailor-mades. As a result, three or four men would get together, each pooling a third or a quarter of his rations for a third or a quarter of a cigarette.

[I felt] uncertainty about the fate of my wife, who was expecting a child, about the fate of my family. The only message I had been permitted to send my wife was a field service card which never reached her—eight months later, after I'd been home already for a month, I received it from the postman myself.

Assassination of Mahatma Gandhi

JANUARY 30, 1948

George Woodcock, author:

To me that event was far more important than the killings of Martin Luther King and Robert Kennedy, and at least as important as the killing of John Kennedy.

I suppose the death of Gandhi had its greatest impact on Indians, and certainly it deeply affected Indian history, since it meant that the one great moral influence which might have turned India—and the Third World in its train—towards a different kind of political life to that of the West was removed.

As a pacifist and an anti-imperialist I perhaps made more of a hero of Gandhi while he lived than of any other person existing in my own world and time. When India exploded into violence at the departure of the British, Gandhi was still there, walking between the warring factions, bringing peace without regard to his own safety. It was the one ray of hope as all one's preconceptions of a free India fell in bloody ruins. And then Gandhi was killed, not by hostile Moslems, but by fellow Hindus. I remember that day questioning my whole philosophy of life, and I questioned it for many months and years afterwards, for the killing of Gandhi suggested that the old Huxleyan idea of "nature red in tooth and claw," of *all* life as an endless bloody struggle, was incontrovertible. It was not until the successes of civil disobedience in the later 1950s and earlier 1960s that I began to shed my doubts of the efficacy of Gandhian methods. Even today, when I see Gandhi's vision as the only possible alternative to the various corrupted Marxisms that shadow our world, the memory of January 30, 1948 still haunts me, and that sense of total defeat as I read of it in the morning paper, sitting drinking strong Italian coffee in the kitchen of the flat of an anarchist girl I loved, up in Chalk Farm on the southern purlieus of Hampstead.

Conquest of Everest
MAY 29, 1953
and
Coronation of Elizabeth II
JUNE 2, 1953

Katharine Whitehorn, journalist:

I was sitting up all night on the pavement to see the Coronation, and you'll remember they came round with the newspapers which we kept on buying to keep the rain off; ALL THIS AND EVEREST TOO said the headline—later claimed progressively around the Daily Express, I understand by (a) the man who actually wrote it (b) the sub-editor to whom he handed it (c) the assistant editor to whom *he* proudly showed it and (d) the editor. Some of this could be slightly untrue but I doubt it. I was deeply miserable at the time because I'd decided to go to Finland—best thing I ever did—and kept thinking Coronation-Everest—how happy I could be about everything if only it wasn't for this blasted departure's birth pains. Later, I found that Gavin Lyall, now my husband, was wandering around in London that evening with no intention of looking at the Coronation, merely being irritated to find that he couldn't get across Oxford Street, to the pavement on which I was sitting.

Sputnik
OCTOBER 4, 1957

David Suzuki, geneticist:

I was a junior in college and had been struck down by the Asian flu epidemic. (As I entered the infirmary, all the other victims hissed at me.) While I was lying there burning with fever, I heard a radio news flash that Sputnik had been launched. It was electrifying—because it really did herald a new age, but also because Soviet science seemed inevitable. I had no inkling of the massive infusion of money into science that would follow as a result, nor did I learn we'd got as far and as sophisticated as we are less than 25 years later.

Isaac Asimov, scientist and writer:

On that day (I was 37), I received the devastating news that Doubleday had rejected the very first straight mystery novel (as opposed to science fiction) I had ever written. It was the first time Doubleday had ever rejected a book of mine (and, as it happened, though I did not know it at the time also the last). I heard the news of Sputnik on the radio while sitting in my living room in a state of shock. In my diary, Sputnik took second place to the rejection.

Six-Day War

JUNE 5, 1967

Sir Isaiah Berlin:

During the Six-Day War I was in London. Like many other decent men and women, and particularly, of course, my fellow-Jews, I felt desperately anxious about the survival of the State of Israel. I had no doubt that Nasser would not have proclaimed a Holy War, and his men not have talked of throwing the Jews into the sea or razing their towns and villages, if they had not made sure of sufficient military backing to crush the Israelis. Whatever in fact may have sparked off the conflagration, it looked to the ordinary man in the British street as if it would be a war of extermination, a second Holocaust. The fact that no other country, nor the United Nations, lifted a finger to help the encircled Israelis looked ominous. I heard the news of the Israeli victory after dinner with the American Minister in London. The British and American politicians present all expressed relief at the outcome; I felt irrepressibly exhilarated, and said to my neighbour, the editor of a well-known newspaper, "It shows that there is a God in Heaven after all," to which he replied, "I suppose I am the only pro-Arab here"—he was indeed a personal friend of Nasser and Heikal. I thought that magnanimity was called for, and as I thought generously, congratulated him on his social courage, surrounded as he was by Zionists and their sympathisers—for the most part gentiles, indeed gentlemanly WASPs of impeccably patrician origin. My friend was genuinely gloomy about the outcome and left early. My wife and I remained till a late hour, and on our way back to our flat, walked on air. There was, even among people who had not until then given a thought to the Middle East, a great wave of sympathy for Israel; nothing that communists and anti-Zionists could say at that moment could destroy the rare pleasure of feeling—even if for what turned out to be a relatively short time—at one with the majority of one's fellow-citizens. Such moments cannot last, though they sometimes, if one is fortunate, return.

David Lancashire, journalist:

We didn't need a prophecy. It was happening next door. Dedee and the kids were at home in Beirut and I was across the border in Damascus, waiting to cover the Syrian front. I was having breakfast in the New Umayyad Hotel with AP's Syrian reporter, the best radio monitor I've ever met. Half a dozen radios were on the table, each broadcasting in different Arab accents, and he was listening to all of them at once. "Wallahi, let's go," he said suddenly. "It has started."

We hustled around the corner to his basement office. He stayed there, listening to his radios, and I went up on the roof. Israeli planes were screeching overhead, bombing the fuel dumps in the desert just outside Damascus. The radios were chortling that the Arabs had already wiped out the Israeli air force. Syrian censors had cut off the phone lines, but unaccountably, the lines to Paris and Moscow stayed open.

For three days I dictated copy to Paris. On the third night they got me. I was arrested by a mob of armed teenagers, along with the only other western correspondent in the country. They blindfolded us, jammed us into a Volkswagen and drove us around town before taking us to an old house where we were questioned for hours. Back into the Volkswagen, on with the blindfolds, another drive, and when we got out of the car we found ourselves at the gate of a prison. With great relief, I might add. At least if the prison authorities shot us they might tell somebody about it; the teenagers wouldn't. We were held in a concrete cell with eight pickpockets and petty offenders, who supplied us with coffee and cigarettes. They were indignant that we had been tossed in with criminals. "It is not proper that you should be here," one said sympathetically. "You are prisoners of war. You are not even Jews." A few hours later we were put in a truck, driven to the Lebanese border and deported to Beirut.

Dedee and our small sons had taken an evacuation flight to Holland her home. "I was so sorry not to have been there," she said later. "I didn't know you were in jail." "Never mind," I replied. "The maid and the dog gave me a terrific welcome home. The maid cried and the dog wet the floor. You wouldn't have done either."

Pierre Mendès-France, politician:

Like the vast majority of Frenchmen of all political persuasions, I followed with great anguish the development of a situation that seemed about to crush the State of Israel and its people. We were deeply offended by the hostile attitude of General de Gaulle and his government. We were all very relieved when we learnt of the lightning and almost miraculous campaign that gave Israel a clear military victory. However, we had other hopes that would—at the same time—be dashed. We had thought that after such a great military coup a real dialogue would finally begin between the rival camps and that eventually this would lead to a lasting peace.

Golda Meir, not yet a member of the government, visited me in Paris at about this time. She was full of hope that a real peace would result, and I am convinced that she considered this a much more important prize than any new territorial acquisitions.

For several days anything might have been possible, but positions on either side quickly hardened and became frozen; distrust and bitterness gained the upper hand. Peace must always be made very quickly.

Gore Vidal, novelist:

Elizabeth Bowen was brought to my flat in Rome. We were all grim: was the Third and last War about to begin? She said, wanly, "And I am writing what I think is my best novel, and it won't be finished." I said that that was precisely my own response to world's end. As it was, she lived to finish *Eva Trout* and I finished *Myra Breckinridge.*

Assassination of Robert F. Kennedy

JUNE 5, 1968

Clarke Blaise, novelist and short story writer:

1968 was the last year of our long studentship. My wife had received travel funds from McGill for doctoral research at the Schiller-Archiv in Marbach, Germany. I flew over with our four-year-old on the Icelandic run to Luxembourg, then got him to Oxford where he was to stay with friends. Bharati stayed that week in Montreal, settling the new baby with a sitter. We met in Luxembourg. We took a luxury train to Paris, enjoyed a fifty-dollar, eight-course dinner in the First Class diner. This was our honeymoon. Two weeks in Paris; two months in the Schwarzwald.

It was May; Paris was brilliant. We took a perfect room on the *rue des écoles.* We ate at the "Hanoi" across the street, feeling liberated. Out early the next morning to buy cheese and wine, we were drawn to the clusters of irate students. *Appuyez les ouvriers!* We accepted their pamphlets but despaired of understanding so much specialized passion. In the middle of a cobblestoned *cul-de-sac* an overturned little Citroën burned almost prettily. Other peoples' riots seemed so decorative; the violence so staged, deaths so avoidable.

A week later the trains, the posts, the telephones, were all closed down. We were effectively trapped. At the Gare du Nord the communists were out in earnest, shouting in our ears, *"Lisez, demandez, l'Humanité!"* Shadier operators whispered in the voice of an older France, *" frontière belge, cinq cent francs."*

Two weeks later, by hitch-hiking and sleeping apart in student hostels, we'd made it to Amsterdam. For the next ten days we subsisted on the landlady's generous breakfasts. Every morning I feared detection, a demand for rent. We sat in the parks eighteen hours a day; even the museums were out of reach. I searched the gutters for change. Our Canadian paychecks had been sent to Paris, and Paris was still in shambles. We couldn't wire Oxford; I couldn't pay for a transatlantic call. I cursed Europe, its inconvenient and inconclusive revolutions. The Paris *Herald-Tribune* was not publishing; we were totally out of contact with American news. I walked three miles every morning to the central Post Office and rooted through bins of mail from France, hoping to find our checks.

At least we'd lived through a bit of European history, I thought; 1968 would be for us a European experience. We, too, had lived through *"les événements"*; mention *soixante-huit* to us and we'd respond like Frenchmen.

Obviously, I'd have to panhandle. Stand in the lobby of American Express where all those undeserving little bastards received money from home. Find a Canadian student and pour out my story. I dreaded it more than being discovered by my landlady.

One cool bright Dutch morning on the Vondel Park, a man showered himself in breadcrumbs. Pigeons seemed to devour him. A young man carrying a pile of hastily-lettered posters ran into the park and dashed from tree to tree, tying a poster around each trunk. It said, KENNEDY ATTENTAT.

I was delighted. California, of course! Bobby must have won. Los Angeles was nine hours behind us; it was roughly midnight there. I rejected the curious coincidence that the word I took to be Dutch for victory was also the French for a serious attack.

Mention '68 to me now and I think of the impossibility of ever entering another's politics, or ever completely escaping one's own.

Susan Clark, actress:

Five years and some months after my debut in London, I was making an interesting movie with a young star named Robert Redford and Katherine Ross and Robert Blake. The movie was *Tell Them Willie Boy Is Here* and in it there is a scene where they talk about the assassination of President McKinley. It didn't seem to have much importance. I, as a

Canadian, had never heard of President McKinley, and the only thing I knew about President Taft, who was the living president in our movie, was he was about to visit the town of Riverside on a barnstorming political tour.

We were doing the interior scenes on the sound stages at Universal Studios in early June prior to our location in Palm Desert for six weeks. The magic of the Kennedy name and his visit to Los Angeles on that fateful day prompted several people to bring their portable televisions, and most of us rushed home that night to watch the convention.

The war in Vietnam was a horrendous, tragic daily news program, and many of us who were Doves marched, wrote letters, campaigned in our own way, but still the violence was half a world away. Now I was watching an assassination on television—the violence had come home!

The next day at the studio our set had a three-minute mourning period for the late Robert Kennedy. We postponed the scene dealing with presidential assassination for a week—none of us could say the lines.

Coming so soon after Martin Luther King's death made the next few weeks unsettling and lonely. I remember sitting that evening in my small apartment in the Hollywood Hills, reasonably pleased with my new life, new city and new job and being reminded of the other Kennedy's death five years earlier. If ever I had believed as a foreigner in the American Dream, the deaths of John F. Kennedy, Martin Luther King and Robert Kennedy ended it.

Arthur Erickson, architect:

We had landed from our sailing yacht in Mykonos and were wandering through the white-washed streets of the town on that sunny June day when a merchant ran out of his shop with wild eyes and shouted "Kennedy!" and made the gesture of a slice across the throat. We nodded assent. He repeated and then said "Americans—crazy!" We nodded assent again shaking our heads sadly and he ran back into his shop. We continued walking, wondering why an event that had happened several years ago should still affect this wild-eyed Greek. But continuing down another street, still speculating on what had so disturbed the merchant and concluding that from some unfortunate experience with tourists he had come to resent all Americans and deem them crazy—another merchant came rushing out of his shop again shouting "Kennedy!" and making the same gesture. This time we were dragged into his shop and seated around his radio to hear to our disbelief and horror the English language broadcast of the second Kennedy assassination. "Yes, America—crazy," we kept saying to every Greek we passed on our way back to the yacht, shaking our heads in sadness.

Gore Vidal:

I was in a hotel at Ostia, losing weight. The ABC TV man in Rome rang to say, "Bobby was shot down." I said, "Good," thinking that he meant that Bobby had lost the California primary. When he told me what had happened, I went back to Rome and taped for TV not an appreciation of someone I disliked, but a heart-felt attack on the National Rifle Association which has contributed so much to violence in the land.

Russians Invade Czechoslovakia

AUGUST 20, 1968

Vladimir Ashkenazy, pianist:

I . . . remember being impressed by the cynicism of the U.S.S.R. (or rather the *degree* of it) when it invaded Czechoslovakia in 1968—and by the utmost hypocrisy with which they accompanied the invasion (as indeed is the mark of their activity all over the world before or since). I was a holder of a Soviet passport at the time and nearly renounced my citizenship on the impulse, full of revulsion with their behavior.

Heinrich Böll:

On August 20, 1968, my wife, my son and I arrived in Prague at the invitation of the Czechoslovakian Writers' Union. The telegraphed invitation had said, among other things, "Our intention is that you convince yourself—on the spot—of the worthy course of our process of renewal so that on your return you can inform the general public of your country." Looking back, the text of the invitation now appears a murderous irony. I had accepted without hesitation because I saw great hope for West and East in the Czech model of democratic socialism; from there, from Prague and Bratislava, what was regarded as Utopian idealism until January 1968—socialist liberty—might have spread to both the East and West.

Here is what I could now "inform the general public of my country": Already that first night the drone of heavy low-flying airplanes had awakened us. At seven o'clock the next morning a friend arrived at the hotel, banged on the door and shouted from outside, "We have been occupied!" Shortly after that we heard the first shots in St. Wenceslas Square. We went there immediately, saw the Soviet tanks—a demonstration of absurd stupidity—and countless people, young and old. What stirred me most was how passionately the people tried to argue with the soldiers, to explain to them and to themselves this incredible chain of events. A single shot from the civilian side probably would have triggered a catastrophe, but that shot was not fired. It was plain to see that we were witnesses to an historic event, the consequences of which cannot be imagined even now. It was also plain that here, socialism, under the central direction of Moscow, admitted its moral bankruptcy, and that we were dealing with the blatant oppression of an entire nation. The model of hope that had been a reality here for eight months had been destroyed.

Josef Skvorecky, novelist:
On that day I woke up at exactly 7:00 a.m. in Munich. We were staying the night with friends, on our way to Paris where a book of mine had just been published. I switched on the portable radio, and that real German voice gave me the nightmarish unreality: *"Heute Nacht had die Rote Armee Tschechoslowakei besetzt."* I felt like a freshly knocked-out boxer. *Finis Bohemiae!* flashed through my mind, and I knew that this was the end of civilization in Czechoslovakia. For me, for my generation, it was the end of everything. Two days later, on the German TV, I heard Kissinger calmly predicting that for two or three months the West would pretend outrage, and after that everything would be back to normal again. I hated him, but he was right. He knew what *Realpolitik* was, and so did I; but I tried to ignore my knowledge. On the same TV screen I also saw a terrified Shirley Temple crossing the border from Bohemia into Germany. A year later, in San Francisco, I saw her still working for the Czech cause, performing in a Czech national costume on the campus at Berkeley. Doubtlessly, it must have fostered, in the minds of the sophisticated flower children, the image of the peasant computer scientists from Bohemia, ten of whom had just defected to somewhere near Menlo Park, California. But then Shirley became a diplomat, and I suppose she donned other national costumes. Kissinger was absolutely right.

The Democratic Convention

AUGUST 27, 1968

Gore Vidal:
Most TV viewers can tell me what I was doing better than I can. That night heated words were exchanged between me and a right-wing publicist named Buckley.

Man on the Moon

JULY 20, 1969

Isaac Asimov:
I was 49. I had driven to Connecticut on that day to visit my son who was at boarding school at that time. I drove home through a light rain and

then spent the evening at the television set, waiting for the initial step on the Moon. Unlike the other events, this one did not come without warning.

Anthony Burgess, novelist:

I was in Malta when the news of the moon landing came through on television. As Malta is small and nationalistic, the news bulletin had to begin with: "Mr Borg-Olivier was among the first heads of state to send congratulations to the U.S. President on the lunar landing." There was, naturally, a dignified picture of Prime Minister Borg-Olivier accompanying this announcement. My son was then aged four. He had learned Maltese and was using it as a first language. He ran through the house shouting: *"Borg-Olivier fuq il-qamar!"* This means: "Borg-Olivier is on the moon!" The next day at infant school, having been taught that Jesus Christ rose from the tomb, or *qumar*, he insisted that Christ rose from *il-qamar*.

Senator Keith Davey, politician:

I was staying at Arundel Lodge in Muskoka. I went to the main lounge to watch the event on television. There were a group of young teenage girls at the Lodge from a religious group. We got talking and apparently one of their beliefs was that there were little green people living on the moon, and they were most interested to see them when the landing was photographed. I asked them what would happen to their faith when they discovered there were no little green men—without hesitation one of them replied, "And what will happen to your faith when there are!"

Sir Alec Guinness, actor:

Huge rejoicings. Sent telegrams to various American friends. In the evening my wife and I sat by a pond in our garden, waiting to see the moon in the water, while our Abyssinian cat stalked a frog.

Sir William McMahon, politician:

For some time I had been interested in the preparations leading up to the effort by the United States to place a man on the moon. As the day drew near I became more and more preoccupied with the potential effect on mankind, the technological and social risks and the scientific discoveries that had been made. So from the time of the launching to the time of the day of return I had been immersed in the flight and its success.

Man had once again established his capacity to handle the most difficult problems of technology and science. New technologies developed which could be put to manifold beneficial use. Mankind was given another opportunity to improve the standards of its peoples. The television coverage was without doubt the most fascinating technical picture of discovery I have seen.

Gore Vidal:

I lay on the floor of my room at the Beverly Hills Hotel, hardly able to breathe from excitement. What other society could have sent to the moon so many Rotarians?

Kent State Shootings

MAY 4, 1970

Dave Brubeck:

This is an event that I am still involved in, because it became to me a symbol of the cumulative agonies of the sixties. Just a few weeks ago I was talking to a man who is still fighting the battle for justice on behalf of the families of those who were slain, and the students, who were maimed. In the wake of Kent State, my wife and I and one of our sons, Chris, were moved to write a cantata called *Truth is Fallen* based on Isaiah 59, "Truth is fallen in the street and equity cannot enter." The bible goes on to say that there was no judgment. None pleaded for truth.

However, I feel that the Kent State and Jackson, Mississippi outrages were turning points in the American psyche. It became apparent to all, through nightly TV news, that the slaying of our young was the end result of the political course we had taken, and when the "silent majority" began to speak, slowly at first, they did call for justice here and in Vietnam. After the assassinations of John F. Kennedy, Martin Luther King Jr. and Robert Kennedy—not to mention Malcolm X and Black Panther leaders—we were inexorably moving, in our cry for law and order, toward a paranoid police state. Because of Kent State we are forewarned.

Nixon's Resignation

AUGUST 9, 1974

Douglas Fairbanks, Jr., actor:

The day President Nixon resigned, my wife and I were in New York. It had been predicted for quite some time, and I seem to recall that the general feeling was not *whether* the president was to resign, but *when*. It was obvious that every possible effort was made to avoid or postpone what must have been, for him, the most deeply traumatic moment of his life. It was also for the world a surprise and a scandal which certainly pleased some, shocked some, and saddened some. I suppose most Americans were, if anything, ashamed that such a thing could happen to the man who combined the offices of Head of State with Head of Government on the one hand, but on the other rather proud and pleased that the mood of the nation and the machinery of our system of government was such that, however painful, this kind of political surgery could be performed without anesthetics and that the patient—the nation— could not only survive, but recuperate without any need to disguise it's scars.

Anthony Burgess:

I had been invited to appear on the Dick Cavett Show in New York, and I had flown thither from Rome. Then the rumours began to flow into my hotel room of the impending presidential resignation. The Dick Cavett Show would not be cancelled, but it would be postponed. Wait, I was told, don't move, wait for another call. And so for all the long time of waiting I was stuck to the television screen, angry at the waste of time. A more permanent and inexpugnable anger at the villainy of all politicians owes its beginning to this experience. I remember the hypocritical Nixon on the screen, but I remember far better the words of Gerald Ford: "Truth is a glue that binds people together." I flew back with those words echoing in my brain. "Truth is a glue," God help us. Or, as I put it in verse:

> "Truth," says the U.S. President, "is glue."
> May God help Ford, the Lord help also you.

The Dick Cavett Show was late recording, and I had a plane to catch. It rained, and I could not find a taxi. I jumped onto the aircraft almost at the moment of the removal of the steps. I almost had a heart attack. I blame the American presidency for it.

Katharine Whitehorn:

Nixon's resignation cheered me up a lot, because it confirmed my feeling that America has the cures to its own diseases, but I can't remember for the life of me where I was when I heard it. Anyway the rat is back again.

The Test Tube Baby

JULY 26, 1978

Susan Clark:

In July of 1978 I was back in London and working there for the first time in eight years. The concept of a test tube baby was a fantasy shared by many young women of my age, particularly professional women who felt that they could handle with help the rearing of a child, but perhaps the pressures of a relationship and a career would prove to be too much and the career or the marriage would end.

Like many young women, we really wanted to make life simple, and it seemed terribly romantic, not unlike Aldous Huxley's novel, *Island*. I and a couple of my friends fantasized about a test tube baby who would be another Mozart, another Picasso, another Shakespeare.

Having grown beyond that stage and realizing children needed more than a dream, this fantasy was brought back to life with the headlines "Test Tube Baby Success—Live in London." I bought all the newspapers I could find and watched eagerly all the in-depth interviews that the young couple and the doctors were subjected to following this world-shattering event.

The young mother looked tired and somewhat puzzled at all this interest. Obviously my fantasy had been shared by millions of women all over the world and doubtless scores of men, too. I remember thinking that I was pleased that the first test tube baby was not the fantasy of a young romantic single woman but the result of a couple obviously in love and desirous of having a family. They appeared to be a very simple, uncomplicated pair, and I will be curious to watch over the years to see if the media is as fascinated with this child at 10, at 20 and 30 and 50 years of age as it was with the birth.

The Collapse of the Shah's Regime in Iran

FEBRUARY 11, 1979

David Lancashire:

The collapse of the Shah of Iran meant only nostalgia, not discomfort. By that time I was back in Toronto, working for the *Globe and Mail*. But I had covered elections in Iran for the AP, I had covered the birth of the Shah's son, and I had covered the start of his so-called White Revolution. I had also written some pieces about royal corruption, which got me on the Shah's black-list and barred me from Iran. The prime minister promised to fix things up, but he was assassinated shortly afterward, and it was years before I got back to Tehran (for the Shah's coronation, as it happened). My reaction at the time of his removal: welcome to the black-list, Shah.

The authors and the publisher wish to thank the following for permission to reproduce copyrighted material. Care has been taken to trace ownership of copyrighted material contained in this book. Any errors or omissions drawn to the publisher's attention will be rectified in subsequent editions.

Clement Attlee, *As it Happened*. London: William Heinemann Ltd., 1954.

H.E. Bates, *The Blossoming World*. London: Michael Joseph Ltd., 1971. Used by permission of the Estate of the late H.E. Bates.

Cecil Beaton, *The Years Between*. London: Weidenfeld & Nicolson, 1965.

David Ben-Gurion, *Letters to Paula*. London: Vallentine, Mitchell & Co., 1968.

Anthony Boyle, *Only the Wind will Listen: Reith of the BBC*. London: Hutchinson & Co. Ltd., 1972. Reprinted by permission of Curtis Brown Ltd.

David Brinkley, "President Kennedy was shot in Dallas, Texas, today," in *TV Guide*, Nov. 25-Dec. 1, 1978.

Cab Calloway, *Of Minnie the Moocher and Me*. New York: Thomas Y. Crowell and Co., 1976. Reprinted by permission of Harper & Row Publishers, Inc.

Emily Carr, *Hundreds and Thousands: The Journals of Emily Carr*. Toronto: Clarke, Irwin and Co. Ltd., 1966. Used by permission.

Charles Chaplin, *My Autobiography*. London: The Bodley Head, 1964.

Winston Churchill, in *The Daily Telegraph*. London, December 9, 1929.

Winston Churchill, *The Grand Alliance*. Copyright 1950 by Houghton Mifflin Company and reprinted by permission.

Kenneth Clark, *Another Part of the Wood: A Self Portrait*. London: John Murray Publishers, 1974.

Janet Flanner, "Letter from Paris," in *The New Yorker*, October/November 1929. Copyright 1929, 1957 and reprinted by permission of *The New Yorker*.

Anne Frank, *The Diary of a Young Girl*. Copyright 1952 by Otto H. Frank and reprinted by permission of Doubleday and Company, Inc.

Michihiko Hachiya, *Hiroshima Diary: The Journal of a Japanese Physician, August 6-September 30, 1945*, translated and edited by Warner Wells. Copyright 1955 by the University of North Carolina Press and reprinted by permission.

Nevile Henderson, *Failure of a Mission, Berlin 1937-39*. London: Hodder & Stoughton, 1940. Reprinted by permission of Raymond Savage Ltd.

Harold L. Ickes, *The Secret Diary of Harold L. Ickes, Vol. II, The Inside Struggle, 1936-39*. New York: Simon & Schuster, 1953. Reprinted by permission of Simon & Schuster, a Division of Gulf & Western Corporation.

Paul Johnson, "London Diary," in *New Statesman*, November 4, 1966.

Groucho Marx, *Groucho and Me*. Copyright 1959 by Groucho Marx and reprinted by permission of the publisher, Bernard Geis Associates, Inc.

André Maurois, *Proust: Portrait of a Genius*. New York: Harper & Bros., 1950. Reprinted by permission of Georges Borchardt, Inc.

Golda Meir, *My Life*. London: Weidenfeld & Nicolson, 1975.

Harold Nicolson, *Peacemaking, 1919*. London: Constable, 1933.

Richard Nixon, *The Memoirs of Richard Nixon*. New York: Doubleday, 1978. Reprinted by permission of Grosset & Dunlap Inc.

Lester Pearson, *Mike: The Memoirs of the Rt. Hon. Lester B. Pearson, Vol. 1, 1879-1948*. Toronto: University of Toronto Press, 1972. Reprinted by permission of the University of Toronto Press, Quadrangle Books, Inc., New York and Victor Gollancz Ltd., London.

Charles Ritchie, *The Siren Years: A Canadian Diplomat Abroad*. Copyright 1974 by Charles Ritchie and reprinted by permission of Macmillan of Canada, a Division of Gage Publishing Ltd.

Eric Sevareid, *Not So Wild a Dream*. Copyright 1946, © 1976 by Eric Sevareid (New York: Atheneum Publishers, 1976). Reprinted by permission of Atheneum Publishers.

Howard K. Smith, *Last Train from Berlin*. New York: Alfred A. Knopf, 1943.

Studs Terkel, *Hard Times: An Oral History of the Great Depression*. New York: Random House, 1970.

Theodor Wolff, *Through Two Decades*. London: William Heinemann Ltd., 1936.

Leonard Woolf, *Beginning Again: An Autobiography of the Years 1911-1918*. London: Hogarth Press, 1964. Reprinted by permission of Mrs. M.T. Parsons and the Hogarth Press Ltd.